Music, Muscle, and Masterful Arts

# Music, Muscle, and Masterful Arts

*Black and Indigenous Performers of the Circus Age*

Sakina M. Hughes

The University of North Carolina Press  CHAPEL HILL

*This book was published with the assistance of the Authors Fund of the University of North Carolina Press.*

© 2025 Sakina Mariam Hughes
All rights reserved
Set in Merope Basic by Westchester Publishing Services
Manufactured in the United States of America

Library of Congress Cataloging-in-Publication Data
Names: Hughes, Sakina M., author.
Title: Music, muscle, and masterful arts : Black and Indigenous performers of the circus age / Sakina M. Hughes.
Description: Chapel Hill : The University of North Carolina Press, [2025] | Includes bibliographical references and index.
Identifiers: LCCN 2024035426 | ISBN 9781469676265 (cloth) |
  ISBN 9781469676272 (paperback) | ISBN 9781469676289 (epub) |
  ISBN 9781469680743 (pdf)
Subjects: LCSH: African American circus performers—History. | Indian circus performers—United States—History. | African American entertainers—History. | Indian entertainers—United States—History. | Circus—United States—History. | Wild west shows—United States—History. | BISAC: HISTORY / African American & Black | SOCIAL SCIENCE / Ethnic Studies / American / General
Classification: LCC GV1803 .H84 2025 | DDC 791.3089/96073—dc23/eng/20240905
LC record available at https://lccn.loc.gov/2024035426

Cover art: Muscular man's back in silhouette by jacoblund; Vintage four string banjo by ozaiachin; A horse lamp in a pink circus tent by heatherdeffense; Alternative dance in the sky by simonapilolla. All from Envato Elements.

*To my Ancestors and to Mason,
who allow me to dig deep and grow toward light all at once.*

*To Black artists and musicians of the tented-show era:
I know paving the road was hard and hellish,
but you made it look and sound so good!*

*To everyone Black.*

*Contents*

List of Illustrations ix

Acknowledgments xi

Introduction 1

CHAPTER ONE
A Circus World 16
*1870s–1920s America*

CHAPTER TWO
For Good Treatment, Equal Justice, and Sure Salary,
Give Me the Circus 33
*Black Musicians Reinvent the Circus from the Inside Out*

CHAPTER THREE
His Skin Is Dark, but He Will Come Out on Top . . .
or Know the Reason Why 63
*Black Labor in and out of the Tent*

CHAPTER FOUR
But Simply a Man Normal in His Environment 94
*Indigenous Americans, Wild West Shows, and
Taking on the Vanishing Race Narrative*

CHAPTER FIVE
Hidden in Plain View 128
*The Circus Towns of Columbus, Ohio, and Peru, Indiana*

CONCLUSION
The Big Black Boom 149
*Black Art on an International Stage*

Notes 155
Bibliography 175
Index 199

*Illustrations*

Gertrude Ma Rainey and her Georgia Jazz Band in Chicago ca. 1924–25  3

Sells-Floto Free Street Parade  18

Wallace Parade in Peru, Indiana  18

Carl Hagenbeck entrance banner  19

Barnum and Bailey Supernatural Illusions poster  19

Furber and Williams's "He's Up Against the Real Thing Now"  25

"Negro Snack Stand," detail  28

"Negro Snack Stand," wide view  28

"Negro Hotel"  29

Tuskegee Institute Glee Club and Orchestra  37

Fisk Jubilee Singers  37

Lowery Band wagon  43

James Wolfscale  43

Bessie Smith  50

Newsprint, Eph Williams Original Famous Troubadors  65

Newsprint, "30 of the Best Colored Artists in the World"  65

Newsprint, Miss Jennie Hale  65

Coy Herndon's New Orleans Strutters  73

Millie Christine  81

Princess Wee Wee  81

Canvasmen: "Colored Brigade"  86

Group Sideshow Canvasmen  86

Society of American Indians  95

Sells-Floto Wild West poster  99

Nabor Feliz portrait  112

"Nabor Feliz Speaking to Children," 1923  112

101 Ranch Indian Real Wild West poster  116

*Wassaja* masthead  123

Marie Louise Bottineau Baldwin  125

Sarah Winnemucca  125

Susette La Flesche Tibbles  126

Sellsville Polkadot School  135

Godfroy family  138

The Hagenbeck-Wallace Quarters  140

## Acknowledgments

In 2023, I went to South Africa for the first time and learned a new word that beautifully encapsulates the experiences of being a scholar and writing a book. *Ubuntu* means, "I am because you are." It describes the writing process—from first drafts to published product—perfectly because it acknowledges the importance of those in our lives who provide guidance, support, criticism, and encouragement. It is one of my most important lessons since I began this project in graduate school.

I want to acknowledge the wonderful faculty at Michigan State University that helped shape me into the scholar that I am today. My dissertation advisor, Dr. Susan Sleeper-Smith, has been an amazing mentor and friend for many years now, and I am so thankful to have been able to work with such a caring person and fabulous academic. I could never list all the things I am grateful for, but I was privileged to be at MSU with Dr. Sleeper-Smith, and I'm thankful for the generous time she spent with me, theorizing and discussing how to write African American/Indigenous American histories that honor all groups involved. Others on my committee—Dr. Thomas Summerhill, Dr. Edward Watts, Dr. Leslie Moch, and the late, great Dr. David Bailey helped me find my voice in telling stories, and I am forever grateful. Dr. Tiya Miles, the outside reader on my dissertation committee, has become a great mentor over the years. She has modeled how to be a scholar and public intellectual, bringing together lost ideas, dreams, hopes, and hidden knowledge in beautiful, meaningful ways, and she has been a longtime supporter of my projects, reading, critiquing, and challenging my work. I was honored to work with amazing scholars at the University of Michigan during my postdoctoral fellowship; among them, Dr. Martha Jones helped me to look deeper at race, politics, and visual culture, and Dr. Kevin Gaines's work in respectability helped to form an important pillar of my study. Even before she was a cheerleader for my work, Dr. Janet Davis provided an academic framework for me to begin my own journey into circus studies. Dr. Janet Zepernick has been a wonderful friend and mentor, reading and rereading chapters during the pandemic. Our meetings were often the highlights of my day during the long months of COVID-19 isolation, and she really helped to keep me going when I thought there wasn't anywhere else to go.

I was lucky to have generous funding from Michigan State University, the Newberry Library D'Arcy McNickle Center for Native American and Indigenous Studies, West Virginia University's Literary and Cultural Studies Program, and the University of Michigan, Du Bois-Mandela-Rodney Postdoctoral Fellowship in the Department of Afroamerican and African Studies. The great network of scholars with whom I was able to work set a very high scholarly bar, and I continue to reach for it. My time with the CIC American Indian Studies Graduate Student Consortium was crucial; especially valuable was my time with Dr. Jacki Rand, Dr. Scott Stevens, and Dr. John Tippeconnic. In 2007 I attended Dr. Tippeconic's seminar on Indian education, and in 2008, I had the great privilege of joining Dr. Rand's seminar entitled "The Indigenous, the State, and Internal Colonialism in a Transnational Context." Both of these seminars have proven critical in my studies. Dr. Scott Stevens, director of the Center, mentored me during my Newberry Fellowship at a time when many of the ideas that would become this book finally started coming together. The librarians, archivists, and staff at the Newberry Library, the Antioch Baptist Church in Columbus, the Columbus Metropolitan Library, and the Indiana Historical Society were crucial in my research and discoveries. Special thanks to Marilyn Van Winkle, archivist at the Autry Museum of the American West, Beverly Parker, interim director at the Miami County Historical Society, Katy Scullin, Ohio Memory program coordinator at the Ohio History Connection, Mark Schmitt at the Milner Library Circus and Allied Arts Collection at Illinois State University, and Peter Shrake, archivist at the Circus World's Robert L. Parkinson Library and Research Center, all of whom have helped me quite a bit over the years. Working on the 2018 PBS American Experience documentary film *The Circus* was amazing and provided me with a chance to meet circus archivist Fred Pfening III, who has been a great resource and cheerleader for my project. I have been ecstatic to work with the editorial staff of the University of North Carolina Press, namely Mark Simpson-Vos, who has mentored me through this process and who has shown unending patience as I navigated revisions, a cross-country move, three bouts of COVID-19, and a broken toe on a different continent!

During the course of this project, I was honored to meet some of the great African American and Indigenous American circus artists working today. They, like marginalized performers during the golden age, see their work as much bigger than their own careers. They understand their work as social justice work, centering the often-ignored humanity and artistry of Black and Indigenous peoples. I owe a big "thank you" to these artists who work with talents like Missy Elliot and 50 Cent but made time to speak with me in between performances. I am indebted to Veronica Blair, an African American professional aerialist, aerial director, circus researcher, consultant, and founder of the *Uncle Junior Project*, which honors Black circus performers. Blair invited me to an international virtual circus conference on Black, Indigenous, and other people of color in the industry in the early months of the pandemic. This conference introduced me to a worldwide network of Black, Brown, and Indigenous artists, who expressed such excitement for my work and gratitude for being centered in this history that I realized how important telling this story would be. They gave me reason to push through many rounds of revisions and reinvigorated my desire to get this book published. During that conference, I met a superstar in his own right, Jonathan Lee Iverson, the first African American ringmaster in the long history of the Ringling Bros. and Barnum and Bailey Circus and a professional who has tirelessly worked to entertain, evoke wonder, and broaden our understanding of the circus arts during his more than twenty years in the industry. Other circus artists who helped me understand the importance of this work are Sam Malcolm, a Paiute-Shoshoni juggler who was extremely generous with his time as he toured across the country, and Pamela Donohoo, artistic director, choreographer, and award-winning performer.

My community of friends has made me laugh and inspired me along the way. My dear friend and SIS, Dr. Nik Ribianszky, has been with me since graduate school, day one. We both wrote our dissertations while raising our daughters, talking shop, and drinking boxed wine (yes, there are some decent boxed wines). Other friends at MSU and the CIC-AIS I am grateful for are Dr. Mary Phillips, Dr. Jenifer Barclay, Dr. C. Joe Genetin-Pilawa, and Dr. James Buss. My year as the Du Bois-Mandela-Rodney Fellow in the Department of African American and African Studies under the leadership of Dr. Tiya Miles at the University of Michigan was a phenomenal year for me—made even more extraordinary by all my friends and writing buddies, Dr. Reighan Gillam, Dr. Elizabeth Hinton, and Dr. Jessica Welburn Paige. I loved being among so much Black Girl Magic, and that year will always occupy a special place in my heart.

I want to thank my Dad, Stacey Anthony Waller, a carpenter by trade, who taught me the meaning and value of hard work. Whether building a cabinet or a story, he taught me that if it's worth doing, it's worth doing right! He also taught me to appreciate excellence and the necessity of frequent, hearty, sidesplitting laughter. When I was a teenager, just starting to get into activism and radical history, I didn't understand how he could laugh at comedians like Mantan Moreland and Steppin Fetchit who leaned so far into anti-Black racial stereotypes. But his laughter was infectious, and I always ended up joining him. My Dad helped me to both appreciate the genius of early Black vaudeville entertainers in segregated America and be proud of the activism that was so important to me. More important, he taught me valuable lessons about pride, work, nuance, and progress that I only fully realized while writing this book. At the end of the day, calling in and calling on are so much more valuable than calling out. If each generation, as Franz Fanon wrote, must find their mission and fulfill it (or betray it), those artists and musicians did an amazing job and left us with music, art, and performance to lift up and be proud of.

My Gramma, Tempie Mae Simmons, passed away the year I started graduate school. Born in Mississippi, my Gramma attended a segregated school that did not go past elementary school. When she was barely eighteen, she made the brave decision to accompany her husband north to Detroit. There, she cleaned houses, raised six children, fished, canned fruits and vegetables from her garden, and forged a way for me to complete a doctoral degree. She has been a great inspiration as I go through life in all my roles—as mother, breadwinner, student, teacher, and historian.

And finally, thanks to my sunshine, the love of my life, my greatest teacher and favorite archival assistant, my daughter, Mason. I've been working on this project in some aspect pretty much the whole time she's been conscious on this planet. From playing tricks on everyone in the office at MSU, to all the times she so willingly accompanied me on research trips, and to recent years as she has become my fresh set of eyes, catching typos and gaps in my arguments. Mason has, throughout the process, kept me busy, kept me sane, kept joy in my life, and been my biggest reason to keep going.

Music, Muscle, and Masterful Arts

# Introduction

In 1904, Lewis Williams, a clarinetist in an all-Black circus sideshow band, responded to an offer to leave his Black employer and join a white-managed troupe. Williams's response, besides being refreshingly audacious, was powerful and highlighted the burgeoning opportunities the circus industry offered African American performers at the turn of the twentieth century. As new circus opportunities developed, Black artists prioritized their own personal growth, as well as the advancement of African American art and society in general. These artists were no longer beholden to the racially biased whims of white managers because they more and more worked for Black companies:

> DEAR SIR: I received your favor and I appreciate your valuable offer, but at present I must decline the same as I am under contract with Mr. Pat Chappelle, and I have no desire to give up my job here for several reasons.
> First. I am a black man, and I am interested in anything that a black man has, and will do all in my power to make it a success.
> Second. I have been with Mr. Chappelle for over four years, and have always found him to be a perfect gentleman; he is always ready to help his people in any way he can; he has helped me and most every one of the company. . . . My third reason is I was learned with this show . . . and I know that Messrs. Rusco and Holland would have never picked me up as Mr. Chappelle did and learn me, so I will frankly say that, if you were to offer me $20 per week, I would consider it an insult . . . and we get the money [so] the colored people do not have to go up the side fire-escape or in back door and set in the gallery to see show. They set where they pay for. I would never persuade a member of a colored man's show to join a show run by a white man, as you know that the white man bought and sold our fore-parents, and I thank the Lord to-day that there are some young Negros in the world that they cannot buy. I am one of them that Messrs. Rusco and Holland can not buy. And, as for yourself, Mr. Blue, I earnestly trust that this will be a lesson to you in the future—to hunt a black man for a white man. . . . I trust, in the future, you will try to get other people

from other places for your white bosses instead of trying to break up a colored show.¹

Williams's letter reveals that he is—and he knows he is—part of something bigger than just a popular entertainment industry. Indeed, his decision to stay or leave his Black employer held great historical, symbolic, and personal importance. He understands that he is working to create space for Black people by expanding artistic opportunities and making well-deserved money, all while demanding respect for African Americans in a way he is aware he would not have been able to do in generations past. His bold missive perhaps seems more at home in subsequent generations of Black activists, but his attitude was not an anomaly at the turn of the twentieth century. In fact, Williams reflects the sentiments of many contemporary Black circus artists. These professional men and women entered demeaning white spaces where they were initially viewed as oddities in freak show tents. Within a short time—about a generation—they developed artistries and work ethics of excellence, leading them to eventually dominate American popular entertainment while demanding the social and economic advancement of all Black Americans. Along the way, they created career and development opportunities where striving artists found spaces for self-expression and self-respect. Williams's employer, Pat Chappelle, was the epitome of this era's Black pride, artistry, and entrepreneurship. The *Indianapolis Freeman* called Chappelle the "black P. T. Barnum," but his talents transcended Barnum's, as he not only rivaled his counterpart's ingenuity and business acumen, but he also did it while Black in a segregated America. Chappelle was the son of formerly enslaved people who had helped build the town of LaVilla, Florida, a thriving African American community. His family established successful businesses in LaVilla and went into local and state politics in Florida and Massachusetts. Chappelle's musical talent was evident from an early age, and with his brothers as business partners, he organized traveling vaudeville troupes, culminating in his announcement of the formation of the Rabbit's Foot Company in 1900. His initial advertisement for the troupe called for sixty high-quality Black performers of all types and ages and promised his future employees that the company would travel "in our own train of hotel cars."² Chappelle and his brothers trailblazed in every venture they touched. That year, *Crisis*, a contemporary Black periodical, reported that Chappelle won a discrimination suit against the Louisville and Nashville Railroads, getting the Interstate Commerce Commission to rule that "Negro minstrels traveling in private cars are entitled to the same treatment as white occupants of such cars."³ During the second sea-

Ma Rainey and the Georgia Jazz Band pose for a studio group shot ca. 1924–25 with "Gabriel," Albert Wynn, Dave Nelson, Ma Rainey, Ed Pollack, and Thomas A. Dorsey. The drummer's identity is unknown. Photo by JP Jazz Archive/Redferns, Michael Ochs Archives via Getty Images.

son, Chappelle boasted that he had successfully "run a Negro show without the help of a single white man."[4] Be it vaudeville companies, parades, a baseball team, saloons and pool halls, real estate ventures, or the many other projects he undertook, Chappelle supported Black talent, encouraged African American entrepreneurship, and centered Black people.

Williams and Chappelle worked their crafts in what historians call the golden age of the circus, an era lasting from the 1870s to 1920. This period of great circus advancement is a microcosm of America and mirrors the great advances in the rest of the United States. America concurrently experienced an age of tremendous industrial growth, commercialization, increasing civic engagement, massive immigration, and overseas expansion marked by land grabbing, genocide, and Jim Crow laws. The American Gilded Age (1877–90) saw rapid economic expansion, and by the 1890s, five transcontinental railroads crisscrossed the nation. Directly following the Gilded Age, the Progressive Era (1890–1920) was a time of social activism and political reform aimed to address the problems the Gilded Age had brought about with its rapid urbanization, industrialization, immigration, poverty, and racial unrest. The idea that some groups were superior to others, once based on slavery, now took the shape of pseudoscience as a means to explain the success and failure of individuals, races, and entire social classes. According to Social Darwinism, a false application of Darwin's 1859 theory of the natural world, evolution was a natural process in society. Social Darwinists believed some races were more fit than others to function in a civilized, democratic society. These periods—the golden age, the Gilded Age, and the Progressive Era—have another name in African American history and among Black communities: it is the Nadir, the time from 1878 to 1924 during which America no longer valued Black people as slaves. It was this period when Black life became all but worthless in mainstream America, and anti-Black violence itself was an integral part of southern white culture.[5] Reactionary white supremacy, a sharp increase in anti-Black violence, and the repeal of the political and legal rights accorded Blacks during Reconstruction years characterized this period. With the 1915 release of America's first blockbuster, the maliciously racist film *The Birth of a Nation*, the Ku Klux Klan saw a revival. Race riots, lynching, and racial violence plagued American cities: white-on-Black lynch mob violence rose from seventy-four reported incidents in 1886 to over six thousand by 1950.[6] White America had an interest in the African American population: Black folks who had emerged from slavery just decades before were still needed as a cheap labor source that would help America become a world economic power. Additionally, white America reasoned that African Americans were both childlike and sensuous by nature, and therefore had a sort of primitive edge when it came to artistic expression and entertainment, and so they increasingly looked to Black people to entertain. Because of this, many reasoned, Black artists could serve up the next big dance, song, or musical style but never reach the sophistication of their European American counterparts. In the American circus, Black artists were confined to performing minstrel shows in sideshow tents. In minstrel shows, Black artists played roles that white Americans paid to see: buffoonish and perpetually failing at imitating the higher class aesthetic of whiteness. Black minstrels were loud and wore oversized suits and ragged top hats, and they spoke in puns that portrayed them as incurably uneducated.

Though it may not be a widely known site of African American civil rights triumphs to those living in the twenty-first century, the circus at the turn of the twentieth century was a symbol of progress and hope for many. It was a location to challenge racial hierarchies and promote skill, entrepreneurship, self-help, and Black culture—without the upper-class elite dichotomies defining high and low art. Supporting Black people's uplift from slavery into professional settings mattered a great deal to this generation. As I will show, African Americans used the circus in many ingenious and surprising ways. A perhaps unintended consequence of their ostracization from the big tent to the sideshow tent was that Black artists had a degree of autonomy, and from the very beginning, they began to alter and transform the industry into something of their own design. African American circus employees saw their work as economic and social uplift, as it granted some men and women more economic freedom as well as travel opportunities. African Americans in traveling circuses preceded the Great Migration by a generation, but their choices may have foreshadowed many of the aspirations of thousands of migrants who came later. This history has been largely lost through the generations, but the evidence is there—through the powerful words artists and their supporters wrote, spoke, and sang—just waiting to be discovered. In examining the careers of African American laborers, artists, and entrepreneurs, some truly amazing stories emerge—stories fraught with danger and discrimination but also with possibilities of wealth, fame, self-determination, and real joy.

This story focuses more on African American circus workers, taken in whole, but the book points to important lessons about how American power structures enable a larger system of settler colonialism and white supremacy to define citizenship and utilize concepts of race to promote white American exceptionalism, a necessary concept in the destruction of Indigenous land, people, and nations. The circus' golden age also coincided with some of the most damning policies against Native Americans. By the 1880s, white Americans largely believed that the days of the so-called Indian threat were over.[7] White reformers, politicians, and the public at large agreed that Native Americans would either disappear from the face of the earth or allow themselves to be culturally transformed into farming, Christian, Protestant US citizens.[8] The Indian Wars and subsequent devastating Dawes Act of 1887 authorized the federal government to divide Native American land into small allotments for individual Indian families and then sell millions of acres deemed as leftover lands to non-Indians, decreasing tribally owned land from around 138 million acres in 1887 to 48 million acres in 1934.[9] This period of great theft gave rise to the infamous Wild West shows, which exploded in popularity. These shows featured white America's wildly distorted portrayals of Native Americans, including bigoted stereotypes and the dying race narrative, purporting that Indigenous Americans were on the verge of disappearing. White America had a vested interest in promulgating false narratives of the vanishing Indian: Indigenous peoples possessed desirable land and resources, and popular entertainment helped spread the fiction that they were disappearing due to their inability to adjust to civilization and modernity. Equestrian and Wild West shows portrayed Native Americans as savages that must be tamed. Their ultimate defeat by the US armed forces was warranted according to this logic, and despite a damning history of violence and deception, white Americans' land-grabbing and genocide were reconciled with the American freedom ideal because Indigenous people were unwilling or incapable of using the land wisely. Thus, their disappearance was inevitable. Adding insult to injury, these shows homogenized Indigenous cultures and perpetuated the myth that all Native Americans dressed in the Sioux battle regalia, wore feathers, and performed violent war dances. Though on very different trajectories, Indigenous Americans also used this limited space to benefit their families and communities. Through travel, lecture, and media attention, Native American artists and entertainers helped galvanize a pan-Indian culture, one that the Society of American Indians worked in very different ways to create.

This work explores the world of African American and Native American laborers, artists, and entrepreneurs in circuses, minstrel and vaudeville shows, and Wild West shows. These venues were inseparable, as entertainers and laborers fluidly moved, season by season, from one to the next, and circuses were home to both minstrel shows and Wild West presentations. African Americans and Native Americans, both in the capacity of laborers and performing artists, played increasingly important roles in these industries. The main argument running throughout this book is that Black and Indigenous people were crucial to the great success of the American traveling entertainment industry at the turn of the twentieth century, and the ways they constructed their interactions with and participation in the industry opened new pathways to social, economic, and political progress for themselves. Although participation in various traveling companies supported white supremacist ideologies of racial hierarchy, their perseverance, activism, resourcefulness, and skills greatly benefited their communities in practical ways. The circus helped coalesce national identities for Black and Indigenous peoples, resulting in explosions of cultural and political expression, including the Harlem Renaissance, and the strengthening of a burgeoning pan-Indian identity. Ideas about Black and Indigenous people also played into notions of gender and respectability. As I will show, both African American and Native American women carved out places for themselves in the postbellum American circus, as blues queens in the ever-popular Black sideshows and as crafters, living exhibits, and family support laborers in Wild West shows. As they built successful careers, disseminated

Black and Indigenous culture, and fought for racial equality in unique ways, they humanized traditionally racist American popular culture. This spreading of culture in the circus industry was a crucial element for the Indigenous and Black people who attended shows across the country and created a large fan culture that provided an important foundation for the recording industry of the 1920s.

Another argument in this book is that the circus provided the social and economic means to sustain robust communities of color in America's heartland. Ragtime historians have shown how turn-of-the-century African American traveling acts were havens for various kinds of performers from musicians and magicians to aerialists and jugglers.[10] Dance-band work, for instance, was attractive to working-class Black men and women who might otherwise have had to push a broom somewhere at a much lower wage, given the economic constraints imposed by racism. Hattie McDaniel, the first Black woman to win an Oscar, echoed these sentiments. McDaniel, who had established an all-Black female traveling minstrel show before her movie acting career took off, famously said, "I'd rather play a maid than be one. Why should I complain about making $700 a week playing a maid? If I didn't, I'd be making seven dollars a week being one."[11] Some circus folks expressed similar sentiments when working with big companies such as the Sells Brothers Circus and the Great Wallace Circus. The Sells Brothers in Ohio and Wallace in Indiana utilized a ready pool of low-wage labor and available lands on which its employees could create and sustain communities and raise their families. Despite racist policies that severely limited their ability to gain education, stable employment, and professional careers, African and Native Americans persisted in the region. I center communities in Miami County, Indiana, and Sellsville, Ohio, from the 1870s through the 1910s to show how the availability of labor catalyzed growth and how the loss of labor dramatically changed the communities. In these two circus towns, African Americans and Native Americans built communities across the nineteenth century, provided the necessary start-up labor for large circus communities, and used circus opportunities to their individual and mutual advantages. In the cases of the Sells Brothers and Wallace brands, employment opportunities for Black and Indigenous people declined after the first decades of the twentieth century. The Black community of the Sells Brothers Circus responded to outside pressures by relocating. The Miami community of the Hagenbeck-Wallace Circus endured financial hardships and continued to lose land, although they remain a presence in current-day Indiana.

This book dialogues with scholarship in many fields, but its most important contributions will be to the fields of Black American history, Afro-Indigenous studies, and circus history. Currently, there are no other monographs that explore the lives of African American and Native American circus artists and laborers. A growing literature looks at the shared histories of Native Americans and African Americans. The "first" and the "forced," these histories of Native Americans and African Americans are inextricably linked. Historians have explored the shared histories of slavery, government policy, education, and Afro-Indian families. The growth of the railroad circus at the turn of the twentieth century reflected and perpetuated American attitudes toward continental expansion and empire building, immigration and class, scientific racism, and gender norms. As Janet Davis observes, the circus in its golden age was bound up in, and pushed forward, the social, cultural, and economic forces that made America modern.[12] The political theorist and American Indian studies pioneer Vine Deloria argues that performance employment might have saved some Native Americans from undue pressures of farming and harsh treatment that many others faced. Many Native Americans used traveling entertainment to gain higher levels of freedom, learn more about the rest of the nation and the world, and operate as a transnational educational platform.[13] Although many of these roles were based on racial stereotypes, Philip Deloria argues that American Indian performers used racial "expectations to gain entrée into positions in which they were able to participate in shaping the particular form of the modern."[14] Wild West scholar Joy Kasson argues that Sitting Bull, who performed frequently in Buffalo Bill's Wild West Shows, would not have chosen the performance over the hunting life. However, given the circumstances and the choice between entertainment and farming, Sitting Bull chose the former. This life afforded him opportunities that were unavailable to him elsewhere.[15] Within the circus and other limiting spaces, Indigenous artists created pockets of dignity for themselves. In doing so, they subverted racial hierarchies and opened doors that were closed to people of color in other professions.

I reference several circus companies throughout the book and place special emphasis on the Sells Brothers Circus and the Great Wallace Circus. The Ringling Bros. and Barnum and Bailey Circus, in its various permutations, has been the focus of several scholarly and hobbyist studies. However less frequently remembered, there were other shows that traveled the nation that were just as influential and beloved during the circus' golden age. The Sells Brothers Circus and the Great Wallace Circus had several variations in name but nevertheless were giant shows in their own rights. The brothers—Peter, Ephraim, William Allen, and Lewis—enjoyed a reputation that admirers characterized as practical, honest, resourceful, and most importantly, up-by-their-bootstraps hard working.[16] The Sells were an influential family long before they established the circus in 1872. In early March of that year, they thanked their loyal business patrons and announced the inaugural tour of the new "Sells Brothers' Quadruple Alliance, Museum, Menagerie, Caravan and Circus, which will take the road about April 20th, giving its first performance in this city."[17] The *Ohio State Journal* gave a warm welcome to the endeavor, proclaiming, "The Sells Brothers' Quadruple Combination is a home institution which will without doubt be creditable to Columbus enterprise. Much money and time has been spent in perfecting the circus organization and collecting animals for the menagerie department, and they ought to have an encouraging start on their travels when they pitch their tent in this city on Saturday next."[18] On April 26, 1872, the paper exclaimed, "We look for a decided sensation . . . on the inauguration of the Sells Brothers' QA [Quadruple Alliance] in this city to-morrow. [The] Sells are well known in Columbus as industrious and energetic in whatever they undertake."[19] The Sells Brothers Circus became one of the greatest circuses of all time and toured for thirty-five consecutive years. During the first five years, the company traveled as a wagon show and made the leap to rail in 1877. With their expansion, they included elephants and Wild West shows, and they hired minstrel acts and Jubilee Singers; they also established winter quarters, called Sellsville, outside of Columbus. In its first decade, the Sells Brothers Circus carried a sideshow that featured a Black band with minstrel and jubilee-style shows. In addition to the six-member Black sideshow band, shows in the 1880s advertised the Georgia Minstrels and Jubilee Singers, a one-man act called E. Duprey, the "White Moor," and a Ute equestrian show that performed under the main show tent.[20] When the show went international in the 1890s, they carried an eight-piece Black band and other African American performers to Australia, New Zealand, and Hawai'i. On average, the Black-managed minstrel show carried ten performers, including a six-piece band. With leader Solomon White, the sideshow band was paid eighty dollars per week with each performer averaging eight dollars per week. By contrast, musicians in the white band who performed in the show's big tent earned ten dollars per week. In 1904, industry legend P. G. Lowery led the eighteen-piece band in the Sells Brothers Circus sideshow.[21] By 1905, the company was under the management of James Bailey, who dismantled the circus and dispersed Sellsville.[22]

Contemporary African American artist Aminah Robinson (1940–2015) painted a vividly personal illustration of Sellsville. Her pieces, such as *Life in Sellsville* (1871–1900), recall her family's experiences in the former circus town and their subsequent move to the Black community known as Blackberry Village. Her work is witness to the stories Sellsville residents passed down to her about life in and around the circus, and she mixed those stories with her own memories of later incarnations of the Sells circus (at that time under the management of the American Circus Corporation and based in Peru, Indiana). "As a young child," she wrote in a reflection on a Sellsville piece, "I would see the Sells Circus unload from the train . . . we would get out of school to help them unload." Robinson's art points to the pride and joy in the African American residents who lived there. However, Robinson also conveyed the hardships faced in later years when the circus came under new management and forced employees to find other work and housing.

Although several circuses and similar traveling shows wintered in Indiana throughout the nineteenth and twentieth centuries, none were as popular or successful at the time as Benjamin Wallace's circuses. Of all the traveling entertainment based in Indiana, no company dominated the railroad circus business or employed as many performers and laborers in the late nineteenth and early twentieth centuries as the Great Wallace Shows.[23] In 1881, Wallace's livery business was a stopover for traveling circuses, and he claimed it to be the "largest livery stable in Indiana."[24] In 1883, Wallace acquired all the assets of a traveling circus when he foreclosed on a failing company that could not pay its livery bill. Wallace bought the animals and equipment from other circuses that were downsizing or going out of business.[25] In 1884, Wallace and Company's Great World Menagerie, Grand International Mardi Gras, Highway Holiday Hidalgo, and Alliance of Novelties hit the road, touring by wagon through Indiana, Southern Ohio, Kentucky, and Virginia. By 1886, the Wallace show traveled by rail, and by 1892, it had outgrown its stables and moved to the new winter quarters on a nearby 220-acre farm, previously owned by Indigenous Miami people, who then went on to work for the circus. In the 1891–92 season, Wallace hired his company's first all-Black sideshow troupe, The Black Hussar Band, which toured with him from 1892 to 1897 and intermittently from 1897 to 1913.[26] From that season forward, he maintained a Black band and other African American acts, including comedians, minstrels, clowns, and vocalists.[27] Many of these acts worked for Wallace for several seasons, enjoying stable employment, national publicity, and relatively safe passage throughout the United States. With a mind on expansion in 1907, Wallace purchased Carl Hagenbeck's circus to combine with his own show. A period marked by a devastating trainwreck followed by a disastrous flood marked Wallace's retirement, but circuses continued to winter on the Wallace compound for generations.

## Chapter Descriptions

Chapter One. A Circus World: 1870s–1920s America

Chapter 1 reinserts African American and Native American labor into a compact historical overview of the American circus. The chapter puts the circus into the context of other contemporary forms of commercial entertainment, such as the medicine show, world's fairs, Wild West shows, and minstrel shows, a venue that first featured white actors in blackface makeup but came to feature African American artists. The transcontinental railroad changed all parts of American life, including circus work and culture: the number of companies on the road, the size, the range of attractions offered, and the number of jobs created all were impacted and increased. Black music, dance, and art culture made advances that still reverberate around the world. Spaces outside circus lots became locations to buy and sell Black food, crafts, jewelry, and clothing. Native Americans' contributions were critical in creating Wild West culture, but white Americans commercialized and used it to make the claim that Native peoples were disappearing from the American landscape. This rigid role made it nearly impossible for Indigenous people to assert the kind of influence on the industry that is seen in Black communities.

Chapter Two. For Good Treatment, Equal Justice, and Sure Salary, Give Me the Circus: Black Musicians Reinvent the Circus from the Inside Out

Chapter 2 explores the talented African American musicians who spread early blues, jazz, and popular dances through sideshow and minstrel work. After the Civil War, African Americans burst onto the American music scene. Like never before, they took jobs as musicians, started community bands, ensembles, and choirs, and used their artistry as both side hustles and as major forms of income. But they did not stop at simply performing music. Artists became managers and show owners, using sideshow companies as springboards to create rich opportunities. For Black performers, this often meant careers as entertainment producers and entrepreneurs in vaudeville and minstrel shows. The minstrel show, local theater, the blues tent, and circus sideshow were all intertwined for these artists, who smoothly transitioned from one venue to the next as the exigencies of the industry guided them. The most lasting contribution, however, was to the blues and to jazz, as many sideshow artists spread the sounds and dances of the blues and early jazz era and moved from circus tents of the 1910s to the recording studios of the 1920s. The stars of the circus blues and jazz tents were both well-known bandleaders and the blues women who would become some of America's first blues recording artists. The Black sideshow was crucial in the development and dissemination of early ragtime, blues, and jazz music. By 1910, every major touring circus company had a Black sideshow band.[28] By 1920, the term "jazz band" was synonymous with the circus sideshow band, and newspapers claimed that circus audiences were "jazz crazy."[29] This chapter argues that African American circus musicians built strong networks, were crucial to the popularization of Black music, and forged pathways from circuses and minstrel shows to the recording industry of the 1920s. This chapter also suggests that the culture built in and around circuses was a crucial element of Black fan culture and the promotional industry that echoes even into the present day. Black circus artists navigated their way through white supremacy culture and African American respectability politics of the day by being excellent in their fields and creating supportive alliances with Black newspapers across the country. Their grappling with these issues presaged the Harlem Renaissance generation of artists, leaders, and spokespeople to take up instruments as well as the struggle toward equality.

### Chapter Three. His Skin Is Dark, but He Will Come Out on Top . . . or Know the Reason Why: Black Labor in and Out of the Tent

Chapter 3 details various forms of African American circus work, ranging from skilled performance artists, also called *kinkers*, to manual laborers. For these men and women, golden age railroad circuses provided opportunities to travel across the country decades before the peak of the Great Migration would take them away from southern agricultural and domestic work. The traveling circus industry created a variety of jobs and had diverse approaches when it came to hiring Black workers. Some were directly related to the circus, including performers, laborers or roustabouts, horse drivers, porters, and animal trainers. Others were supportive personnel and ranged from carpentry and farming to food production and animal breeding. As Jim Crow bigotry became the norm, circuses excluded Black artists from main tents. Kinkers not associated with show bands after the turn of the century had trouble finding work, but a few managed to eke out a living bouncing from circus to vaudeville acts to minstrel shows and to whatever kind of travel or local work they could find. Work in unskilled labor was also quite precarious. Although the most likely job for a Black man in the circus was unskilled labor, there were occasional positions as porters, drivers, animal trainers, carpenters, and blacksmiths, and work in food production and animal breeding. Complicating this dynamic was the violence that Black artists and roustabouts faced both from outside the circus and from inside the circus from hostile coworkers.

Chapter Four. But Simply a Man Normal in His Environment: Indigenous Americans, Wild West Shows, and Taking on the Vanishing Race Narrative

Chapter 4 explores Native Americans' roles as Wild West Indians and other circus performers. The Wild West show phenomenon has its conceptual roots in America's Indian Wars as well as perceptions of other peoples across the globe whom Americans and Europeans perceived to be uncivilized. This chapter explores representations of Indian show warriors and their implications for the white supremacist imagination of the late nineteenth and early twentieth centuries. This chapter argues that circus and Wild West shows reflected and re-created racist and imperialist representations of Indigenous peoples even as Native American people themselves created ways to amplify their voices through travel with the shows, appearance on lecture circuits, and by gaining great artistic skills. Wild West shows were owned and managed by white men, and Native American performing artists were never able to wrest control from these owners as African Americans did in some ways. Dehumanization of a static, uncivilized, dying culture was the primary objective in Wild West shows. Indigenous performing artists were often at odds with middle-class thought leaders who criticized their involvement in these demeaning exhibitions. However, Indigenous performers gained access to national and international travel, educated Americans while on lecture circuits, and helped create a national pan-Indian identity that would, in conjunction with groups like the Society of American Indians, influence the creation of the American Indian Movement.

## Chapter Five. Hidden in Plain View: The Circus Towns of Columbus, Ohio, and Peru, Indiana

Chapter 5 shows how circus work enabled African Americans and Native Americans, in many ways, to hide in plain sight from racist interference of neighboring whites, allowing them to work, raise families, and participate in a version of the American dream. The Sells Brothers Circus winter quarters was a thriving community that employed hundreds of people. African Americans in Sellsville built institutions and created self-supporting networks once they had access to employment. Through nontraditional work in an industry known for its theatricality, Black Americans built a community that embodied the American working-class ideal. When the circus town folded, the Black community lost its structure, and many residents relocated or were forced to move into segregated, low-income housing. Next, the chapter turns to the small but organized Indigenous Miami community that persisted in Indiana, despite the devastating removal policies that other Indigenous villages faced across the Old Northwest. Here, Native American laborers used the circus winter quarters to remain in their homes, hiding in plain sight and maintaining stable employment opportunities. Miami people's legal victories, which leading families shrewdly negotiated, enabled their continued presence in the late nineteenth-century Midwest. From the 1880s, the Great Wallace shows, later renamed the Hagenbeck-Wallace Circus, maintained quarters among the Miami community until 1913. This chapter shows how Native Americans used circus employment in their neighborhoods to create a broader range of economic and cultural opportunities.

When I first embarked on this journey to uncover the lives of African American and Native American traveling performance artists, I almost immediately hit a bump in the road. Planning my first trip to a major American circus archive, I called ahead to announce my upcoming arrival. The conversation went well until I said that I would be researching Black and Indigenous people. At that point, the archivist laughed and said, "Why, there were no Black or Indian people in the circus!" Only slightly discouraged, I responded that I would be coming just to see what I could find. Interestingly, within those archives was a small treasure trove of material on African Americans and Native Americans. It was in no way a comprehensive look at the subject, but it provided many fruitful leads. How the information of what was housed in the archive had escaped the archivist's knowledge, I am unsure. But I have a strong guess: Black and Indigenous peoples' histories are often written out of American history books, and this history was no different. Whitewashed and forgotten, these stories can not only give Black, Indigenous, and people of color a sense of their own contributions to the United States but also give all Americans a fuller and more truthful understanding of our roots as a diverse nation—a nation that would not exist without people from many cultures and races, especially the original caretakers of the land and the millions of Black people who literally built the country and made America a world superpower. And that is the main argument of this book: that though routinely written out of histories, circuses were important to African Americans and Native Americans and, by the same token, African Americans and Native Americans were crucial to the rise of the American circus in its golden age. As in all other aspects of American life, Black and Indigenous people were present, sometimes as participants, sometimes as leaders, but always the vanguard, as creatives, creators, and catalysts for progress that pushed America to a more honest appraisal of itself.

CHAPTER ONE

# A Circus World
## 1870s–1920s America

Before the arrival of the mammoth circus during its golden age (1870s–1920s), advance men plastered towns with thousands of magnificent, colorful posters announcing the coming of the much-anticipated show. Once on location, shows gave a free but majestic parade down the main throughway of the town. This great circus day parade was important to both the townspeople and the circus company itself. First, it was advertising for the show: circus impresarios knew that townsfolk judged the quality of circuses on the grandeur of their parades. The parade allowed townsfolk a glimpse of the exotic sites and exciting sounds that they were in store for if they were lucky enough to have a ticket for the big show. Even more, it was a holiday for towns and cities across the country. Schools let out, and places of business closed for the day so that everyone could partake in this most wondrous of events. The parade itself was a breathtaking exhibition. Bizarre animals from around the world were on display. Elephants, rhinoceroses, giraffes, and hippopotamuses inspired amazement and awe. Big cats, clowns, the circus band, minstrels, dancing ladies, men on horseback, and grand pageant spectacles stirred feelings of patriotism, childlike wonder, and historic heroism.[1] Outside the circus, long, snaking lines welcomed those who had not bought tickets in advance, and once inside the showgrounds, crowds wandered around a tented city that could cover as much as ten acres.[2] On the noisy midway, vendors sold lemonade, snacks, roasted peanuts, and candy. Game booths enticed patrons with gaudy prizes, and dime shows promising nude women lured men to "Gentlemen Only" cooch shows.[3] The sideshow tent opened to a band—increasingly a Black band during the circus' golden age—and so-called freaks of nature, which were both a big part of circus publicity and one of the reasons it was not always considered family friendly. The standard sideshow usually included some combination of "born Freaks" and those who made themselves unusual by tattooing or developing a rare skill. Also on display were snake charmers and other novelty acts and "exotics" from around the world, such as "Fiji cannibals" and Zulu warriors.[4] Next, audiences made their way to the menagerie tent, often attached to the big top, where patrons saw big cats, bears, llamas, pigs, horses, chimps, peacocks, and a wide assortment of animals both indigenous to North America and from the far off lands of Africa, Asia, and Europe in displays that were considered educational even by local religious leaders. The beginning of the main event was marked by a grand march of animals and performers into the big tent. The procession was followed by an array of spectacular artists performing death-defying trapeze stunts, trampoline and gymnastic feats, stilt-walking, clowning, juggling, and dazzling animal acts. The concert, or after show, which often charged an additional fee, consisted of minstrel shows, Black bands that were barred from the main tent show, and rambunctious Wild West exhibitions. When all was said and done, audiences went home, and circus workers began to prepare for another day of wonder and spectacle.

The American circus was an amalgamation of several different types of spectacle and performance, including equestrian acts that dated to European circuses and newer American attractions that evolved during this ever-commercializing period of US history. In its broadest form, the circus incorporated into its oeuvre dime museum curiosities, the minstrel show, vaudeville, Wild West shows, animal menageries, a variety of specialty acts, and freak shows. Unsurprisingly, the circus was the most popular form of public amusement in the United States from the early nineteenth century until the dawn of the television era.[5] It grew from single-building productions during the evolutionary era to small wagon outfits in the antebellum era to the great railroad spectacles of the circus' golden age. Often neglected in the many generations of circus literature, from memoirs to academic works, are the contributions of African American and Indigenous American peoples. In the 1920s, the Black circus artist and wire-walker Frank Kirk complained that the full history of the circus was not being told. He added, "Why not write these interesting things without waiting to make a controversy out of it?"[6] Kirk lamented the vast number of African Americans in the industry who could not get long-term jobs or were not acknowledged, supported, or promoted by the majority of circus owners. Black and Indigenous performers were in circuses from the very beginning of early America. Through music and minstrelsy, equestrian shows, and Wild West exhibitions, Black people played important roles in helping shape the circus world. As the nineteenth century progressed into the twentieth, Black and Indigenous performers were largely pigeonholed into certain aspects of mainstream American circuses but left their marks despite those limitations. Simultaneously, Black music, dance, and art culture made advances that took the country by storm and reverberated around the world. Native Americans' contributions were great, but white Americans commercialized and utilized them in entertainment differently as a way to show a people disappearing

Sells-Floto Free Street Parade. Circus World–Wisconsin Historical Society.

Wallace Parade at the corner of Broadway and Canal, Peru, Indiana, 1901. Courtesy of the Miami County Historical Society, Inc.

Carl Hagenbeck entrance banner. Circus World–Wisconsin Historical Society.

Barnum and Bailey's Supernatural Illusions, "A Novel and Entrancing World of Magic Art," 1893. Circus World–Wisconsin Historical Society.

from the American landscape, making Indigenous people's influence on the industry a more fraught and challenging endeavor.

The roots of the American circus reach across the Atlantic to England, where Philip Astley is widely considered the founder of the modern circus in 1768. Astley was a cavalryman who fought in the Seven Years' War (1756–63) and was called one of the finest horse handlers of his generation. Upon his discharge from the military, Astley and his horse, Gibraltar, performed trick riding in London in the 1760s. By 1768, Astley brought in musicians, juggling acts, clowns, and acrobats to cover the interludes between the horse riding acts in his trick riding displays, built an arena for his performances, and charged admission.[7] With this combination of acts, the modern circus was born, positioning trick riding as the central element.[8] A little over two decades later in 1792, John B. Ricketts introduced the first large-scale, multi-act circus to America. Ricketts, a Scottish trick rider, opened a riding school in Philadelphia and began exhibitions, which were a precursor to the great American circuses of later years. He performed equestrian acts for the first month of his operation and then employed several performers later in the spring of 1793, including a roped dancer, a balancing and juggling act, and the equestrian pantomime. Ricketts is said to have met President George Washington at one of his performances in 1793. In this legendary show, Ricketts toasted the health of "The Man of the People" and met the approval of President Washington.

With such accolades, Ricketts emphasized the wholesomeness of his act and aimed at the broadest possible audience. He asked parents to bring their children to the circus. His efforts were successful; the *Federal Gazette* and *Philadelphia Daily Advertiser* reported on May 17, 1793, "There never was any place of polite entertainment so generally esteemed by all ranks of people as this circus, which has been crowded with, from six to seven, and sometimes twelve hundred spectators, old and young, grave and gay; every day since it has been opened, and every person goes away perfectly satisfied and delighted."[9] From 1793 to 1800, Ricketts went on to perform in every major eastern American city, erecting circus buildings as he toured. Although he increased the spectacular elements of his productions, his programs always maintained some equestrian character. Using this strategy, Ricketts proved that a variety show produced on a large scale could attract a steady audience while competing with established theater companies.

African Americans were involved in American circuses from the beginning, and they excelled in their careers. An equestrian and acrobat, "The Young African," also called Pitre or Peter the African, appeared in circus advertising in 1807,[10] and in 1811, he was one of three circus trampolinists.[11] A contemporary of Pitre, Master Duffee was an early Black equestrian and vaulter. He was an apprentice on the Pepin & Breschard Show in 1809 and worked with Cayetano Mariotini's group on the East Coast in the spring of 1810; he returned to New York City in time to rejoin Pepin & Breschard for the company's opening on June 21.[12] In publicity bills, Duffee is shown leaping over a hoop and whip, dancing the hornpipe, and dashing around the ring on the tips of his toes. In August 1815, Master Duffee was with a small troupe performing in Chillicothe, Ohio, where he "rode on his head with his feet in the air" and executed the "Lion's Leap" through a hoop and over two swords. During his career, he traveled from the East Coast to as far west and south as New Orleans, where he performed on his trick horse, Colin.[13]

The antebellum wagon circus and small-scale rail shows were different in character and in target audience from Rickett's largely equestrian performances. These new shows leaned more toward the variety of performances, such as clowning and freak shows, that were once interludes between horse acts. In 1825, New York circus men J. Purdy Brown and Lewis Bailey introduced the canvas tent, the first ever to house a circus.[14] In 1834, at least five companies simultaneously carried the first known bandwagons. Street parades also evolved during this period into a major component of Circus Day, and circus bands were popular and greatly anticipated. In 1847, the circus chariot appeared, and circuses added ornamental bandwagons. The famous steam calliope made its debut in circus parades in the 1850s. First emerging in the 1830s, the early railroad circuses were smaller than their wagon show counterparts because rail travel was difficult and expensive in the antebellum period. Prior to the movement toward gauge standardization that began with the Pacific Railway Act of 1863, the 66,171 miles of railway track in the United States were of twenty-three different gauges, and transporting stock and equipment from the railroad to the circus grounds was a time-consuming process. Moreover, all railroad expenses, including wages for the train crew, had to be paid up front—very different from the wagon shows, which had their own transportation and had fewer advance expenditures.[15] Nevertheless, several railroad circuses traveled on two cars: one a sleeping car, the other a baggage car with animals, both wild and tame, several small cage wagons, seats, tents, and other equipment.

In the five decades following the Civil War, the American circus industry experienced tremendous development in the number, size, and quality of circuses and the range of attractions offered. This change was ushered in by the completion in 1869 of the standard gauge transcontinental railroad, which made it possible for the American circus to become a coast-to-coast operation, beginning with the first transcontinental tour of Dan Castello's Circus and Menagerie. With rail cars adapted to circus needs, companies carried a wider variety of animals, performers, and equipment, allowing the shows to become bigger and more elaborate. Trained wild animal shows came into being in this period, and the enlarged big top gave performers more room to maneuver; this allowed circus acts such as the flying trapeze artists to increase their troupe size and expand their repertoire. The railroad circus also created numerous jobs. Some were directly related to the circus, including performers, laborers or roustabouts, horse drivers, porters, animal trainers, calliope drivers, and musicians. There were also jobs in supporting trades such as carpentry, blacksmithing, farming, costume design, tent making, food production, animal breeding and capture, and printing. In addition, the biggest circuses maintained their own railcars, railyards, and rail operators. The largest circuses relied on a wide variety of industries, employed hundreds of people, and influenced local economies as they passed through towns and cities across the country. The railroad also altered the territories in which circuses fought for market dominance. In his memoir of his days as a bareback rider for the Sells brothers, Orin L. Hollis wrote that in the 1873 season, the company traveled by wagon and limited its tour to Ohio and Kentucky. That season, the show covered 1,741 miles.[16] With the transformation to rail travel in 1878, the Sells Brothers Circus expanded its territory in the Midwest and sometimes ventured farther south and east. During the 1884 season, for example, the show covered 11,537 miles by rail from Columbus to New Orleans. Expanding overseas in 1891, the Sells took their company to western states, then to Hawai'i, New Zealand, and Australia. During that season, the company covered 41,145 miles over land and sea.[17]

Though the 1880 federal census failed to record the extent of Black artists in show business, the 1880s was a decade of heightened popularity for Black minstrels and there was a dramatic increase in the size, number, and quality of these Black companies. There were better educational opportunities for African Americans, and minstrel companies were able to hire better-trained musicians who could read and write music. Almost all the companies carried a band and an orchestra. Black companies also shifted their focus in the 1880s from depictions of plantation life to a wide variety of entertainment that included dramatic actors for one-act sketches, comedians, wire-walkers, acrobats, magicians, ventriloquists, hoop rollers, jugglers, trick skaters, and cyclists. This new industry focus created demand for a wide variety of Black performance artists. The increasing emphasis on the one-act sketch had opened more opportunities for Black actors to develop their abilities in writing, scoring, and staging, all of which would be required to produce the first Black musical comedies that appeared at the end of the 1870s.[18] Through these developments, several Black showmen emerged as national stars, achieved great monetary success, and began touring Europe, the Pacific, and Africa.

The Gilded Age and Progressive Era were epochs of exhibition, and circuses were just one venue that allowed Americans to take pride in the nation's economic and territorial expansion, view new artistic and material resources, be fascinated by tremendous feats of strength and human ability, and gaze upon the so-called exotic. This was the heyday of public expositions, festivals, and extravaganzas: regional, national, and world's fairs presented the wonders of the modern age to large numbers of paying attendees. Exhibitions crisscrossed and dotted the American landscape: world's fairs and exhibitions, medicine shows, animal menageries, race plays, freak shows, magic shows, Wild West shows, and minstrel shows awed audiences in big cities and remote towns alike. The biggest and most successful circuses brought together as many of these popular forms of entertainment as possible. These exhibitions often included and influenced each other, but the real glue that bound them was white supremacy. At each of these venues, crowds got the unified message that there was a racial hierarchy and that white Americans occupied the top echelon.

World's fairs and exhibitions, for instance, did not travel; rather, they remained in their grandiose locations around the country for months at a time. Crowds of spectators—nearly 100 million between the mid-1870s and 1916, to be specific—visited these exhibitions throughout the country in cities such as Chicago, New York, Saint Louis, Atlanta, San Francisco, and Omaha.[19] World's fairs created and re-created popular racial imagery. They drew upon and reshaped other sources of entertainment such as the menagerie, the minstrel show, the circus, and the Wild West show. World's fairs purported to be as educational as they were entertaining. As with so many American institutions, Black people navigated the rocky terrain of racial bigotry while creating spaces for themselves. Though world's fairs blatantly promoted racial hierarchies, African American artists had some opportunities to appear before the American public while maintaining their professionalism and dignity, both in white shows and in all-Black extravaganzas. P. S. Gilmore's World Peace Jubilee was in Boston in 1872, and 1876 witnessed the celebration of the centennial of American independence; exhibits included a plantation scene featuring Black folk songs by formerly enslaved and freeborn Black singers. The 1893 celebration of the 400th anniversary of the European discovery of America in Chicago attracted more than twenty-seven million people. August 25 was designated "Colored American Day" and included the tenor Sidney Woodward, the mezzo-soprano Desseria Plato, the poet Paul Lawrence Dunbar, and the violinist Joseph Douglass, Fredrick Douglass's grandson. Just two years later, the all-Black extravaganza, *Black America*, presented an outdoor pageant with five hundred casted performers and sixty-three male quartets. It was a musical and financial success.

Racial hierarchy was on display at the minstrel show, America's first and most popular form of entertainment from the nineteenth century. This tradition lasted into the mid-twentieth century, though relics of it are still seen in modern movies and television shows. The minstrel show consisted of a variety of skits, dancing, and musical performances that demeaned and dehumanized African American people. These shows, starting in the 1830s, were first performed by white actors in blackface makeup. After the Civil War and into the golden age of the circus, more and more African American actors, barred from other stage work, began performing in blackface. These shows categorized Black people into damaging stereotypes such as Sambo, Zip Coon, Uncle, Mammy, Jezebel, and Sapphire. Sambo is a perpetual child, incapable of the adult world, and Uncle and Mammy lovingly cater to white people's every need. The Zip Coon stereotype is a lazy, easily frightened, inarticulate buffoonish character. Jezebel is lascivious by nature, and Sapphire is emasculating, loud, rude, stubborn, and overbearing. The stereotypes that minstrel shows portrayed were some of the only "contact" many whites had with Black people and culture. Put together, they were dangerous, dehumanizing, and wildly popular. By the 1910s, many circuses had their own minstrel show acts in their sideshow tents, and many of these shows traveled as stand-alone acts. Although the minstrel show perpetuated horrible stereotypes about African Americans, it served a great purpose for white Americans; that is, the minstrel show assisted in maintaining social order, reassuring white people that they were on the top of the social hierarchy and that Black people would forever be inferior.

A typical minstrel show of the era started outside the tent with an open-air concert and a ballyhoo, a boisterous, attention-grabbing demonstration. Inside, the show started with a tambo-and-bones-style show. These often featured comedians, comic songs, instrumental numbers on the violin

Furber and Williams's "He's Up Against the Real Thing Now," 1898. Music Division, The New York Public Library Digital Collections

and banjo, ballads, and a pair of characters—Mr. Tambo, on the tambourine, and Mr. Bones playing the bones or a pair of clappers. The second part of the show was the olio, or medley, which consisted of individual acts that concluded with a hoedown in which every member did a specialty number while the others sang and clapped. The third part was often a musical farce comedy. African American minstrel performers, while working in blackface, became successful purveyors of authentic contemporary Black vernacular music and dance. They gradually transformed the stereotypes of minstrelsy into vehicles for the development of racial self-referential humor and the advancement of modern African American popular music.[20] Louis Chude-Sokei writes, "The notion of minstrelsy and its discourses of authenticity were so formalized and institutionalized that the very notion that a black performer could *outperform* a white performer in a white form such as minstrelsy was unimaginable. Yes, the idea that a *Negro could play a Negro better than a white man* was both ludicrous and heretical."[21] The idea that blackface performers could benefit African Americans seems contradictory on many levels. However, when viewed in terms of a labor market, African Americans emerged as victors in an industry that at one time both demeaned and excluded them from performance roles. Black minstrel performers featured representations of non-American Black characters in exotic cultural spaces, usually Africa or the Caribbean. The presence of Black-on-Black cross-culturality in minstrel shows slightly predates W. E. B. Du Bois's pan-African conferences and Marcus Garvey's pan-African movement in Harlem. These African American performers impersonated African and Caribbean peoples and reimagined Africa as a creation of Black popular culture without white Americans' associations of backwardness, primitiveness, and superstition.[22]

Black sideshow performance artists performed alongside so-called human oddities and sideshow staples, such as fat ladies, human skeletons, and conjoined twins. Though they remained in the sideshow tent, Black acts became anticipated components of major circuses. During the decades following Reconstruction, the Black sideshow companies worked hard to make their trade a staple in the industry. The band generally performed on a high platform directly behind the sideshow tent entrance, so that only a thin canvas separated it from the outside public. Circus managers did this to entice visitors inside. The number of Black and Native American entertainers grew exponentially in the latter decades of the nineteenth century. With the addition of the Black sideshow band, the Wild West exhibition, and the concert (or after-circus show), it was now the music of the Black bands that encouraged people to pay the higher entrance fee to attend the circus.[23] Ticket sellers were generally positioned in close proximity to the band on the other side of the canvas. The band stage was also used for the minstrel and vaudeville acts, which, along with the band, performed continuously throughout the day and night. The sideshow, also called the annex company, rotated band performances with stand-up comedians, jugglers, and other performance art to keep a continual cycle of onlookers entertained. Although some Black performers wrote to the Ringlings to inquire about employment in the early decades of the twentieth century, the only known Black performer they hired before 1920 was "the Nubian," who was part of the great Charles and Ernie Clarke riding act in 1917. The advantage the Nubian had was that he was presented and marketed as an exotic, foreign Black man, not an African American, whom white circus artists may have more readily accepted.

African Americans of the Gilded Age and Progressive Era displayed their own cultures on circus day outside the circus lot as well. From foodways to crafts to music, Black circusgoers set up itinerant stands to sell foods, drinks, liquor, games, jewelry, and clothing, and they provided a host of other goods and services, including musical performances.[24] This area, like the circus itself, was filled with the sounds of proprietors shouting their wares, calling to people to buy their products. This "outside show" was often as spectacular an event and as socially interactive as the circus itself, and the cultural exchange was immense.[25] African American stands ranged from simple cloth-covered tables to elaborate wooden-framed booths with canvas awnings. Whiskey stands, popular among consumers of all backgrounds, sold liquor from tables where customers purchased drinks by the cup.[26] In some towns in the South, the Black majority could not buy from the stands inside the circus itself,[27] but the popularity of the Black-run stands, which could number in the hundreds, especially in the South, impressed circus proprietors and managers. In the 1895–96 season, for example, the Ringling Brothers Circus dedicated several pages of its route book to descriptions of Black patrons and their circus stands in various towns across the country.[28] Accounts by white circusgoers also described the sights, sounds, and tastes of the Black snack stands and testified to the racial mixing that occurred.[29] African Americans, who were often bound to their locales or were too religious to enjoy the circus itself, found a social space in the outside area around these stands, and circus proprietor John Robinson noted that the visiting, or social interaction, done at snack stands by African Americans was just as important to the Black population as the circus itself. Here, Black people interacted with hundreds of others who came from miles around to see circus activities.[30] The activities around the show exposed everyone involved to a wide range of peoples and cultures from across the country, and audiences included a wide cross section of American society.[31] For many circusgoers, the sheer variety of people on a show lot made it a noteworthy experience, and through all this social mixing, circuses and other tented shows became places where African American cultural traditions were affirmed.[32]

Indigenous Americans experienced a very different reality when it came to entertainment and the American imagination. Unlike African Americans who were in some ways able to steer representations of Black people toward the positive and the modern, Native American entertainers would be stuck in American popular culture as a vestige of what was and largely saw their cultures mocked and fabricated in medicine shows and Wild West shows. Medicine shows capitalized on America's stereotype that Indigenous people had great knowledge of herbs, botanical cures, and all things natural and close to the earth. These shows flourished in the 1880s and 1890s after the Kickapoo Indian Medicine Company and Hamlin's Wizard Oil Company

"Negro Snack Stand." *Ringling Brothers Route Book, 1895–1896.*

"Negro Snack Stand." *Ringling Brothers Route Book, 1895–1896.*

"Negro Hotel."
*Ringling Brothers Route Book*,
1895–1896.

established factories on the East Coast. They sent out up to thirty troupes each to sell their products and entertain small-town America. Medicine shows ranged in size, from two-person shows to productions containing several tents of musicians, dancers, actors, minstrels, and comedians. They followed generally the same format. The show began with a ballyhoo, or call to begin, which might have included a parade or a concert. The show went on to feature a comedian or a comical play. Next, the so-called doctor would appear and give a lecture on the pills, tonics, and other recipes he was peddling. Finally, the troupe gave the sales pitch wherein they sold as many items to the townspeople as possible.[33] In all of these forms of traveling entertainment, owners and managers hired racial and ethnic minorities to create the most exotic and unique show for audiences. Native Americans and African Americans were often hired as ballyhoo men, those who called attention to the start of the show through songs, jokes, and instrumental music. Not all medicine shows included Indigenous people, but many falsely claimed that the members of their troupes were authentic. The acts were invented for entertainment rather than for disseminating Indigenous cultures.

With the golden age of the circus came the advent of the Wild West show, and many circuses, encouraged by the success of these events, added larger and more magnificent displays of Native American riding, skills, and culture. Though earlier shows, like the P. T. Barnum-produced buffalo hunt held in

*A Circus World* 29

New Jersey in 1843 and the increasingly popular rodeo, hinted at Wild West exhibitions, William "Wild Bill" Cody was the first to fully capitalize on popular fascination with the West. American expansion had begun a century before and was reenergized by the completion of the transcontinental railroad. No venue captured this sentiment more directly than the Wild West show, which celebrated the conquering of the western frontier and the expansionist designs of white Americans. They were open air shows from the 1880s to the 1930s that depicted archetypical cowboys and Indians—both real Native Americans and actors—who traveled with circuses and as stand-alone shows. Despite the ideological implications of these shows, Native Americans willingly took part in the Wild West shows. Much like Black Americans who participated in minstrel shows due to lack of work elsewhere, many Native Americans saw shows as an opportunity and chose to display parts of their cultures to white audiences over facing the dire conditions on impoverished reservations.[34] Hundreds of Native Americans worked for more than one hundred Wild West shows from the 1880s to the 1930s.[35] While employed, they traveled nationally and internationally. This afforded them sightseeing opportunities, often comparable or sometimes better wages than they could make in reservation jobs, and the opportunity to bring their families on the road.[36]

Native Americans, too, gathered at circuses and Wild West shows. American Indian actors, crafters, and artists met with Indigenous showgoers after performances. Native American groups sometimes traveled several miles to attend tented shows. The *Indianapolis Freeman* reported that in Chamberlain, South Dakota, Indians had made a large encampment for two days waiting for the circus.[37] In 1896 in Ashland, Wisconsin, a local paper reported that Bill Cody's Wild West show was an opportunity for peacemaking between some historical enemies, the Lakota employees, and the 500 Ojibwa attending the production. Cody and the federal agent with the Ojibwa helped arrange a meeting, at which the Native people held a powwow and smoked the peace pipe. The route book observed that it was the first time in almost forty years that "these two old enemies have met on friendly terms."[38]

## Conclusion

A 1902 *New York Clipper* article reveals the excitement around the arrival of a circus and the reverence afforded the circus operations. It compared the era's mammoth circuses to a militaristic feat of great industry and resourcefulness and conjured images of the Industrial Revolution and American growth, development, and expansion. The article announced that there would be "an army of mechanics and laborers" at Madison Square Garden that would "get the place in shape for the great Forepaugh-Sells Bros.' Circus." From the anticipation of the street parade that would "be one of the most gorgeous pageants ever seen in the metropolis and will rival the Mardi Gras procession of New Orleans," to the eagerness surrounding the grand entry, the *Clipper* article boasted that this would be the most "imposing spectacle of the kind ever attempted."[39] The article went on to say that the "impression of a well-oiled machine was no stranger to the Sells Brothers" because the "whirr of industry resounds throughout Sellsville . . . , and in every department, from dawn till dark, there is the greatest activity in making preparations for the opening of the approaching season." The article marveled at the "Great Twentieth-Century Colossus" and reported that a visit to Sellsville was "like a visit to a great naval plant when the preparations for the late Spanish-American war were at their height."[40] This imagery positions the Sells brothers, and indeed all the great circus impresarios, for comparison to the great leaders of industry of the Gilded Age and Progressive Era. The militaristic precision, the expansiveness, the hard work put in by countless workers. These images reveal the power of the American railroad circus at the height of its popularity. Although the circus began as an equestrian exhibition, by the mid-nineteenth century, it had become much more than a trick horse show. Over the nineteenth century, the circus transformed into a transnational popular amusement that evolved into a distinctly American cultural form. The majority of American circuses were small railroad operations or wagon shows, but the largest and grandest among them were characterized by transcontinental railroad travel, sprawling three-ring canvas big tops, some of which could hold over ten thousand people, a parade, grand entry, sideshow, menagerie, and the after-show concert, all held in tented cities across the country. During the last decades of the nineteenth century and the first decades of the twentieth century, the circus symbolized an age of opulence and magnificence that grabbed the imaginations of rural and urban folk across the nation. During this golden age, circus performers were household names, circus posters covered city walls, and traveling exhibitions by circus impresarios such as P. T. Barnum, James Bailey, and the Ringling Brothers attracted millions of spectators a year.

It is common knowledge that as the United States expanded its railroads, American circuses expanded their scope in all directions across the United States and eventually around the world. But another phenomenon, lesser known, was at play. As American circuses extended their range, so too did

African American and Native American entertainers of all sorts travel to every part of the country and exponentially grow their audiences. During the golden age of the circus, every major circus operation had a Black band and minstrel show, and many had some form of Wild West production. For African Americans, this meant that at every stop along the circus route, audiences of all varieties and colors imbibed the latest African American entertainment, from trapeze artists and acrobats to comedians, jugglers, and musicians. As the subsequent chapters will show, the circus industry conveyed different messages about Black and Indigenous peoples' involvement in the shows of the golden age. African Americans made a mark in the early republic and remained an important role as purveyors of the latest music and dance. Their art ushered America into the Jazz Age, albeit while facing limitations of racial prejudice and nasty stereotypes. Indigenous peoples were relegated primarily to Wild West shows and other roles that reinforced narratives about savagery and the disappearing, uncivilized Indian. These ideologies were reflected in each of the components that constituted the golden age of the circus.

None of these areas of entertainment had a more profound effect on the American cultural landscape than the music performed in these tents. Indeed, not only did the work of Black circus musicians pave the way for the blues and jazz scene that produced groundbreaking Black recording artists, but circus work served as both a music academy and launch venue for many artists. They honed their craft, composed the lyrics and melodies of hundreds of popular tunes, and built professional networks, all while disseminating Black music to town after town across America and eventually, the world. Similarly, Native American entertainers—trick horseback riders and actors—traveled with circuses and Wild West shows that increasingly crossed the nation and the globe. Wild West showmen recruited Native American performers to lend legitimacy to their displays, but Indian performers were not helpless victims. They created spaces for Native Americans to educate white Americans about their cultures in ways the showmen did not always control.[41] The result was that circus managers, eager to meet the bottom line and fill their own coffers, inadvertently made way for an extremely talented and inventive generation of artists who seized somewhat precarious opportunities to spread their cultures and change the world.

CHAPTER TWO

# For Good Treatment, Equal Justice, and Sure Salary, Give Me the Circus

*Black Musicians Reinvent the Circus from the Inside Out*

There was real magic occurring inside the circus sideshow tent. Just a generation after the Civil War, African Americans burst onto the national and international music scenes. In various burgeoning styles and increasingly varied venues, Black musicians claimed an industry from which slavery and racial oppression had once barred them. Black artists built careers in the new context of the postbellum era in minstrel shows and a wide variety of other interconnected entertainment spheres. Eventually, all of America came to be steeped in Black music. In the circus, Black sideshow musicians brought the music and dance of the wider Black world to eager attendees on a daily basis. In 1910, an *Indianapolis Freeman* reporter wrote, "Have you noticed that nearly every circus on the road has a colored aggregation taking care of the sideshow? Dear colored performer, please take care of the opportunity given you and don't squabble yourself out of a job."[1] Black sideshow work could be lucrative for skilled musicians, was extremely competitive, and for many, was a godsend in terms of opportunities for African American musicians to develop their talents. Similar to classical artists—from musicians and dancers to architects and sculptors—Black traveling show artists set aside time for local musicians, providing lessons on both the business and artistic side of the industry. In the classical music world, these sessions would be referred to as "master classes." Classically trained Black musicians would have been familiar with this tradition, and newspapers advertised these events with pride and excitement. In 1913, an *Indianapolis Freeman* correspondent referencing the bandleader extraordinaire P. G. Lowery and his training at Boston's prestigious New England Conservatory of Music noted, "P. G. always freely shares his schooling, which he paid very dearly for in Boston."[2] Lowery's sideshow band solidified its reputation as a traveling conservatory for Black musicians that built credibility, respectability, and community among African Americans across the country. These artists were crucial to the development and dissemination of early ragtime, blues, and jazz music. By 1910, every major touring circus company had a Black sideshow band.[3] By 1911, the *Indianapolis Freeman* reported that there were at least four hundred musicians and other performers in Black circus bands and minstrel acts nationwide. By 1920, the term "jazz band" was synonymous with the circus sideshow band, and newspapers claimed that circus audiences were "jazz crazy."[4] Audiences of all colors and backgrounds came to expect Black sideshow bands at prominent circuses and Wild West shows. Black women participated in circus minstrel shows as callers, dancers, and, very importantly, blues singers. These musicians' influence reached beyond the circus. Many famous jazz men and blues queens of the 1920s got their starts in minstrel tents and sideshow productions. As the twentieth century progressed, African American women found their niche in blues tents, concert halls, and eventually, the record industry. This chapter argues that African American circus musicians developed styles and built strong networks that expanded the boundaries of an already established tradition of Black musicality and created pathways from sideshows and other tent shows to the recording industry of the 1920s. This chapter also suggests that the culture built in and around circuses was a crucial element of Black fan culture and the promotional industry that echoes even into the present day. To build this Black fan culture, African American circus artists navigated through white supremacy as well as Black respectability politics of the day by being excellent in their fields and creating supportive alliances with Black newspapers.

Black circus bands emerged from a long tradition of African American musicians. Among other enduring and culture-shifting musical traditions, Black Americans had established an excellent band tradition before the Civil War when almost every town had its own military-style band. Each Black Civil War regiment had its own band, of which several developed into highly celebrated groups. For example, Joseph Anderson (ca. 1816–73) trained regiments of bands during the Civil War, and Pedro Tinsley (1865–1921) kept the tradition alive, leading his own Tinsley's Colored Cornet Band during the 1880s. Black male instrumentalists dominated the concert stage, and the most celebrated was Thomas Green Bethune, widely known as Blind Tom. Black boys' brass bands were popular in the 1890s; one of the first was the Brister's Boy's Band out of Cincinnati. Society dance orchestras were perhaps more common than brass bands in the postwar years. There were also philharmonic societies, musical associations, chamber ensembles, and choral groups. Countless itinerant and local Black musicians played organ or piano in churches, opera houses, dancehalls, pubs, and any local events needing musical accompaniment. Black composers at the 1897 Nashville Exposition contributed over 450 compositions to the Negro exhibit. Afro-Caribbean practices that persisted in children's play included chants and verbal contests and the use of simple instruments such as the diddley bow and other single-stringed bowed instruments that had changed little since their transition to the Americas from central Africa.[5]

Black musical styles in the postbellum period reflected the multiple forces influencing African American life in the latter part of the nineteenth century. Many Black churches, for example, continued the practice of the ring shout, a form of musical and kinesthetic religious celebration that includes call and response, dance, and Indigenous African and Christian influences. Other Black congregations rejected the ring shout and adopted the European-influenced worship music of middle-class churches. Formerly enslaved people continued to sing about their experiences, but many Black spirituals were simplified, keeping only hints of the pentatonic scales, syncopation, and heterophony that were characteristic of traditional southern Black singing.[6] The groundbreaking Fisk Jubilee Singers, the first African American vocal ensemble to appear in a formal concert setting, simplified traditional spirituals and arranged them in multipart harmonies that reflected European classical music as part of their project to replace the minstrel stereotype with dignified Black performances. At the same time, African American artists built a parallel tradition of secular popular music and stage shows that encouraged African Americans to associate music less often with the church.[7] Prison songs, for example, arose from the disproportionate number of Black men behind bars after the Civil War. Railroad songs, the most famous of which was the "Ballad of John Henry," also abounded, reflecting the impact of the railroad on Black people. On the concert stage, the last quarter of the nineteenth century saw the rise of several Black prima donnas who gained international fame; the Hyers Sisters, for example, were among the first of these post–Civil War rising stars. Several male artists also won critical acclaim, including Sidney Woodward, a concert tenor who made his 1893 debut in Boston. However, male singers at the top of their fields generally found it more difficult to succeed in the concert world than their female counterparts, so they were more likely to join ensembles, minstrel troupes, or touring concert companies.[8]

Following quickly on the popularity and success of ragtime, other new styles of nonreligious music were brewing in Black America, and African Americans were turning up to support their favorite artists as they never had done or could have done before. By 1910, the blues was the most sought-after secular music in the African American rural South.[9] The blues initially featured an individual with instrumental accompaniment, typically a singer playing a guitar. The singer's inventiveness was a hallmark of the blues: the songs are subjective and relay the singer's perceptions of and reflections on the world. The vaudeville circuit was a huge factor in the commercialization of the blues. The Theater Owners Booking Agency (TOBA) was established in 1909 by S. H. Dudley, a pioneering African American theater owner; TOBA's new white owner, Milton Starr from Nashville, later reorganized and expanded the company in 1920.[10] TOBA maintained a network of theaters for Black audiences in the South and sent a variety of road shows along the circuit throughout the year. Some performers expanded their tours beyond the South and visited the Northeast, Midwest, and West, but the so-called chitlin circuit remained central to their careers. Performers criticized TOBA for low pay, poor accommodations, and arduous travel schedules, and they famously described its acronym as standing for "Tough on Black Asses." Nevertheless, TOBA gave artists steady work, and for African American audiences, the constant stage offerings provided regular exposure to some of the most talented Black dancers, musicians, and comedians. Female blues singers were among the leading attractions on the TOBA circuit. This structure provided some safety for women performers on and off the stage, as well as a regular income and commercial promotion. In the South and elsewhere, TOBA raised Black America's expectations for high-quality entertainment and provided fertile fields for future innovations and entrepreneurs in African American music.[11]

The 1870s through the 1890s were especially momentous decades in the history of African American music: for the first time, popular performers created their own stage identities as Black composers, and producers mounted their first major stage productions.[12] The Hyers Sisters kicked off the era of the Black musical comedy with *Out of Bondage* in 1876 to great success, foreshadowing the popularity of these types of shows in the last quarter of the nineteenth century. *The South Before the War*, with a mostly Black cast, made its New York debut in 1893 at the London Theatre.[13] *A Trip to Coontown*, the first show written, directed, and performed exclusively by African Americans, appeared on Broadway in 1897, then in 1898 came *Clorindy, or the Origins of the Cakewalk* and *In Dahomey* premiered in 1903. Typically, a big show opened each year in New York or another large city, then went out on the road to play cities, towns, villages, and hamlets all over the country in the same fashion as minstrel troupes, medicine shows, and circuses. Most locales, no matter how small, had an opera house where productions could be staged and a village square for the concerts that advertised the shows.[14]

The postbellum shift from white-owned minstrel companies to Black-owned companies was a game changer for Black talent. Having placed a

Tuskegee Institute Glee Club and Orchestra. The New York Public Library Digital Collections, https://digitalcollections.nypl.org/items/510d47de-4d37-a3d9-e040-e00a18064a99.

For seven years the Fisk Jubilee Singers gave concerts in this country and in Europe and secured funds sufficient to erect Jubilee Hall. The New York Public Library Digital Collections.

foot in the door of entertainment, Black artists began the process of humanizing their characters and bringing their own flare to the industry. Vaudeville and minstrel companies such as The Smart Set, Littlejohn's, and the Russell Brothers employed hundreds of Black artists and were the trailblazers of Black entertainment companies. Charles B. Hicks, whose career probably started in circuses and white minstrel companies before the end of the Civil War, organized the Georgia Minstrels in 1865. Often identified as white because of his light complexion, Hicks is generally credited with being the first to introduce Black entertainers into the mainstream of American show business.[15] Besides the Hyers Sisters from California and the Fisk Jubilee Singers, the Luca family toured the northern states before the end of the Civil War. Both circuses and Wild West shows drew from this growing pool of Black talent to develop Black sideshow acts. Importantly, the appearance of African American blackface minstrels signified a shift in popular entertainment created for and by African Americans. Black artistic communities coalesced around musical performance and re-created popular entertainment by infusing into it the exciting new rhythms of ragtime and blues music. Musicians performed the latest ragtime, blues, and jazz tunes. There were reports of the blues in vaudeville acts as early as 1910, but documentation of blues singing under minstrel show tents was not in widely distributed Black newspapers until 1914.[16] This music reflected the excitement and cultural change of the era. Ragtime in particular signaled a cultural shift in America from the relatively rigid behavior and morality dictated by the Victorian middle class toward more relaxed social relations and, in some white circles, toward a new respect for African American music.

## Bandleaders

African Americans in the postbellum, pre-Harlem generation dispensed ragtime, blues, and band music culture and formed a bridge from the era of demeaning, white-written "coon" songs to the era of "race records," which paved the pathway for African American vaudeville, Broadway, and film employment.[17] The fabulous successes of the Black recording industry were due to the hard work and dedication of talented artists, and sideshow bandleaders made important contributions as well. As sideshow acts increased in popularity and size, bandleaders gained more prominence and were responsible for advertising new positions for Black musicians and educating and training them in the skills of running a successful sideshow business. Bandleaders continuously placed ads in national Black newspapers, including the *Indianapolis Freeman*, the *Chicago Defender*, and the *Kansas Herald*. Industry journals and race papers could not ignore the skill the new generation of Black bandleaders brought to the craft, and they closely chronicled these men's careers. In forging new industries and creating new Black businesses, traveling entertainers were a source of pride for Black audiences who attended their performances and read news updates about them. In 1891, the *Indianapolis Freeman* reported that in Columbus, "The past week has been one of enjoyment among the colored people of this city. The first thing occurring was one of the most successful concerts we have attended for quite a while. Those taking part in the concert were . . . a band organized for the purpose of traveling with Sells' Brothers circus."[18] The Sells band and its accompanying ensembles included a star lineup of African American musicians from around the country.

P. G. Lowery's (1869–1942) lengthy career as a musician and bandleader in many ways exemplified African American ingenuity and perseverance inside the circus industry around the turn of the twentieth century. He was born in Kansas to a musical family and received his first instrument, a drum, as a young child.[19] He was classically trained at the New England Conservatory and became the first African American to graduate from that institution. In adulthood, he both collaborated with circus managers and fought their unfair policies. He built several successful and highly popular traveling circus annexes and sideshows. Most notably, he educated hundreds of Black musicians while he kept multiracial audiences in awe of his expertise on the cornet and as a band director. In 1890, under contract with the Sells-Forepaugh Circus, Lowery hired a company of twenty-three musicians and performers to create a band and minstrel department. His success with Sells opened doors for many other Black circus performers, as other circuses followed suit. By 1911, the *Indianapolis Freeman* celebrated Lowery and the business he had inspired:

> The present outlook is that there will be more circuses carrying colored companies this season than ever before. Most of the circuses offer engagements to both ladies and gentlemen in their band and minstrel departments. This branch of the profession was first introduced in 1899 by Prof. P. G. Lowery with the Forepaugh-Sells circus in Madison Square Garden, New York, New York with a company of twenty-three musicians and performers. He then opened an avenue that is now offering engagement to over four hundred musicians and

performers. Previous to this time the circuses only carried a band of not exceeding ten pieces.[20]

Although Lowery was not the first Black sideshow bandleader, he was crucial to popularizing the Black band and making it an expected and beloved part of the American circus experience. For several years, he divided his time between his own companies, the Sells Brothers Circus, the Great Wallace Shows, and eventually the Ringling Bros. and Barnum and Bailey Circus. Circus managers valued Lowery and took special steps to ensure the safety of his sideshow performers by providing him with his own rail cars.[21] In 1910, the *Indianapolis Freeman* declared, "The branch of colored show business known as circus minstrels and vaudeville had its beginnings with P. G. Lowery, the renowned cornetist and bandmaster . . . in 1899."[22] He enjoyed fame on a national level: "Since Lowery's initiative . . . no less than fourteen white tents are giving employment to big colored companies. . . . Something like three hundred people—performers and musicians—are employed in this phase of the show business. The number promises to increase."[23] The Lowery Band consisted of nearly two dozen members and sometimes grew to dozens more for important engagements. They toured with the Wallace Circus from 1905 through 1913, and by the 1913 season, Lowery was listed on the first page of the Hagenbeck-Wallace Circus route book alongside the individual "Head of Departments" as "director of the sideshow tent." Other members of the "Executive" and "Business" staff included the equestrian director, the musical director, the general press agent and representative, and the official announcer.[24] Eventually, the Black sideshow band, accompanied by a comedy or variety act, was a staple in the Wallace shows. The Lowery Band was advertised on a larger-than-life canvas alongside the main entrance "essential" acts, such as the equestrian show.

As Black sideshow acts increased in number, so did Lowery's popularity. One correspondent in Harrisburg, Pennsylvania, wrote, "The Barnum and Bailey show, also the 101 Ranch, were in our city with colored companies . . . but as soon as Lowery's band played their first number one could see a vast difference in Lowery's band and the bands with other companies. . . . When hearing Lowery's band, one can easily tell they are from the Lowery school."[25] In 1916, the *Indianapolis Freeman* asserted, "P. G. Lowery's band is known as the 'School of Music.' The best musicians in the profession are from the Lowery School."[26] Lowery became a national celebrity, and local papers celebrated his return whenever his tour brought him back to his hometown. One of the local papers bragged, "A Greenwood boy is the leader of the band with the great Hagenbeck-Wallace show which will be here next week. . . . He speaks a good word for the show and says he has an excellent band. Lowery is well known in Eureka and his musical ability is nowhere more appreciated than here. He has had the reputation of being the finest cornet soloist in the US and when he had visited at Eureka he has never failed to draw a large audience."[27] On another occasion, the local paper wrote, "Lowery now with Wallace circus writes that he expects to spend Sunday, September 20 with his mother at Reece. . . . He will be glad to see old friends. He has charge of a company known as the Dixie Minstrels and says it is a first class company with a good band."[28] Throughout his career, newspapers followed his tours closely. Lowery tended to speak very highly of the industry. He said of the circus, "Good people, good treatment, and great show."[29] In his early career, he praised the circus life and the opportunities made available to African American entertainers. Lowery asserted, "It is generally understood by the public at large that circus people have a tough time. I deny the assertion and will say for good treatment, equal justice and sure salary, give me the circus."[30]

Lowery also used the circus to create better working conditions for Black employees. In 1904, he protested the demeaning messages of the minstrel show with his own vaudeville show, which subverted common racial stereotypes. He strengthened Black management by training young leaders. Lowery also formed a labor alliance with some of the foremost Black show managers seeking to protect African Americans "by demanding first-class accommodations and keeping the salaries up to standard."[31] He was a savvy businessman and shrewd negotiator as well. In 1915 management of the Hagenbeck-Wallace Circus demanded that Black performers add manual labor to their duties, raising and tearing down tents in addition to their artistic work. Lowery refused, publicized the dispute, and took his troupe to a smaller show called Richards and Pringles' Georgia Minstrels. The Black sideshow industry leaders as well as the Black public supported his move. The *Indianapolis Freeman* provided an explanation: "He refused the engagement because the manager requested his men to double canvas. P. G. informed the manager he would leave . . . and the same was heartily endorsed by his band and every band director in the circus business."[32] Doubling canvas meant that in addition to their regular duties in the sideshow tent and on parade, Lowery's men would have doubled as roustabouts, driving and pulling stakes and getting white tops up and in order; if Hagenbeck-Wallace, by that time owned by the American Circus corporation, not Benjamin Wallace himself, had convinced Lowery's prestigious organization to double canvas,

*Give Me the Circus*

many other circuses may have followed suit.[33] Lowery's shrewdness paid off, and the Black performers' strike cut deep into Hagenbeck-Wallace's profits. At the end of the 1915 season, management asked Lowery back under better conditions.[34] A writer for the *Indianapolis Freeman* exclaimed, "I am proud to know that the Hagenbeck-Wallace management are forced to seek Prof. P. G. Lowery's services to regain the patronage of old that they have failed to get this season without him and his classy company of musicians and singers."[35] Though Lowery's perseverance and success were causes for celebration in the African American community, circus life was still one fraught with unfair treatment from inside the industry and sometimes mortal danger from the outside public at large. Indeed, Lowery's experience with Hagenbeck-Wallace simultaneously illustrates the challenges and the triumphs of life in traveling shows for people of color. In 1920, P. G. Lowery's troupe broke the big tent race barrier and became the first African American band to play for the main show in the Ringling Bros. and Barnum and Bailey Circus. Ringling, along with every other major circus, had banned Black performers in the main tent up to that point.[36]

James Wolfscale (1868–1921), born in Chillicothe, Missouri, was another sideshow musical giant who enjoyed great popularity and helped spread dance band music. His father Dennis, a formerly enslaved farm laborer, and his mother Esther, a housekeeper, raised James and his older brother and three younger siblings.[37] Before joining the circus life, Wolfscale worked with P. T. Wright and the McCall's Minstrels. Starting in 1890, he worked with Sells and Gray, Sells and Downs, Cole Brothers, Jones Bros. Wild West, the Forepaugh Sells circus, and finally, the Barnum and Bailey Circus. By 1894, Wolfscale's Algerian Band and Jubilee Singers, described as "a Zulu band of ten pieces that performed along with the freakshow," was performing for the Sells and Renfrow's Circus California tour.[38] In 1895, this Sells syndicate held its winter quarters in Topeka, Kansas, a location close to Wolfscale's own home. During the offseasons, he toured on the vaudeville circuit. In 1895, Wolfscale's band was the leading musical act with Caldwell's Minstrels. Between 1900 and 1905, Wolfscale led bands for various Sells circuses, joining Sells and Gray in 1900 and Sells and Downs from 1902–5 and surviving the Sells and Downs train wreck in 1902. In 1903, his band was called the J. E. Wolfscale Vaudeville Co., and he toured with several companies including the Jones Bros. Buffalo Ranch Wild West Show in 1911. Wolfscale quickly rose to fame after joining the Barnum and Bailey Circus and over the subsequent six years, expanded his annex show by adding comedians, dancers, and coon song shouters. His band was featured in the Barnum and

Lowery Band wagon. Circus World–Wisconsin Historical Society.

Portrait of James Wolfscale. Public domain, via Wikimedia Commons.

Bailey spectacle Cleopatra. Wolfscale's band appeared as Egyptians mounted on camels. According to the *New York Age* and the *Indianapolis Freeman*, this was the first band in America that attempted to play while mounted on the backs of camels.[39] In the 1913 season, Wolfscale's band was said to be the "most popular band in the parade because they give the people what they want, besides playing heavy marches and all the popular songs and latest rags on parade."[40] During the 1914 season, he led a 32-piece band with two parade bands in a forty-two-week season.[41] This was the largest Black band in the circus business and the crowning achievement in Wolfscale's career.[42] Wolfscale and his wife, Littela Decosta, lived in Chicago where Decosta managed Harriet Thompson, also known as Little Princess Wee Wee, a featured sideshow performer in Wolfscale's show whom the couple helped become an accomplished song and dance artist. Princess went on to join the Whitman Sisters Company in 1925 and met President Coolidge. Also accompanying Wolfscale's company in the Barnum and Bailey sideshow around the period of 1913 to 1915 was William Henry Johnson, or Zip the What Is It.[43] Barnum and Bailey cut Wolfscale's band to twenty for 1915, and this may have been the reason he threatened not to tour with the circus that summer but ultimately went back to Barnum and Bailey and kept his two parade bands.[44] When Lowery joined Barnum-Ringling, Wolfscale moved on, but the two remained friends and kept an open correspondence through the *Indianapolis Freeman*.[45] Wolfscale toured with several other companies in subsequent years, including John Robinson Circus and Leon's Southern Minstrels.[46]

Wolfscale's work was important to the dance scene in the pre-Harlem and Harlem eras. His son, Roy, who had traveled with his father in circuses, decided to go a different route for the 1916 season. He instead went on to join John Wickliffe's Ginger Band of Chicago (a jazz band), and he "was present for their historic 1916 engagements at Schlitz Palm Garden in Milwaukee and the Gruenwald Café in Minneapolis, which introduced audiences to a new style of dance music."[47] During that season, Wolfscale eliminated the minstrel show and added a vaudeville act and popular dance music. "Dance craze" songs were prominent in the repertoire, and crowd favorites were "Dancing the Jelly Roll" and "Walking the Dog." The dance music was a sensational hit, and "Walking the Dog" inspired other dance craze hits that introduced American popular culture to jazz.[48]

Although Lowery opened the doors to Black circus work via the minstrel show, other Black bandleaders moved the needle forward by rejecting the minstrel show altogether. Professor R. Roy Pope was widely known as the "Hoosier cornetist" who refused to be relegated to minstrel shows. He was a hometown hero in Indianapolis and a person who brought the Black community great pride.[49] Pope worked his way through the industry and landed a position as bandleader for the sideshow tent of the Ringling Brothers Circus. The *Indianapolis Freeman* boasted, "Although not a graduate from college, he is one of the best colored musicians on the road and a gentleman."[50] As a young boy, he came under the tutelage of musician and professor Bradshaw and was quickly declared a prodigy, first on alto saxophone and then on the cornet.[51] After that, he "elevated himself to be manager and bandmaster over a company of sixteen people traveling with the largest show on earth. He is considered the pride of Indiana, having made a good record and still maintaining the respect and good will of all."[52] In 1910, Pope was lauded as the youngest bandmaster in the circus business.[53] In 1911, one of Pope's decisions made a statement:

> The coming season, beginning in March, will bring to the profession another new idea in the musical line. Three seasons ago the Ringling Bros.' circus did not carry any colored assistants in any line. This aggregation, known as the largest and greatest on earth, will by persistent efforts of the efficient band director and cornetist, Prof. R. Roy Pope, carry an exclusive concert band without minstrel and without women. Last season Prof. Pope was the first of band masters to discard women performers and this season he takes the initiative in eliminating the minstrel part. The band will be composed of fifteen select musicians who will render daily programs, and afternoon concerts only.[54]

With the greatest number of Black circus artists on the road, Pope took advantage of the popularity and power of the Black band and moved instead to leading a singular band with no demeaning minstrel show. His decision to omit female performers most likely reflected a desire to promote a clean, family-friendly image that did not include some of the suggestive performances and bawdy, blue humor common in acts that included women. There was also a sentiment around the turn of the century among some that blues was a man's province, and women should stick to spiritual music and more domestic tasks. A few years later, this sentiment was echoed in a letter Herbert T. Meadows, amusement editor of the African American newspaper the *St. Louis Argus*, wrote to the *Indianapolis Freeman* asking, "What has become of our art?" He further complained: "We are disgusted with the burlesquing of our good women. We want no more. . . . We can get along

*Give Me the Circus* 45

without smutty and suggestive remarks. We have too much respect for our mothers, sisters and sweethearts to introduce them to this degradation. What we do want is clean comedy, good music, new songs, new jokes, and novelties of artistic value."[55] Respectability politics no doubt played a role in Pope's decision and attempt to gain more respect for Black men as true musicians, at the expense of female artists. However, this attitude would not stop the talent and determination of the era's blues queens who, despite respectability politics, rose to the top of the blues charts and garnered national and international fame.

From these sideshow tents emerged a generation of blues and jazz artists who went on to have successful recording and touring careers in their own rights. The lengthy list of jazz musicians who cut their teeth in circus bands supports the possibility that circus bands engaged in improvisation during performances. William Phillips, whom the *Indianapolis Freeman* referred to as "King" by 1909, played with touring companies throughout the teens, including A. G. Allen's Minstrels and W. C. Handy's circus band.[56] He became well known as a composer and was popular among circus and vaudeville bands. In 1915, R. Roy Pope's band featured three of Phillips's pieces: "The Florida Blues," "Eagle Rock Rag," and "High Ball Rag." Wolfscale's band also featured "The Florida Blues" in 1915.[57] From 1919 to January 1920, Phillips was a sought-after musician in Chicago, working as Sidney Bechet's replacement in King Oliver's jazz band after Bechet left for a European tour.[58] Receipt of an invitation from King Oliver, a renowned jazz musician, testifies to Phillips's reputation as a gifted improviser before 1920. Clarinetist Buster Bailey, who played with the King Oliver and Fletcher Henderson bands, remembered Phillips as "one of the first jazz clarinet players I ever heard."[59] Another clarinetist, Garvin Bushell, spoke of playing arrangements of popular songs and blues during his time in the Sells-Floto Circus: "When we arrived in a town we'd ride on a wagon for the parade and play 'Beale Street Blues' or 'The Memphis Blues' or 'The Entertainer' in fast tempo, or else some old military marches. Other bands played them two to the bar, we'd play them four to the bar. . . . We played 'Rubber-Necked Moon,' out of the Smart Set show, 'How Do You Do, Miss Mandy?', and 'Snag It,' which Joe Oliver used to play."[60] Great jazz men including Wilbur Sweatman, Willie "Bunk" Johnson, Willie Hightower, Alvin "Zoo" Robertson, and Buddy Petit all spent time touring with circuses. Decades after circus bands had faded from popularity, Garvin Bushell remembered, "There were some great black clarinet players with circuses in those days. Percy Glascoe from Baltimore was one, and Fred Kewley from Detroit was another. Outside of players in the Jenkins' Orphanage Band, Kewley was the best black clarinet player in the country. . . . Those guys had a style of clarinet playing that's been forgotten. Ernest Elliott had it, Jimmy O'Bryant had it, and Johnny Dodds had it."[61] Bushell's memories of circus clarinetists specifically associate them with later, more well-known jazz musicians, further strengthening the idea that music resembling early jazz was present in the music of Black circus bands.[62]

## Blues Women inside and outside the Tent

Commercial female blues singers were the first to become nationally known through recordings; Mamie Smith (1883–1946) was the pioneer, recording "Crazy Blues" in 1920, the third one of her songs sold to Okeh Records to become a hit. Both blues and jazz, as Amiri Baraka observes, are the results of social and psychological changes within the African American community as it moved toward the mainstream of American society. This movement tended to have very significant results: Black people's idea of America as the place to live was broadened; there was a realization by more Black people "of a more human hypothesis on which to base their lives."[63] As Angela Davis observes, like most forms of popular music, African American blues lyrics talk about love, but what is distinctive about the blues, particularly in relation to other American popular musical forms of the era, is their intellectual independence and representational freedom.[64] One of the major ways in which blues lyrics deviated from the era's popular music was their provocative and pervasive sexual—including homosexual—imagery.[65] The blues developed a tradition of openly addressing both female and male sexuality and revealed an ideological framework that was specifically African American. Formerly enslaved Americans' economic status had not undergone a radical transformation; they were no less impoverished than they had been during slavery. Emancipation, however, radically transformed their personal lives: formal restrictions on travel were removed, education was more attainable, and sexuality could be explored freely by individuals who now could enter into autonomously chosen personal relationships.[66] Therefore, it was the status of their intimate relationships that saw a revolution: "For the first time in the history of the African presence in North America, masses of black women and men were in a position to make autonomous decisions regarding the sexual partnerships into which they entered. Sexuality thus was one of the most tangible domains in which emancipation was acted upon and through which its meanings were expressed. Sovereignty in sexual matters marked an important divide between life during slavery and life after emancipation."[67] Emerging during the decades following the abolition of slavery, the blues gave musical expression to the new social and sexual realities encountered by African Americans as free women and men. Moreover, up to 75 percent of blues songs were written from a woman's perspective.[68] The representation of love and sexuality in women's blues often blatantly contradicted mainstream ideological assumptions regarding women and being in love. The poetic content also challenged the notion that women's place was in the domestic sphere and rarely made direct mention of motherhood or marriage.[69]

Some of the most famous blues women recording artists of the 1920s made their start on the Black vaudeville stage as well as in minstrel shows and blues tents. These traveling tent shows heavily influenced the big circus tents across the country. By 1920, all African American minstrel shows were expected to carry at least one blues singer, and throughout the period, every major circus was expected to carry a minstrel show, which usually included a blues singer. Although contemporary blues men often performed as blackface comedians, blues women, also known as coon shouters and blues queens, were pioneers of the record industry. Patrons in the South came to expect the blues through greats such as Gertrude "Ma" Rainey (1886–1939), who also traveled with tented troupes including the Rabbit's Foot Minstrels. Said to be the first singer to use blues as a part of her act in minstrel shows, Ma Rainey appeared in a local Georgia talent show when she was fourteen. This performance propelled her into show business. In 1904, she married Will Rainey, a comedy singer, and together they created the song and dance routine Ma and Pa Rainey: Assassinators of the Blues for the Rabbit's Foot Minstrels.[70] She was a contralto, with a deep, powerful, earthy voice that captured the mood and essence of Black rural southern life and gained her great popularity in the South. She had a straightforward style as she described the drudgery, pain, and joys of human existence. Rainey traveled with several of the most popular minstrel shows other than the Rabbit's Foot Company, including Tolliver's Circus and Musical Extravaganza, the C. W. Parker and Al Gaines show, and Silas Green from New Orleans. Paramount Records signed her in 1923, and this propelled her career again, this time as a national celebrity. Paramount announced her as "discovered at last . . . Mother of the Blues."[71] Newspapers heralded her coming, and she added northern cities to her circuit. Her gold-plated grin and gold necklaces became her trademarks in photographs announcing her arrival across the country.

Other artists followed in Ma Rainey's footsteps. The unsurpassed superstar of the blues, Bessie Smith (1894-1937) began singing for the Florida Blossom Minstrels in 1912. Smith was born in Tennessee and through her many talents became the most famous blues singer in the 1920s and 1930s. She started dancing on the tented show circuit when she was about fourteen years old and spent the next decade traveling with various tented shows, including the Rabbit Foot Minstrels with Ma Rainey and the Florida Cotton Blossoms. She joined the TOBA circuit for five years and sang in clubs in Atlanta, then New York and New Jersey.[72] The year 1922 found Smith back in the South and pursued by Columbia Records talent scout Frank Walker. She signed with Columbia in 1923 and is still revered today as the "Empress of the Blues" and one of the best singers in her generation. Her first recordings, "Down Hearted Blues" and "Gulf Coast Blues," sold a million copies within the first year.[73] Another blues queen Ida Cox (d. 1967) is a shining example of an artist who started in tented shows and went on to have a stellar recording career. Born in Knoxville, Tennessee, sometime between 1888 and 1896, Cox left home at the age of fifteen. The "uncrowned queen of the blues" got her start with White and Clark's Black and Tan Minstrels and moved on to the Florida Orange Blossom Minstrels, the Silas Green Show, and the Rabbit's Foot Minstrels. Critics and audiences alike found that she had a powerful voice. She went on to record for Paramount Race Records in the 1920s.[74] Ads in African American newspapers attest to her popularity with such hits as "Lawdy, Lawdy Blues" and "Mama Doo Shee Blues." A huge success that catapulted her career came in Jack Goldberg's *Raisin Cain*, a show produced by the latter in New York about 1927 and had its first showing at the Lincoln Theater in Kansas City, Missouri, in 1928. That year, the *Inter-State Tattler* labeled her the "Queen of Blues" and went on to report that she was "singing a mean blues show."[75] Black newspapers reported big audiences showing up for her shows: "The house was well filled for four performances of Ms. Cox and her players."[76] In a 1932 interview, Cox said, "I sing the blues because that is what the public demands."[77] And she gave the public what it demanded: her show, *Cain Raisers*, a seventeen-member group, opened in Chicago in 1926. In 1939, Cox was compared in importance to Bessie Smith: "Ida Cox, whom some critiques of modern music claim was the first great blues singer and even the predecessor of the great Bessie Smith, will have a truly merry Christmas this year" when she will "put her heart in her songs on the stage of Carnegie Hall."[78]

Contemporaries called Lizzie Miles (1895-1963) the "queen of blues singers" and described her voice as lusty and needing no mic.[79] Known as the

Portrait of Bessie Smith. Library of Congress, Prints & Photographs Division, Carl Van Vechten Collection, [reproduction number, e.g., LC-USZ62-54231].

"Creole Songbird," Miles entertained audiences from the early 1910s until her death in 1963. During that time, she sang with many of the great jazz bands, including Kid Ory, King Oliver, and Jelly Roll Morton in the top clubs of Chicago, New York, and Paris. Between 1922 and 1939, she recorded more than seventy titles.[80] Miles started singing at backyard parties when she was a young girl in New Orleans. In 1914, she joined the Alabama Minstrels. Her husband, J. C. Miles, a native of Indianapolis who had worked for the Alabama Minstrels since 1912, sent show updates to the *Indianapolis Freeman*. He wrote that the show during the 1914 season was "doing fine business throughout the Virginias, Carolinas and Tennessee. We closed our tent show season at Norfolk recently, and are now playing the finest and best theaters throughout these sections."[81] That year, Miles and her husband opened with the Jones Brothers and Wilson's Three-Ring Circus, and Miles was the only woman in the group. They toured with the Jones Circus, subsequently named the Cole Brothers Circus and Five-Car Show through the 1915, 1916, 1917, and 1918 seasons. When the circus went to the winter quarters in the off-season, the Miles couple divided their time among family in Louisiana and Indiana and kept busy with minstrel show work.[82] Her successful circus career spanned until 1918, when she became sick with that year's infamous flu, an epidemic that killed millions worldwide, including her husband. The death of J. C. was also the close of her circus career, and Miles went on to work in clubs in the 1920s.

Miles remade her image in the 1920s as seen through the many newspaper spots advertising her records and shows throughout the country. A 1922 advertisement in *Billboard* proclaimed that her song "Sing Em" was a "Sensational fox trot" with "a dance orchestra."[83] *The Negro World* featured Miles in a Victor Records advertisement among the "Special List of Blues."[84] The advert read, "Those are popular hits sung by popular colored artists who have won fame and recognition for themselves as musical entertainers. There is side-splitting comedy, dance music that won't let your feet keep still, and entertainment galore in this special list. You'll want one of every record in it."[85] A midwestern paper advertised Miles in the repertoire of Okeh Records as a race artist along with other well-known blues queens.[86] In 1924, papers celebrated, "Lizzie Miles, the Creole Song Bird, at The Capitol, makes a decided hit every time she sings 'Fooling Me,' and 'Louisiana.'"[87] She was "ever increasing her popularity."[88]

A momentous leap in her career came in 1924. The *New York Age* announced, "Miss Lizzie Miles, Creole Songbird, Plans Foreign Trip: Will Invade European Countries, with letters of Introduction from Russian Opera Singers."[89]

> Miss Lizzie Miles, Creole Song Bird of the Columbia Phonograph Company of New York and London, will soon be hailed as Mademoiselle Lizette for in a few weeks she sails for Paris, thence to the capitals of Europe and near East. Mlle Lizette, or Miss Lizzie Miles, so impressed members of the . . . Russian Opera Company with her songs . . . paying high compliments to her high degree of musical culture. PP. Andrew Salama, director of the Russian Opera Company was so kind as to give Mademoiselle Lizette as he chose to address her, letters of introduction to prominent and influential men and women living in the principal cities in Western and Central Europe, and he has been instrumental in the arrangement of her banking connections in Russia, which country is her destination.[90]

African American artists who ventured to Europe often reported back to the Black newspapers their impressions of the continent, and Lizzie Miles was no exception. She wrote her impression of Paris in the *New York Age*. She reflected, "Sightseeing is wonderful, skirts are very short," and, "The place has a liberal colored patronage despite the fact that they get French cuisine rather than southern home cooking."[91] She finished off her letter with, "All in a gay Paris."[92] Later, the *New York Age* reported that "Miss Lizzie Miles is Mont Martre's Smart Entertainer: She is on Program In Paris Cabaret with 9 Russian Singers and Dancers." Miles reported that she was singing in one of Mont Martre's smartest cabarets and had been rechristened by director Alexander Schayinsky as *Le rose noire* (the black rose). She announced she had met many people and made many friends in western Europe, and that Paris was a very nice place for one with plenty of money to come and spend a wonderful time.[93] Back in Harlem in 1925, Miles continued to grow in popularity. She performed at the Capitol Club "with her stunning Paris creations and those snappy songs that she sings" and was a "superb attraction."[94] The *New York Inter-State Tattler* carried an ad for the Capital Club in Harlem that called her show "high class entertaining."[95] Miles, along with Louis Armstrong and many other greats, performed on programs such as the Sport King's Pajama, Overall, and Gingham Frolic at the Renaissance Casino.[96] In 1932, Warner Brothers featured her in a short film.[97]

Miles made a career comeback in the 1950s along with the jazz revival that was widely taking place. One reviewer wrote that she was "going strong at the age of 58."[98] During this period, she played clubs in San Francisco and Los Angeles. In 1957, she was included in *Capitol's History of Jazz* record along with legends such as Leadbelly and "Some of Capitol Records most ambitious jazz efforts of the past."[99] At this time, the "Salty Dog" and "A Good Man Is Hard to Find" were causing a lot of excitement among fans of R&B and pop. According to *Billboard*, "Lizzie really belts it out on this side breaking into New Orleans French for some of the lyric. A good performance."[100] On October 17, 1958, she appeared on the Robby Troup Show on *Stars of Jazz* on KABC-TV in Los Angeles.[101] One *LA Times* reviewer wrote, "Lizzie is 60, and we don't know where she was. . . . She's great and sounds durable, like she'll be around a while. We don't know where she's been all our life, but we're going to make up for it . . . if we have to go to Bourbon Street in New Orleans where she sings 'Basin Street Blues' first in English and then in French and each time it's inky blue."[102] Miles's voice rang through the paper's description, "Each song was a work of art, which is to say a labor of love, a piece of the heart. . . . She's got a voice like a growl trumpet," and "Sometimes she puts you in mind of Cootie Williams; sometimes it's Louis Armstrong but it's freewheeling, like a trumpet, and has its virtuosity . . . and she's all heart, all beat, all swing, and all blues. . . . She snarls out a passage and then blows it out like Louis about to bust a gut . . . and she croons it out and wails it out, and belts it out, for sheer joie de vivre."[103] Critics in the 1950s and 1960s gave Miles much respect, ranking her with the likes of Bessie Smith, as a classic blues singer.[104] Then in 1963, "The music world lost one of the oldest established jazz stars last week with the death of Lizzie Miles in her native New Orleans."[105] During her life, she sang with a variety of jazz artists, including Jelly Roll Morton and King Oliver. Miles had a varied career but like many great jazz and blues singers, she owed her start to the circus.

The Question of Respectability

In this era, Black artists were relegated to the sideshow tent, known for its so-called human oddities: spectacles such as the bearded lady, little people, and people with physical disabilities filled the sideshow tent for circus goers to gaze upon. This tent's success was based on othering people of different races, abilities, and appearances and perpetuated ideas about the exotic, strange, and uncivilized outsider or social other. African American artists—sometimes classically trained—found themselves in this tent, classified as just another oddity to be demeaned. Some found this kind of work demoralizing and pursued careers abroad or joined army bands to display their skills. When Black entertainers began applying burnt cork in minstrel shows, they did so conscious of the social implications of their actions, fully aware that the "Negro being performed and constructed via white Blackface minstrelsy was an explicitly racist and politically unnatural fiction."[106] Instead of giving up on the American entertainment industry, they engaged in the form to erase the bigotry from within. The first African American blackface minstrels overwhelmed and overcame a white-dominated field within a relatively short period. By 1915, the most popular minstrel shows were already well-established institutions: Allen's New Orleans Minstrels originated in Chicago in 1899, the Rabbit's Foot Company began in 1900 in New Jersey, and Silas Green from New Orleans opened around 1904.

African American moral leaders, who were compelled to help lower socioeconomic Black people out of poverty and into middle-class respectability, censured blackface minstrel shows and their buffoonish, anti-Black imagery. Black leaders voiced hatred of minstrelsy from the very start of its popularity. In 1848, when performing in minstrel shows was exclusively a white occupation, the previously enslaved great orator Frederick Douglass called these performers the "filthy scum of white society, who have stolen from us a complexion denied to them by nature, in which to make money and pander to the corrupt tastes of their fellow white citizens."[107] Later in the late nineteenth and early twentieth centuries when Black Americans dominated minstrel acts, the highly esteemed author of *The Souls of Black Folk*, W. E. B. Du Bois, decried minstrelsy as inauthentic and degrading, a view many Black writers shared.[108] Herbert T. Meadows of the *St. Louis Argus* wrote that many did not criticize Black vaudevillians in their early stages, allowing time for the performers to develop and refine their art. But by 1904, it was time to take a look at the progress. He continued, "After months of fostering and petting, we find only an indolent lot of careless, unappreciative individuals, who have apparently made no progress whatever and the very fact of this lack of advancement has caused a stagnation that is becoming disgusting and driving vaudeville patrons to exclusive picture houses. The eccentric corked comedian would be an occasional pleasure, but a continuous string of these freaks with their nonsensical 'stale' jokes has become monotonous."[109] Class also played a role. African American leaders often countered anti-Black stereotypes by emphasizing class differences among African Americans and encouraged conformity to middle-class values among the lower classes.[110] Uplift during Jim Crow was a top-down social movement in which the educated Black elites felt that they carried the burden of leading the Black lower socioeconomic classes into a modern way of life and full citizenship.[111] Some Black leaders envisioned themselves as intermediaries between white and Black America.[112] Black churchwomen engaged in service projects that encouraged respectability and middle-class behavior among recent migrants from the South who retained rural or lower-class habits of speech, dress, worship, and other distinct cultural patterns.[113] In her 1904 presidential address to the National Association of Colored Women, Mary Church Terrell admonished her peers, insisting that the Black elite were not living up to their calling to uplift the less educated, lower-class members of the race.[114]

An important tool for elevating Black America was imagery, and African American leaders used photographs to create a counternarrative to popular derogatory imagery. Douglass famously sat for dozens of photographs in which he never smiled in order to display his humanity and unwillingness to put whites at ease. Subsequent images of African Americans as people of science, culture, elite education, and superior refinement challenged racism and "race science" through competing evidence.[115] Du Bois and collaborating photographer Thomas Askew organized 363 photos for the 1900 Paris Exhibition in a collection entitled *Types of American Negroes, Georgia, USA* This collection responded to displays of people of color at similar exhibitions, circuses, and fairs that advanced pseudoscientific, eugenicist, and criminological claims of racial inferiority.[116] In contrast to typical exhibits, which featured so-called native village scenes with people of color in their so-called natural habitat, Askew's photographs show a middle-class Black ideal of culture and dignity. Anchored in a patriarchal model of an African American elite and envisioning restrained and disciplined African American manhood and domestic womanhood, photographs showed Black men, women, and children in a dignified light: they were modest and reserved, often posed with classical instruments, books, and architectural props.[117]

Racial uplift and the respectability culture that grew up around it have always been contested in African American society, as creative people have pushed the boundaries of what is respectable and progressive. African American circus folk were some of the early challengers to reformist attitudes that portrayed religious morality as the only pathway to stability and middle-class respectability. They broadened the importance of Black culture, music, and the joys of having a good time. In photographs of his band, Lowery exuded pride, and throughout his career, he took dozens of photographs, both portraits and group photos that projected industry professionalism. In these photos, Black men are distinguished by their instruments and wear professional uniforms. Though minstrelsy was a part of the Lowery show, his photographs provide a stark contrast to contemporary minstrel images that did not separate the artist from the bulging-eyed, blackface character they portrayed. In Lowery's photos, actors display self-respect and a seriousness about their craft, and they do not appear in blackface. This choice humanizes and professionalizes the men who played the roles of minstrels. Three women in one photograph are soubrettes who sang every genre from opera to ragtime and challenged contemporary gender expectations. They, too, are professional musicians sitting among the uniformed men.

## Centrality of African American Newspapers

The story of Black traveling musicians cannot be told without the thousands of stories, editorials, reviews, and advertisements published in the Black press, which chronicled their careers in vivid detail. African American newspapers, often called race papers at the time, evolved inclusive perspectives on Black circus artists and ideas of respectability. Race papers educated, entertained, and created a sense of solidarity among Black people. They disseminated the information that leaders discussed at race conventions and raised issues of local and national importance that ranged from anti-Black violence to education to views on US foreign policy. *Freedom's Journal*, established in 1827 in New York City, is generally credited with being the first African American paper.[118] I. Garland Penn's *The Afro-American Press and Its Editors* documented ten race papers across the country in 1870, but by 1880, Penn identified thirty Black newspapers, including the *Indianapolis Leader* and *The Colored World*. By 1890, there were 154 Black-run newspapers.[119] In 1888, Edward E. Cooper, formerly of *The Colored World*, founded the *Indianapolis Freeman*. Cooper, the only Black graduate of Indianapolis High School in 1865, claimed that his paper was the "first and only illustrated journal of the Afro-American race."[120] The *Indianapolis Freeman* had wide distribution and grew to have correspondents in several cities across the country. Cooper aimed to appeal to Black Americans everywhere on matters of current interest and to report news from places that would have otherwise had no public voice. Penn praised the *Indianapolis Freeman* saying, "Success with it has been simply phenomenal. . . . As a literary paper it keeps pace with the educational and literary progress of the race. As an illustrated paper it portrays the Afro-American as he is, and not as so often represented by many of the white journals."[121] Other contemporary writers called the *Indianapolis Freeman* "the *Harpers' Weekly* of the colored Race."[122]

The importance of African American newspapers to the Black circus industry and the entertainment careers they fostered cannot be overstated. In addition to bringing Black news to readers across the country, the *Indianapolis Freeman* became famous as "central headquarters" for anything and everything related to professional Black entertainment—from operatic and classical musicians to circus sideshow and minstrel performers. By 1891, African American showmen called the *Indianapolis Freeman* "the Colored *New York Clipper*," the Black alternative to the most popular weekly mainstream entertainment trade paper of the era.[123] These publications reflected a variety of views on cultural expression and uplift, especially in the realm of music and performance. In the decades following Reconstruction, African American papers included entertainment news and encouraged readers to attend ballets, operas, and symphonic orchestra performances as markers of middle-class status and tools for educating children. For many educated African Americans, music played a critical role in facilitating a respectable Black culture and racial uplift. Classical music embodied the middle-class ideal of gentility and challenged white cultural supremacy by showing that Blacks, too, appreciated respectable music.[124] Black musical clubs supported Black ensembles and orchestras and encouraged African Americans to attend music conservatories in Europe. Harriet Gibbs Marshall received classical training and went on to found a conservatory for Black musicians.[125] The nationally distributed *Chicago Defender*, an influential antiracist weekly Black newspaper established in 1905, reflected some assimilationist aims in promoting excellence in European art forms to its African American readers. Cultivation of European classical music was thought to be an ideal vehicle for practicing genteel behaviors. It showed that the listener and performer were members of an elite group and instructed the less fortunate in proper values and conduct.[126] But in spite of this strong support for classical music, Black media reactions to Black sideshow musicians and other traveling popular entertainers were positive. Many editorials disapproved of negative stereotypes in the entertainment industry; however, race papers celebrated the artistic accomplishments of African American musicians and artists and created a culture of celebrity around successful Black figures. Classically trained African American musicians often found work in minstrel shows, though, as they sometimes lamented in papers, they preferred to find work in orchestras. They published open letters that described how they negotiated race during their performances, passing as white, Native American, or Latino in order to find work. When they did, and especially when they became successful or famous, editorial and entertainment writers applauded their fellow African Americans for overcoming obstacles and in some cases beating a racist system. Writers respected musicians and performing artists, whether active on the opera stage or in a circus sideshow stand. When an individual overcame adversity, Black papers lauded them and held them up as examples of race pride. The *Chicago Defender* came to reason that to support Black artists in their endeavors was, in fact, a matter of racial uplift.

Those with the highest readership—such as the *Indianapolis Freeman*, the *Chicago Defender*, the *Christian Recorder*, the *Kansas Herald*, *Negro World*, and the *New York Age*—reached millions of African Americans and served to unite disparate cultures across the country. Papers like the *Indianapolis Freeman* and the *Chicago Defender* had wide readership beyond municipal or state boundaries. Because Black Americans across the country read them, these publications became a great publicity engine that made important and lasting connections between cities, industries, classes, and Black cultures. Black papers also fed African Americans' imaginations and raised excitement about the fun of the circus. For African Americans, the circus was not just for entertainment. Black journalists wrote story after story praising Black circus artists. In doing so, they helped unify Black American culture, encouraged Black pride, promoted Black businesses and self-determination, and in all ways portrayed Black excellence. Black bandleaders advertised their tour dates, when they were hosted by the town's notable Black citizens, and what new, special treats Black audiences should expect. For their part, bandleaders also communicated with each other and with families through open letters to the paper, wrote of their challenges and triumphs, and encouraged readership. Bandleader James Wolfscale sent praise of the *Indianapolis Freeman* on more than one occasion. In one letter, he wrote, "Some of the most pleasant hours spent by the company this season were spent during the day each week we received this wonderful journal, and every professional member of our race should be proud of this paper, the greatest Negro theatrical journal of the age. May your great success continue. Prof James Wolfscale and Band, Barnum and Bailey Circus."[127] Newspaper coverage enabled readers to follow the careers of their favorite musicians and hometown heroes, creating a platform for fan culture as well as providing a medium of communication for music industry insiders. Black bandleaders used entertainment sections in papers like the *Indianapolis Freeman* and the *New York Age* to keep in touch with each other, send messages and greetings, show pride in each other's work, and share updates and planned itineraries. For example, the Bismark Ferris band went to work for Buffalo and Pawnee Bill's Wild West Show, and in 1911, Ferris announced that there were twenty people in his company, "the largest of its kind on the road" that year.[128] He wrote, "The show did a wonderful business. Among our new instruments purchased in the past week" were baritone, cornet, clarinet saxophone, snare drum, and bass drum.[129] These communications alerted bandleaders when one of their kind was having business troubles, when they were back in business, when members were in ill health, and where and with whom they would be staying on the road.

Black audiences came to understand the importance of their viewership and support of Black artists in shows through a variety of publications, but two names in the paper business stand out as real friends of the circus artist who helped to set audience expectations. Coy Herndon, a circus hoop roller who funded his way through chiropractic school, wrote the regular column, "Coy Cogitates" for the *Chicago Defender*.[130] Always a cheerleader for the race and the industry, he spoke often about his Black counterpart at the white publication *Billboard*, J. A. Jackson. Jackson, the first African American to write for *Billboard*, had a running page in each issue devoted to Black artists and musicians. He kept the page full of new performers and their movements from blues tent to circus sideshow to minstrel show to the recording industry. Jackson also applauded his friend Herndon by regularly writing articles about his performances and amazing biography and encouraging the young man to finish college and chiropractic school.[131] These two men cheered on Black artistry from their typewriters and set audience expectations by constantly reporting on the next new thing. Coy was clear about his purpose: it was much more than entertainment; he said Black artists helped Black folks "forget for a while" the pain of everyday life and experience real enjoyment.[132] Shows were for Black people to showcase their talents, educate their communities, and instill Black pride.[133] Furthermore, Coy urged Black performing artists to support each other and never say bad things about another performer or show.[134] Herndon wrote in a way that let Black readers know they had just as much talent as—or maybe even more than—white circus men. He portrayed Black show owners as "race men" who were professionally, creatively, and intellectually on equal footing with white show owners and who sometimes visited the Ringling winter quarters in Florida to discuss business.[135] He included stories about Black show owners and printed their earnings and salaries, once saying that the Silas Green show made over $150,000 (or $3 million in 2024 currency) in three years.[136] Herndon told Black people that there were alternatives to the prescribed life that society had meted out to them. When shows traveled in the southern states, he wrote that good weather meant good cotton crops, which meant money in Black folks' pockets to buy tickets and have a good time in the sideshow tent.[137] Having the pleasure of being hosted by a town's notable Black citizens—be they doctors or dentists or lawyers—was a special treat that Herndon and Jackson kept in their columns. They not only name-dropped, they advertised and applauded Black professionals for doing great work in their communities across the country.[138] Jackson's and Herndon's columns reveal that contemporary artists and entertainers understood a wide variety of tented shows as related, interconnected, and complementary of each other. Whether minstrel shows, circus sideshows, Wild West shows, vaudeville, burlesque, or the blues tent, all the Black artists smoothly moved from one venue to the next, shaping their skills to fit each new act. The columns reveal that there was ample competition from various traveling companies, and people of all races regularly packed all-Black shows.[139] Herndon explicitly encouraged Black talent, letting local folks know when musicians and artists were holding lessons to educate a new generation as they traveled, and he urged Black people to get into circus ownership for themselves. His case in point was the white rags-to-riches story of Jerry Mugivan, who started as a candy seller in a circus and went on to own the American Circus Corporation and several circuses of his own.[140] Herndon asked if a poor white man could do this, why not a Black man?

One last expectation that Black circus audiences had was that circus folk would stand up to white power, and they looked forward to hearing about those who did. Readers could especially rely on Herndon to call out white circus men who crossed the line or acted disrespectfully. In 1922, an enraged Herndon exposed a circus that broke a contract with him and his partner. Herndon wrote that his act would have been the first Black act of its kind to perform under a white circus main show tent. After signing the contract, Herndon and his partner purchased new costumes, turned down several offers to join other shows, and wasted time, money, and emotion on a company that ultimately canceled the contract due to white performers' refusal to perform under the main tent with Black men. Herndon wrote that this kind of racism—both from the bigoted performers and the show managers who capitulated to their unreasonable requests, prioritizing racist views over Black people and professionalism—was "simply an injustice that should find no approval in the circus, the most democratic institution in America."[141] Herndon went on to say, "In view of the years of loyalty the Negro has given the amusement business, the easy response of Colored musicians, performers and laborers to discipline and the long-time connection of the Negro with the show world, it is unfair for anyone to deprive another of the opportunity to follow his profession because of a difference of race."[142] In another issue, Herndon made public that Mugivan's circuses had a habit of covering up Black shows' posters in every town where they performed together.[143] Mugivan wrote back the very next week with an apology and a promise that this was not intentional and would not happen again.[144] Clearly, white show owners took Herndon and his readers seriously. In a time of high racial violence when many African Americans remembered slavery firsthand, this was a powerful show of Black power and Black pride. Black circus patrons across the country looked to these artists to entertain but also to stand up to the white power structure and embody the burgeoning spirit of the New Negro that fueled the Harlem Renaissance.

## Conclusion

Turn-of-the-century African American traveling acts were havens for various kinds of performers, from musicians and magicians to aerialists and jugglers.¹⁴⁵ As they traveled, African American performers recruited artists for their shows across the country and created networks that spanned the United States and sometimes crossed overseas. They networked for purposes of education, professional advancement, and mutual aid. Though their employers may have taken some measures to protect them against racial violence on the road, employees took their own measures to ensure safer and more comfortable travel. They created valuable connections along circus routes that made the traveling life throughout racist America more tolerable and used the circus to springboard careers. Some Black musicians used their experiences in white-owned companies to raise capital for their own shows, launch new companies, and provide safety nets for each other in difficult times.

As African American leaders fought racial discrimination and searched for venues through which to assert their voices, Black traveling show entertainers broke racial barriers as they built careers. Lowery opened the doors for Black musicians and actors in the circus, which in turn opened doors for Black artists in dance bands and the record industry. By the middle of the 1910s, blues was the major attraction that sustained the popularity of African American entertainers under the sideshow tent.¹⁴⁶ Musicians with circuses and Wild West shows were important in shaping the coming renaissance in African American culture. African American musicians and bandleaders paved the way for the boom in Black music, dance, and fan culture during the Harlem Renaissance and the many generations to come. The phonograph, also popularized in the 1890s, was an important technological innovation, helping to transform the careers of many African American musicians. Bert Williams and George Walker, for example, paid careful attention to recording as a component of their careers and were among the first performers of any race to use records to extend their fame. Black traveling performers of this era made some of the earliest sound recordings decades before the explosion of the race records associated with the Harlem Renaissance and the New Negro movement. Williams, perhaps the most famous African American minstrel performer, was one of the first Black artists on record and was the only recorded Black voice consistently available before the Harlem Renaissance. However, many musicians, both men and women, got their start in the circus and other tented shows, a testament to the importance of the industry to Black excellence in the world of Black recording. The first documented recording of an African American female singer was on February 14, 1920, in New York City. Mamie Smith had made her way up as a vaudeville and cabaret singer and sang "You Can't

Keep a Good Man Down" and "This Thing Called Love." In August of that same year, she recorded "Crazy Blues" and "It's Right Here for You." Demand for this record skyrocketed in the Black community, and Okeh Records realized there was a huge market among Black people for blues and jazz. In the summer of 1921, the company established Okeh Original Race Records, and the likes of Louis Armstrong, King Oliver, Sippie Wallace, Lonnie Johnson, and Sara Martin were recorded. The artistic seeds they planted have lasted through to the present day. Artists, bandleaders, and entrepreneurs like P. G. Lowery, James Wolfscale, Ma Rainey, and Lizzie Miles introduced America to Black star culture, without which Harlem would not have been the same, and the paths for icons from Ella Fitzgerald and Louis Armstrong to Beyoncé and Jay-Z may have been very different.

CHAPTER THREE

# His Skin Is Dark, but He Will Come Out on Top . . . or Know the Reason Why

*Black Labor In and Out of the Tent*

In 1901, Prof. Eph Williams returned to the United States from his European tour to perform with his circus, the Great Northern Railroad Show, for over 2,500 people crowded under his big top tent. This show in Milwaukee kicked off his midwestern tour and carried with it an all-Black cast with over seventy-five performers, including acrobats, opera singers, and comedians, as well as a menagerie of horses, ponies, and dogs. Ephraim Williams, an African American entrepreneur and Wisconsin native, owned several traveling troupes during the golden age of the American circus. Whether he was the first Black circus owner was under some debate: the *Indianapolis Freeman* reported that he was the first African American circus proprietor, though his *Billboard* obituary claimed that four others came before him.[1] Born in the middle of the nineteenth century, Williams had humble beginnings as a shoeshine boy and later became a bartender and barber at Milwaukee's Plankinton Hotel.[2] This was a relatively high paying job for a Black man in the 1880s Midwest. In his spare time, Williams took up horse training. Several circuses and equestrian shows wintered around and stopped in Milwaukee as Williams came of age, and as a young man, he sought out opportunities with some of these local shows. He soon became an accomplished horse trainer and magician and saved enough money to invest in his own circus company in 1885. Williams later partnered with Frank Skerbeck, a German trapeze artist and sword swallower, and opened Professor Williams' Consolidated American and German Railroad Shows in 1893. He based the show in Medford, Wisconsin, and used fifteen railroad cars during the touring season.

Williams's circuses were a hit. The Medford newspaper wrote, "It is beyond question that with the company selected for this year, Prof. Williams need not turn out of the road for any show going. . . . His skin is dark, but he will come out on top yet, or know the reason why."[3] In 1893, Prof. Williams' Consolidated Railroad Show traveled on five cars, had a fifteen-cage menagerie, and boasted fifteen performers. In 1898, with one hundred Arabian horses and twenty-six employees, Williams was the only Black circus owner in America. Business was up and down at the turn of the twentieth century. However, early on he established an all-Black tent show called Silas Green From New Orleans, which played one-night stands throughout the South. Through Silas Green, Williams worked with legends such as the blues singer Bessie Smith. By 1910, he had a new show called Professor Eph Williams' Famous Troubadours. Called "the dean of Negro showmen," Williams was worth over $100,000, not including his valuable show property at the height of his career.[4] "The Eph Williams show did turn-away business through Georgia," according to one show correspondent.[5] The *Cleveland Gazette* reported that "Mr. Eph Williams is the only member of the race engaged in the circus business. He owns 103 trained horses, besides other trained animals, and travels in the northwest."[6] Another observer wrote, "Eph Williams' Silas Green Company showed at Aiderson, West Virginia . . . giving a good performance. Some people say the white people won't go to a show owned and operated by negroes, but Saturday night there were three whites to every negro in its audience."[7] Racially mixed crowds met him across the country.

Williams was called by contemporaries the Black Barnum but surely faced issues and difficulties Barnum never imagined. To be a Black businessman with white employees in nineteenth-century America would have presented unique challenges and difficulties. Being a Black circus worker was often dangerous during this era, including in the upper Midwest where all-white communities could turn violent and deadly. At the time, Black men were largely relegated to hard labor or cast in minstrel shows that reinforced stereotypes. Williams challenged the era's norms and provided an uncommon opportunity for Black opera singers, comedians, and other circus artists. Williams died a rich man in Florida in 1921, but his Silas Green show would go on to be the longest running tent show in US history, running from around 1904 to 1957.[8]

This chapter argues that the African American artists, entrepreneurs, and unskilled laborers during the golden age of the circus found ways to open opportunities for themselves that had previously been closed. The great railroad circuses provided travel opportunities across the country and into cities for Black workers in the circus industry before the Great Migration would take them in large numbers out of the South. The traveling circus industry created a wide variety of jobs for a wide range of performers and laborers. Most, such as acts under the big top, or a show's large main tent, uniformly excluded African Americans. However, Black workers found an increasing, though still restricted, range of opportunities in some areas. During the early

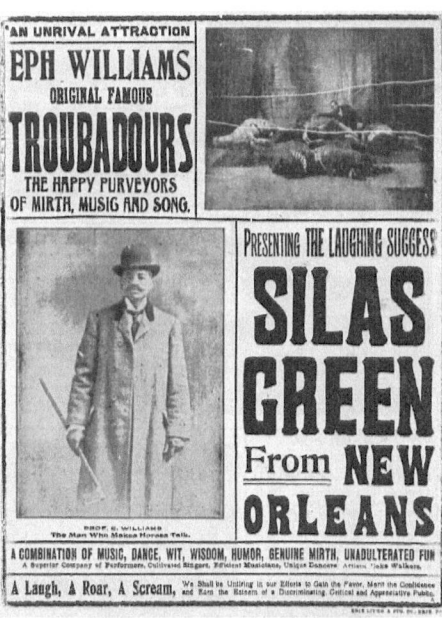

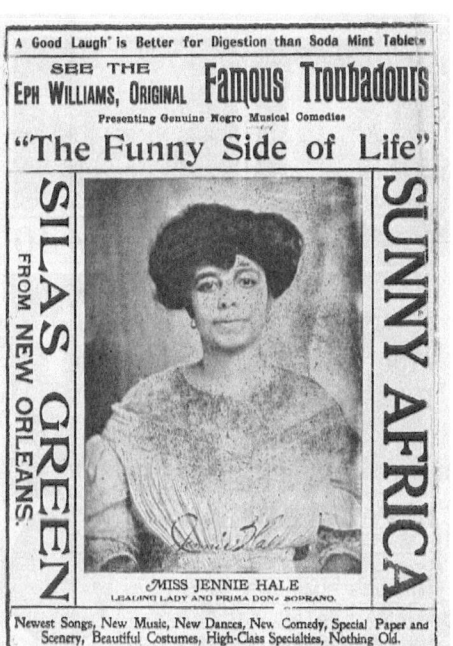

Eph Williams Original Famous Troubadours. Erie Litho & Printing Co. A courier for Eph Williams Original Famous Troubadours presents the "laughing success" Silas Green from New Orleans, "30 of the Best Colored Artists in the World," and singer Miss Jennie Hale. Circus World–Wisconsin Historical Society.

antebellum period, Black circus artists occasionally performed under main tents. As that period came to an end and Jim Crow took hold, circuses excluded Black artists from the main tents. Wanting to capitalize on the popularity of Black music—from ragtime and marching music to blues and jazz—white circus proprietors hired Black bands to play in sideshow tents, also known as the "kid tent" or "freak show tent." These bandleaders often brought entire companies with them, including actors, comedians, tightrope walkers, and a variety of performers also known as kinkers. Kinkers not associated with bands after the turn of the century often had trouble finding work, but a few managed to make a living bouncing from circus to vaudeville acts to minstrel shows to whatever kind of travel or local work they could find. Work in unskilled labor was also quite precarious, but it did exist. Although the most likely job for a Black man in the circus was unskilled labor, there were occasional positions as porters, drivers, animal trainers and breeders, carpenters, blacksmiths, and food producers. The biggest circuses maintained their own rail cars, rail yards, and rail operators and relied on a wide variety of industries. They employed hundreds of people and influenced local economies as they crisscrossed the country. The availability of positions for Black laborers, like skilled artists, depended heavily on circus managers' attitudes about race.

At the beginning of the twentieth century, African Americans across the country were engaged in a struggle for full citizenship and recognition and were against white control over employment opportunities, including in skilled work sites.[9] Some 90 percent of African Americans lived in the South in the year 1900, the vast majority of them working as domestic laborers or in agriculture, picking cotton or tobacco or harvesting rice, and highly educated African Americans discovered that doctoral degrees or upper-class associations did not guarantee careers befitting their education. Even in the more commercial and industrial regions outside the South, African Americans found professional employment in strikingly low numbers—around 4 percent in many midwestern cities, for example.[10] Access to skilled working-class employment was limited by the refusal of labor unions to admit Black members, with the result that Black men were largely excluded from the forms of industrial labor that created economic opportunity and mobility for working-class white men. The *Indianapolis World* commented on the situation: "The greatest enemy of the Negro is the trade unionism of the North. The door of every factory in every state, city and town is closed against your boy because he is black."[11] In its laws, in its labor practices, and everywhere in society, America reinforced its unwillingness to promote people of color to full citizenship or enable them to enjoy equal protection and access to the American dream.

The circus world was thoroughly embedded in and reflective of these American values, so most Black circus artists did not achieve anything close to Eph Williams's success. Instead, Black artists found opportunities in American circuses limited, and the work they did find was most often defined and circumscribed by race and by the attitudes of white audiences. In 1916, Al Wells of the Wells and Wells comedy trapeze act wrote, "Colored novelty acts have never had the chance that our white brothers have had, nor do they get the salary."[12] However, failing to find work for his African American troupe, Wells learned to manipulate white audience expectations around race to bring in business. He changed the group name to Los Cubanos, The Three Garcia Brothers. White audiences, it seemed, were fascinated by the opportunity to see "real" Cubans, and Wells's troupe worked steadily following the name change.[13] Moreover, performers maintained certain illusions on and off the stage to advance their careers and protected the racial identities of their coworkers who performed race.[14] But although the ability of some Black performers to bend racial categories helped advance their careers, over the course of the nineteenth century and Jim Crow era, Black artists had drastically fewer opportunities than white kinkers, who were seen as athletes and artists of great skill, dedication, and intelligence. And no matter how well they were received in the ring, Black performers could not escape dangers on the road as they traveled across the American landscape.

## Zulus and the African Prince

The Zulu craze in American circuses had its roots in the 1879 Battle of Isandlwana in South Africa where Zulu king Cetshwayo's troops vanquished the British. This devastating defeat of British powers by Indigenous troops possessing much less military technology fascinated Americans. There had been a long lead-up to this battle, but when diamonds were discovered in Zululand, tensions reached a new level. As white traders, missionaries, prospectors, farmers, and government officials made deeper inroads into Zulu lands, violence targeted Zulu autonomy. By the 1870s, the Zulus had become barriers to the exploitation of natural resources and the spread of white settlement.[15] As violence increased, Zulus won skirmishes and often eluded imperial troops. After their defeats, Britain poured military might and resources into the South African campaign. Britain successfully dissolved and reduced Zulu homelands, destroyed their military autonomy, attempted to wipe out their cultures, and promoted factionalism. In a generation, the Zulus became a major source of wage laborers in South Africa.[16] Zulus became a spectator favorite in the midst of the Anglo-Zulu Wars and in the aftermath of the Battle of Isandlwana, when the American press featured the exploits of King Cetshwayo's regiments in their victory over the mighty British forces."[17] African Americans as faux Zulu warriors, along with actual British units, were star attractions in the frequent reenactments of the battle of Rorke's Drift, another major engagement from the Anglo-Zulu War. This reenactment, at a time when western European nations were in the midst of conquering virtually all of Africa, was a celebration of white British imperialism that symbolized European victories over African states during the ongoing scramble for Africa."[18]

Circuses displayed Zulus in the freak show tent as representatives of primitive cultures. In this context, the shocking displays of alien cultures perpetuated a narrative of Indigenous people as freaks.[19] Americans took their cue from the British when it came to depictions of Zulu warriors. In British images of the Anglo-Zulu War, Zulus, much like the British soldiers' horses, are depicted "with dark skins, bulging eyes, flared nostrils and elongated, muscular limbs."[20] Although the British army appeared in the press as an orderly, cohesive, well-disciplined unit, Zulus often appeared as part of the African landscape.[21] In displays and exhibitions across the United States, Zulu warriors embodied the image of the Black brute, a caricature that became increasingly popular after the Civil War and extremely popular after the debut of the virulent racist film *The Birth of a Nation*. This caricature played on and contributed to stereotypes of Black men being sexually ravenous needing to be tamed and civilized. In 1893, the southern essayist Charles H. Smith argued that Black men could not help but attack white women and children, writing, "A bad negro is the most horrible creature upon the earth, the most brutal and merciless."[22] His contemporary Congressman Clifton Breckinridge also argued that the Black man was "the worst and most insatiate brute that exists in human form."[23] The effects of this stereotyping were extreme violence against Black communities, resulting in thousands of anti-Black lynchings during this period.

P. T. Barnum offered Queen Victoria's government $100,000 to exhibit the captured King Cetshwayo for five years. The queen was not amused and did not agree to this proposal. However, W. C. Coup's United Monster Shows put three of Cetshwayo's nieces (whom he billed as the chief's daughters, true Zulu princesses), a baby, another Zulu chief, and twenty-three warriors who had surrendered to British authorities in South Africa on display.[24] This attraction was a hit. Soon, just about every circus showman incorporated a Zulu act. Later, in the 1880s, Barnum called for people of all the "uncivilized" races in existence to appear in his show.[25] One person to enthusiastically answer this call was American-born Canadian William Hunt, also known as "The Great Farini." Hunt, a circus performer and promoter of human exhibitions in Britain, brought Zulus to the United States. Barnum's wish was fulfilled. He billed Zulus and Australian Aboriginal peoples as the "last of the living cannibals," along with Native Americans, Muslims, and others who performed in a number of exhibitions.[26]

But there were not enough authentic Zulu warriors to go around, and many African American performers were dressed in something approximating white people's distorted perception of how an African warrior looked. In fact, circus man Gil Robinson observed that most of the Zulus who were exhibited with traveling shows were manufactured.[27] These men faced dangers ranging from their true identities being exposed to physical and emotional harm. William Huggard, a Black sixteen-year-old, posed as a Zulu for the Jay Circus at Proctor's Pleasure Palace, and his job was to sit in a cage eating raw meat.[28] Thomas Morris, another African American Zulu impersonator, was put on display in an iron cage, and his primary function was to shock audiences by ferociously gnawing and tearing apart live chickens that were tossed into his cage. He would dramatically suck the blood from the animal, as audiences imagined uncivilized Zulus did in their natural habitat.[29] African Americans impersonating Zulus were sometimes outed as imposters. One American showman of the O'Brien Circus recalled of the 1882–83 season, "In the sideshow we had a big negro whom we had fitted up with rings in his nose, a leopard skin, some assegais and a large shield made out of cow's skin. While he was sitting on the stage in the sideshow, along came two negro women and remarked 'He ain't no Zulu, that's Bill Jackson. He worked over here at Camden on the dock.' Poor old Bill Jackson was as uneasy as if he was sitting on needles, holding the shield between him and the two negro women."[30] Socially awkward situations like this one may seem insignificant; however, there were many dangers for Africans and other people enclosed in human zoos to navigate. There was the demoralizing and sometimes dangerous use of wire fences and cages to separate performers and audiences. Indigenous people were also trafficked, captured, and kept in service against their will and forced into lopsided contracts and prostitution. The performers and their bodies, dead and alive, were examined and photographed by anthropologists as a part of some circus acts.[31] For Indigenous Zulu reenactors, signs of cruelty and oppression were visible in the poor living conditions and the deaths of performers from disease and suicide.

The Zulu character took on other meanings among African Americans. In some circuses, when finished with the backbreaking work of setting up the lot, Black manual laborers received a "Zulu ticket" from management that enabled them to get a costume from the wardrobe department and join the opening parade. The men wore an imagined costume of a Zulu chief and received an extra twenty-five cents.[32] African Americans, besides often portraying Zulus in carnivals, fairs, exhibits, and on the lecture circuit, also created differing images of Zuluness during Mardi Gras celebrations, barnstorming baseball exhibitions, and serialized accounts in Black newspapers. By the turn of the twentieth century, Mardi Gras performers in New Orleans had created their own mythical Zulu history and wardrobes.[33] In 1910, a group of African American laborers belonging to a club called the Tramps began marching in the Mardi Gras parade as the Zulu Krewe, and in 1916 they established the Zulu Social Aid and Pleasure Club. Many maintain that current Mardi Gras Zulus are a vestige of a past that celebrated racist blackface depictions of African Americans popularized at the height of blackface minstrelsy. However, these performers have argued that the Krewe's formation was a social commentary on white domination and stereotypes of African people and people of African descent.[34]

An outgrowth of the Zulu was the "native prince" character. These men had the imagined characteristics of nonwhite royalty, often blending several cultures into one wardrobe. Cultures contributing to this composite character in the eighteenth and nineteenth centuries might include African, Native American, Mexican, Peruvian, Chinese, Indian, and Polynesian, which were exchanged for one another. These so-called native princes toured the country and made their way to European cities to perform at parties of wealthy hosts. Native prince characters were popular in England and the United States, but Americans would have been familiar with performers such as Okah Tubbee, a Barnum employee and formerly enslaved man who claimed to be the son of a Choctaw chief, and even Abdul Rahman, not a performer, but an actual university-educated prince from Guinea who was infamously kidnapped from his home and sold into slavery in Natchez, Mississippi.[35]

Another famous performer, Prince Oskazuma, sometimes "Askazuma," began performing as a Zulu but became one of the renaissance men of the circus' golden age. Born in 1865, Oskazuma toured as a lecturer on African customs, claiming to be a native of South Africa and educated in Great

Britain.[36] By 1894, Prince Oskazuma, "African Warrior, Lecturer, Mimic, Fire Friend," was touring with the Sells and Renfrow Circus,[37] and during its 1895 season, the Great Wallace Circus featured his sideshow acts. Oskazuma worked for several circus companies as a Zulu prince, worked with and managed Native American performance troupes, and performed with a show called Sweeney and Royer, a "Negro Knockabout" act. During the 1901 season, he toured with the Buffalo Bill Wild West Show and spent many years touring with various circuses and Wild West shows thereafter. One paper said of him, "The famous black scout, Prince Askazuma [sic], is a wonder in the sideshow. He holds his audience spellbound. As an announcer and ballyhoo man he cannot be beat."[38] Oskazuma developed a special relationship with the Native Americans on the Wild West tours and gained the names Hawk, Cherokee Charlie, and the Black Scout.[39] During the 1917 season, Oskazuma signed an agreement with Indian agent Francis Nelson to manage a troupe of Lakota Sioux performers. The agreement charged, "Hawk [sic] to book and handle all Sioux Indians and make contracts for them, with medicine shows, vaudeville houses, parks, fairs, expositions, Wild West, circus and carnivals and any outdoor engagements. Francis Nelson is Indian agent and superintendent of the Indians with the Big Jess Willard and Buffalo Bill Show. Mr. Nelson is a nephew of Frank C. Goings, mayor and chief of police of Pine Ridge Agency, S.D., and the Sioux Indians are particular friends of the Black Scout and have adopted him in the tribe."[40] Oskazuma was involved in a diverse range of activities from promoting boxing matches to philanthropic activities.[41] He recounted his early career with the John Robinson Show in 1880 where he "worked in the cookhouse, loaded the train and led hay animals with John Robinson in 1880. While resting, I played the tuba in the sideshow band. I did Zulu and fire-eating with Powman's and with the Sells show in 1889. My salary was $8 a week. But I thank the old-timers for an education in showmanship. I was an employee of Drew & Campbell's Sideshow with Buffalo Bill was an attraction with Major Lillie's Far East."[42] He helped organize fundraisers and benefits for the American Indian Brotherhood, a retirement home for black actors, and an orphanage band.[43] In 1914 he was the minstrel show manager and assistant managing director of Young Buffalo's Wild West Shows, the first African American to hold that position in the show.[44] Later in the 1920s, he toured with another troupe of Native American performers.[45] In October 1921, J. A. Jackson, the African American reporter who was a pioneer in his own right as the first Black correspondent for *Billboard*, printed a letter from Prince Ozkazuma, in which the prince wrote,

I am one of the older all-round novelty acts in the business. I am known as Prince Askazuma, the human volcano. In conjunction with the fire act I do magic, fancy paper tearing and over here I am specializing in buck and wing dancing. This dance and the American Indian dances in costume make the natives sit up. I conclude my performance with the breaking of a hundred pound rock on my head. . . . Why don't some enterprising Negro organize a real Oriental circus? Our people have some great novelty acts, wire walkers, trapeze acts, both bareback and cowboy riders. This seasoned with a bit of music would be a winner.[46]

Prince Ozkazuma's pride in himself and the work of other African Americans comes through these letters and his lifetime of work and service.

## African American Kinkers

Although Zulu acts were popular in many traveling circuses, other African American skilled performing artists saw their performance opportunities wax and wane. After the Civil War, Black artists were mainly limited to the periphery in sideshows. Early nineteenth-century opportunities for acrobats, aerialists, and animal acts were all but gone by the turn of the twentieth century. In Jim Crow America, Black artists had almost no opportunities in the main tent to showcase their skill. The circus industry's exclusion of African Americans from the role of big top kinkers, a term originally specific to acrobats but eventually applied to any performer, was a great contrast to the level of equality and dignity afforded to the majority of international circus artists, save African and Australian Aboriginal peoples.[47] Contortionists and acrobats from Asia and the Middle East not only performed in the shows, they headlined on showbills, were paid well, and were treated in a similar manner to their white counterparts. In many cases, their white counterparts helped provide funds to aid in their recovery from injury and welcomed them as participants in Independence Day celebrations.[48] Circuses would not feature African Americans in the main performance, although often had a handful of white men performing in blackface.[49]

Despite the limitations, some African Americans rose above challenges, made a living, and enjoyed successful careers in tented shows. Black artist Louis Willis (1851–81) was advertised as "Contraband Lewis," "The Nonpareil Lewis," and "Lewis the Moor" and was mentored by John Wilson, a white bareback and four-horse rider in the John Robinson Circus.[50] Willis worked for the John Robinson show, and according to Gil Robinson, won great success in Russia.[51] In the early 1870s, he was a household name in African

Theater poster for Coy Herndon's New Orleans Strutters. American Museum & Gardens.

American homes in the South.[52] He was called the "Colored Boy Rider" from 1866 to 1873 and again from 1875 to 1879, sometimes being listed as just "Equestrian."[53] Another Black artist, Signor Dehl Montarno, likely came to the United States from England with Howes' Great London Show in late 1870. He sometimes went by the name Dellah Montarna or Sargano, and his real name was William Dellah.[54] Montarno got his start in 1867 and became known as the greatest tamer of all time.[55] He was billed as the "Black animal trainer" and as a "cannibal Hottentot" who exhibited a pack of hyenas for Howes' Great London Show in 1871. Montarno died in a bear cage in Staffordshire, England, performing with Bostock and Bailey's Menagerie in March 1892. It was reported that he made a misstep as the door closed behind him in the bear cage and the animals seized and mauled him.[56] There were a number of Black elephant trainers in the late nineteenth century. Bill Badger, Sidney Rink, and Eph Thompson worked on several circuses and Wild West shows. Badger worked on the Barrett Show in 1887, Forepaugh-Sells show from 1892 to 1900, and other shows after 1900. Company route books bring

*He Will Come Out on Top* 73

his career in the circus world to light: the 1893 Sells Brothers route book showed that Badger was the head of the elephant department with one assistant and five elephants in the show. In the 1898 Forepaugh-Sells route book, Badger was assistant to Patsy Forepaugh, and in 1900, he was assistant superintendent of elephants.

Eph Thompson is considered by many one of the best elephant trainers ever to live.[57] In 1880, Thompson worked ten elephants in ring three while Forepaugh Jr. worked fifteen in ring one. He worked closely with the Forepaugh show during the remainder of the 1880s and trained John L. Sullivan, the famous boxing elephant. This was a sensation in the middle of the decade.[58] During the match, the elephant wore a boxing glove on the end of its trunk and would punch Thompson, often knocking him over. After leaving the Forepaugh-Sells show in the late 1890s, Thompson followed the rising numbers of African Americans who headed to Europe seeking a more liberatory artistic, intellectual, and personal experience. England, France, and Germany were all particular draws to African Americans who saw Europe as more racially egalitarian. As W. E. B. Du Bois wrote, race was the greatest issue of the twentieth century, and measures of freedom and equality were complicated matters on both sides of the Atlantic. This was the height of European nations' colonizing, terrorizing, genocidal campaigns in Africa, accompanied by their growing practice of exhibiting Africans and Asians in zoos, fairs, and other exhibitions around the globe. Nevertheless, many African Americans felt that in Europe, "they could shake off their feelings of defeat, shirk off the burden of responsibility for their race, and live on a continent with no cultural expectations of them."[59] Paris, for example, was hugely popular for Black artists of all sorts as it provided a vibrant, cosmopolitan space to gather, network, and create. Unlike the United States, Paris "allowed boundary crossing, conversations and collaborations that were available nowhere else to the same degree."[60] Thompson and his "somersaulting elephants" were hugely popular in Europe. In 1908, he was reported to be worth $250,000, virtually all of his wealth earned in European circus lots and variety show halls.[61]

A wide variety of artists with physical disabilities and differences found their way, or were kidnapped and forced, into the circus freak show tent. One of the most famous of the Black circus sideshow freaks was Zip the What-Is-It? Zip, born William Henry Johnson (1842–1926), exhibited at sideshows across the country. He owned a farm near Nutley, New Jersey, as well as other property. Many thought he had mental disabilities due to microcephaly, but his colleagues, such as the circus aerialist and original Disney

Tinkerbell Tiny Kline, remembered him as being without any disabilities.[62] Hailing from Brooklyn, Johnson had a remarkable career spanning nearly seven decades. He had a cone-shaped head and started his career as a "missing link" or "wild man" in 1859 with Barnum. Barnum announced that a group of naked subhumans swinging about in trees had been discovered in the Gambian jungle, and Zip was the only survivor of the voyage to America. During his career, he worked for various shows, including Barnum's American Museum, Sawyer's Cabin Singers, Ringling Bros. and Barnum and Bailey Circus, Cooper and Bailey, and Pawnee Bill's Wild West Show.

Another popular Black circus act was that of the "giant." Black men large in stature were advertised as Arabian or African. The Dahomey Giant act held a special place in the American pop-culture imagination and harkened back to the slave-trading nation of Dahomey. Located in western Africa, present-day southern Benin, Dahomey warriors, often the infamous female soldiers, kidnapped people from neighboring nations to sell to European slavers. The game-changing 1903 all-African American ragtime comedy, *In Dahomey*, and other similar contemporary shows were wildly popular. Innovator and partner to Barnum, W. C. Coup was instrumental in transforming the wagon show to the rails and famously added a second and third ring to his show. Coup wrote that the Dahomey Giant in his show was really a big African American man whom dime store proprietors had decided to introduce as a wild monster from Dahomey in Africa.[63] Coup remembered that this Dahomey Giant actor worked with an African American sideshow troupe whose specialty was to pose as representatives from a range of peoples from around the world, including Maori people from New Zealand, Aboriginal people from Australia, and African peoples.[64] Managers hired a theatrical costume designer to make the actor a costume, and a false cablegram was issued, purporting to be from the Great Farini, which stated that the giant had sailed with his interpreter from London and would arrive in Boston. Coup wrote that the man in the act was well educated but pretended not to know English and, therefore, could not converse with the reporters. His interpreter, on the other hand, "managed to fill them up very comfortably."[65] Another Black circus giant was Big George Bell, who signed on with the Ringling Brothers show for the 1912 season. That year, Big George received twelve dollars per week, a uniform, and revenue from photograph sales; in the next year, his pay was raised to fifteen dollars per week (and to twenty dollars per week the following year) plus photo revenue,[66] with the provision that he received seven dollars per week on the road and an extra dollar per week at the close of season. It was a common practice for Black and Native

American workers to be paid this way, supposedly because if they were paid their full wages each week while on the road, Black and Indigenous performers would spend all of their money on alcohol. It seems possible that this practice may also have been intended to discourage these less-affiliated workers from leaving the show before the end of the season, or even to save on the cost of their wages during the season when transportation and other expenses would be at their peak. To compare, the contract for James G. Tarver, a white giant on Forepaugh-Sells in 1911, got twenty-five dollars per week and split revenue from picture sales with the show.

## Women in Shows

The absence of women in the antebellum circus reflected the absence of women in the public sphere in general. The dominant ideology of the nineteenth century identified separate spheres for men and women. The public sphere, outside the home, was where men engaged in paid labor, entertainment, and all aspects of social and political life. Women's activities were expected to be confined to the private sphere, within the home, and to be concentrated on domestic responsibilities and child-rearing. To appease public sentiment, circuses during this period deemphasized the role of women players and sometimes excluded them altogether. Men also constituted the vast majority of the circus audience. Churches often protested the circus' celebration of the body and were wary of its connection to theater. For a woman to not only shed the chains of the domestic sphere but also to engage in paid labor that involved travel, public performance, and baring parts of her body that should, by contemporary standards, be covered, was considered by many to be deeply immoral and contributed to unfavorable attitudes about circus artists. Antebellum audiences targeted women as disrespectful and objected to their costuming, which included stockings under knee-length skirts—far from conforming to the heavily corseted, long-sleeved, floor-length dresses of the period. Purity reformers frequently claimed that all female entertainers were prostitutes because they exposed their bodies for pay. Women audience members were also viewed with suspicion. Some communities went so far as to ban or heavily tax circus troupes. Connecticut, Barnum's home state, outlawed the circus altogether until the 1840s. The state legislature cracked down on performers and forbade unusual feats of the body for monetary gain. During the Second Great Awakening (late eighteenth and early nineteenth centuries), clergymen in Rochester, New York, led the movement to close a circus building and turn it into a soap factory, hoping to make it a much cleaner locale. From 1824 until the early twentieth century, the Vermont legislature taxed the circus so heavily that it resulted in a virtual ban, as the fees were prohibitive for most circuses to pay.[67]

As the nineteenth century progressed, women's presence in the circus—as both performers and spectators—expanded just as more working-class women left domestic service to work in other industries, and political activism gave middle-class women opportunities to participate in the public sphere. Concurrent with the growth of corporations and service industries during the Gilded Age, young women began to work as office clerks and in retail sales at department stores. At the same time, middle-class women became more involved in the public sphere through progressive activism to eradicate poverty, deal with social inequality, and gain the vote. These women also now had disposable income and partook in a variety of public amusements. Simultaneously, a physical-culture movement that lauded strong, healthy bodies gained momentum. In the milieu of women's physical-culture movement, audiences read circus women's meager dress as a function of wholesome athleticism. Physical fitness advocates argued that women's bodies should be free of tight, cumbersome clothing, and an anticorset movement began in the 1830s and gained wide acceptance among the athletic, physical-culture advocates in the late nineteenth century.

By the beginning of the twentieth century, Victorian distinctions between the public and private spheres were crumbling; as a result, the circus evolved into a family entertainment, and female acts became increasingly visible and socially acceptable. Circus proprietors hired women to sell their productions as decent: posters portrayed well-attired white women and families as part of the turn-of-the-twentieth-century audience. Showmen, aware of circus women's transgressive potential, repositioned strong, athletic, traveling women into traditional gender categories—as models of domestic womanliness and objects of titillation. Contemporary women generally wore full skirts and long-sleeved shirtwaists, and anything short of that coverage could be considered nude, including the wearing of leotards, tights, or short-sleeved dresses above the knee. But the distinction between respectable nudity and salacious nudity was often created by racial stereotypes. White women were presented as models of civilized, athletic womanliness. Gender, race, class, and representations of empire aided in creating an irresistible, sexually charged performance under the guise of "clean family fun."[68]

White women became a big part of circuses across the country and were afforded opportunities that other women of their era did not have. They were hired as performers, seamstresses, and costume designers. They occupied segregated train cars and had strict rules about visitors and many other aspects of their lives. However, in a time when the cult of domesticity still heavily influenced American lives, circus women had freedoms that most could only dream of. They left home, traveled the world, and earned as much as men, sometimes outearning them. White circus women enjoyed a great degree of financial success and personal freedom compared to their domestic or factory-based counterparts. They eventually joined the ranks of the suffragist movement and formed formal organizations to support votes for women and to boost the number of female kinkers in the business. In 1912, female kinkers formed the Barnum and Bailey's Circus Women's Equal Rights Society. The group had elected officers, and eventually, new leadership changed the name to the "Suffragette Ladies of the Barnum and Bailey Circus."[69]

Shows did not hire African American women to perform under the main tent.[70] The Black women who did make it into the circus did so under the cover of sideshow annex companies and independent minstrel shows that the circuses hired as a group for a set salary each season. These shows, under the guise of being educational in the realms of natural history and biology, allowed spectators to be entertained by so-called steps on the evolutionary ladder. The popularity of the classic freak show was "accompanied and in part engendered by a scientific interest."[71] Women of color, or white women in black or brown face, were often presented as living, educational artifacts, whose nudity was a part of their racial authenticity. Racial color defined the degree of nudity that was deemed appropriate for display. *National Geographic*, for example, first published bare-breasted Black women in 1896. White readers accepted these photos of women of color as educational, but photographs of topless white women were considered immoral and lewd. Names like Sarah Baartman, Miss La La, and Joice Heth would have been familiar to American and European audiences in the nineteenth and early twentieth centuries. Baartman was a South African Khoikhoi woman who was exhibited all over Europe as the "Hottentot Venus." Hottentot was a word Dutch colonizers used to describe Baartman's ethnic group, and women from the group became scientific and erotic curiosities to Europeans who were fascinated by their bodies. In the hands of the white men who took her to England and France, Baartman lived a miserable existence, being collared, treated as an animal, and exhibited at rich people's parties. She was penniless and survived as a sex worker until her death in 1815. Heth was an enslaved woman owned by Barnum and presented as George Washington's 161-year-old mammy nursemaid. Barnum exploited the blind Heth in life and death: he allowed crowds to touch her body as she told stories about the young Washington. When she died, Barnum held a public autopsy so that onlookers could see inside her body. Barnum had fed the press the rumor that she was an automaton and sold tickets to eager crowds to assure them that she was, indeed, just a very old Black woman. Miss La La had a somewhat happier and more successful life. Born in 1858, her mother put her in a European circus when she was nine, and La La trained to become an expert aerialist. She toured and later married the African American contortionist Emanuel Woodson, with whom she had three children. In her lifetime, she traveled the world, was painted by Edgar Degas, and became famous for her trapeze and human cannonball acts, as well as acts involving being hoisted 200 feet in the air holding on only by her teeth.

Women writers, producers, and performers originally managed burlesque shows, another contemporary entertainment popular for comedic and bawdy scripts that parodied operatic narratives and Shakespearean theater while challenging gender roles and expectations. As these shows came under sole male management, women's performances moved from comedy and social commentary to be explicitly sexual. With this turn toward male management, the burlesque show devolved into an increasingly disreputable vehicle for display of the voiceless female body in stylized erotic cooch dancing and striptease. Introduced at the 1893 Chicago Exposition, the explicit displays of feminine sexuality of the cooch dances graduated to the shimmy in the Jazz Age to the striptease of the late 1920s and 1930s. The cooch dance, interestingly, entered the burlesque performances in an attempt to popularize the new field of anthropology.[72] Just as African and Native American exhibits encouraged visitors to compare more primitive branches of the human evolutionary tree with the most advanced white civilizations, cooch dances served as a reminder of the atavistic nature of women in a semicivilized state: the cooch dancer was constructed as an uncivilized exotic or ethnological other, solely existing to arouse and appease male observers.[73]

Black actors, both men and women who were singers, comedians, and other types of artists, worked in variety shows and, after the turn of the century, as novelty acts or featured guests in white burlesque shows. It was common for white burlesque shows to use Black acts as added attractions, and many hired Black acrobats, jugglers, and animal trainers. The Gilded Age and Progressive Era saw Black women billed as "Jungle Fever," "Voodoo Ladies," and "Sepia Beauties." J. A. Jackson wrote about new Black burlesque shows as "high class" actors.[74] But Jackson also did not shy away from speaking out when he felt women pushed the envelope or crossed the line of respectability. In Baltimore, a club owner kicked out the George Lynch Trio because the singer, Gertrude Brown, offended the audience by inserting "smutty verses in her rendition of 'He May Be Your Man.'"[75] The theater apologized to the audience, and owners assured the clientele that smut would not be tolerated—and once an act made the mistake, they were not afforded the opportunity to do it again.[76] Coy Herndon described audiences' expectations of the cooch show: as men entered the fairgrounds, they were greeted with, "Right over this side folks, I have here ten beautiful girls who dance like only the Sultan of Turkey likes it." Women were directed to another part of the fair, and men were told that "the girl show is strictly for men, where they shake it up and shimmy like jelly on a platter, and oh how scant they are dressed."[77] Herndon wrote that the shimmy shows, which were followed by rigged games where Black people lost money, were there solely to bring in money to the greedy show owners. He suggested that Black fairs' primary reason for existence should have been to "show our achievements that others may profit by them, and to gain money should be the least consideration, compared with wholesome amusements."[78]

Some Black female kinkers practiced their artistry on their own terms and made successful careers. Successful Black women achieved greatness despite garnering less attention than their male counterparts in popular publications. The growing number of blues queens in sideshows and other tented companies also aided women's progress. Reflecting on the industry, Herndon wrote, "Men and women are made for business" and advertised, applauded, supported, and encouraged Black women performers in the *Chicago Defender*.[79] Clearly, these acrobats, wire walkers, and contortionists maintained loyal fan bases, as evidenced by their loving, if smaller in volume, coverage in Herndon's *Chicago Defender* column and "J. A. Jackson's Page" in *Billboard*. Herndon wrote about Mamie Smith's 1923 tour with vaudeville and sang praises of Ethel Waters's musical and dance talents.[80] He propped up women musicians, pianists, and cabaret all over the country, especially highlighting the Midwest and the East.[81] Skilled artists like Maxine Lopez, Jewell Cox, Mamie Williams, Ada Booker, and Princess White were comedians, dancers, contortionists, singers, and soloists whom Herndon showcased in his column.[82] Herndon also encouraged his readers to support female artists. When Minnie Lee Brown, a chorus girl with the Joseph Jones Show, fell ill, Herndon kept fans updated through his column.[83] When Nellie Worther, whom Herndon called "the Race's greatest woman contortionist" and who performed in the wildly popular The Smart Set Minstrel Show,

Millie Christine, the Renowned Two-Headed Lady. Conjoined twins and sideshow performers Millie Christine greet several guests in a formal parlor setting. Circus World–Wisconsin Historical Society.

Princess Wee Wee, ca. 1915. Library of Congress. Copyright by Charles E. Ridenour, theatrical photographer, Philadelphia, Pennsylvania.

fell ill with a diagnosis of cancer, Herndon asked fans to write to her in her Greenville, Mississippi, hospital room.[84]

A handful of Black circus women made it to superstardom despite social restrictions and physical disabilities. Millie and Christine McKoy were perhaps two of the biggest Black circus stars of the late nineteenth century. They were twins joined at the base of the spine and sharing a pelvis, but both had two arms and two legs. Born into slavery in North Carolina in 1851, the sisters and their parents, Jacob and Monemia, were owned by a blacksmith named Jabez McKay. The sisters later changed their names to McKoy. When they were ten months old, McKay sold the twins, who had been attracting crowds of onlookers, to a traveling showman for one thousand dollars. Eventually, a man named Joseph Pearson Smith came into possession of the girls and hired them out as the "Carolina Twins." While appearing in P. T. Barnum's American Museum in New York City at the age of three, the girls were kidnapped and taken to England. Smith eventually regained custody of the girls and took them and their parents and siblings to Wadesboro, North Carolina. There, Millie and Christine learned how to read, write, sing, dance, and play piano. Smith's wife taught them to deliver recitations in German and French.

In the postbellum era, Millie and Christine remained with the Smiths and came to have successful careers, performing song and dance routines as the "Two Headed Girl" or the "Two Headed Nightingale." In 1871, they met and performed for Queen Victoria who gifted them diamond hair clips. They continued to perform for nearly thirty years. By 1885, they were making six hundred dollars weekly.[85] The twins retired to a large home in North Carolina after their trooping days ended. They earned an estimated $250,000 across their career, a hefty sum for a sideshow performer, Black or white. Throughout their career and retirement, Millie and Christine gave financial support to Black schools and churches. In the 1880s, they founded their own school for African American children in Whiteville, North Carolina. Owning property and publishing their own autobiography, Millie and Christine's lives were exceptional as formerly enslaved women and because of their congenital anomalies and extraordinary life story. Many children in similar positions did not survive childbirth, let alone achieve the degree of autonomy the sisters possessed. Other enslaved performers in circus freak shows, such as Heth, endured the demeaning gaze of onlookers and intrusive and graphic examinations. As they matured, Millie and Christine resisted these kinds of intrusions, and despite the exploitative elements of freak shows, they possessed a degree of agency over their lives and shared body unknown to most enslaved people.[86]

Another superstar, Princess Wee Wee, also overcame many challenges at the intersections of race, disability, and gender discrimination. Born Harriet Elizabeth Williams, Princess performed as a professional little person and was billed the "Animated Chocolate Éclair." She worked at the Dreamland Circus and with Barnum and Bailey. J. A. Jackson wrote of her in *Billboard*:

> Princess Wee-Wee, the two-foot, six-inch midget, attracted probably as much attention as any one feature at the opening performance of the big Ringling Bros.-Barnum and Bailey Circus at the Madison Square Garden on March 26. In private life she is Miss Harriet Thompson, the daughter of Mr. And Mrs. James Thompson of 1704 Preston Street, Baltimore, Md. She spent the winter in Cuba and barely had time for a brief visit to her folks before opening with the circus. She recently told a reporter for The Baltimore Afro-American that she would not consider marriage until she found a suitor of her race and of a size that would permit her being the boss.[87]

Michael Mitchell has observed that these kinds of exhibits gave audiences comfort during an era when the world seemed to be moving "too fast and far for a comfortable understanding of the present or impending future."[88] Circuses helped to assuage social anxieties around industrialization, urbanization, immigration, calls to abolish slavery, and later civil rights and women's rights. As Jenifer Barclay observes, "Ubiquitous depictions of enslaved people with disabilities and attempts to connect blackness to the supposedly piteous, heinous, or comedic spectacle of disability were conscious and unconscious, ill-intentioned and well-intentioned."[89] Social constructions of disability and its intersection with gender and race also played an important role to reinforce white superiority and to sustain and legitimize existing social hierarchies and power relations.

## Laborers

In the circus industry, the movement from the antebellum era to the great railroad outfits of the golden age opened the door to Black men's employment in the industry. Although Black workers were often excluded from professional, skilled employment, their labor was needed for industrial work in increasing numbers during the Jim Crow era. Much of this labor was, in essence, still using the Black body as a workhorse, doing manual, backbreaking work, but it contained the suggestion of new possibilities in the associations made possible by urban life. Similarly, the advent of gigantic railroad shows like Barnum, Ringling, Sells, and Wallace created new opportunities for Black laborers. These big circus companies needed much of the same things giant manufacturing concerns of the North required: massive amounts of cheap, unskilled labor. Circus companies gave Black workers the most labor-intensive positions as roustabouts (unskilled general labor), razorbacks (loading and unloading train cars), canvasmen, and hostlers (horse handlers). These employees helped to raise and lower tents, cleaned and fed animals, and performed the manual labor that provided the foundation on which the circus was built. Expendable and easily exploitable, they had a very high turnover rate, and many deserted and others were terminated mid-season.[90] Barnum and Bailey gave bonuses of one hundred dollars to canvasmen who remained for an entire season.[91] These employees were usually the last to eat and sometimes responsible for their own sleeping arrangements. Some slept with the animals whose cars they cleaned, others slept under the open sky or under rail cars to escape inclement weather.[92] Henry Ringling North said that it was financially impossible to give the required number of men permanent employment when the circus spent five months in winter quarters. "Therefore," he wrote, "each spring we had to recruit a whole new army."[93] North went on to say, "They were mostly men who lacked either the capacity or the desire to hold permanent jobs. Rootless, reckless, and feckless, owing no loyalty to us—why should they—nor, in most cases, to families or communities."[94] This may have been a popular opinion of Black laborers, but these men understood the exigencies of the industry and the precarious positions they were in, and they took the jobs that were available to them. Black working men almost always earned less than their white counterparts. In 1902, the Walter L. Main salary list recommended, "If you go south and use Darkies, pay 'em $2.00 a week; the lowest wage otherwise was $3.00 a week."[95] Circus managers' attitudes toward employees of color could vary widely, ranging from violently exploitative to somewhat, or relatively, fair.

Challenges to African American performers and laborers developed in the early decades of the twentieth century, even as racist imagery of Dutch, Irish, and Jewish people declined.[96] As late as 1896, Barnum and Bailey would not hire Black men. In fact, when Bailey and the Sells brothers bought out the Forepaugh-Sells show in 1896, Bailey sent Ephraim Sells a telegram ordering that no Blacks should be hired on the canvas crew. After the death of Peter Sells in 1904, Lewis Sells began the process of liquidating the family business until his own death in 1907. One canvas man, Bill "Cap" Curtis, recalled that when James Bailey joined Sells management, he ended the Sells brothers' practice of hiring Black canvasmen to raise tents.[97] George Bowles, a press agent for The Barnum and Bailey Circus, explained that in 1903, the circus hired African American canvasmen to work in a segregated area only in response to a shortage of white workers:

> Times were so prosperous that any man with a good pair of biceps could not only get a job, but would have people bidding for his services, and many employers who wanted husky boys overbid the circus. . . . These desertions were so frequent that the circus for about six weeks was constantly in more or less trouble. We sent everywhere for men. . . . The problem was solved only when, for the first time in the history of the circus, Mr. Bailey imported a large force of Virginia Negroes, who were greatly pleased with all the excitement and novelty of circus life. He tried to avoid this move, but there was too much doing for white men, to leave any other recourse.[98]

Bailey's policy toward African American employees was more characteristic of circus owners at the turn of the century than was the Sells brothers'. Over the subsequent two decades, the circus changed ownership from Bailey to the American Circus Corporation, originally owned by Jerry Mulligan, Bert Bowers, and Ed Ballard but purchased by John Ringling in 1929.

Historians do not know much about these manual laborers of the circus. Trade papers, such as *Billboard* and the *New York Clipper*, as well as owner and performer memoirs, are full of anecdotes about showmen's and performers' lives, but there are no equivalent sources on the working men and women of the golden age of the circus. At best, their stories may be pieced together through contracts, newspaper articles about crimes or accidents on the road, isolated comments in route books, and contemporary pop culture references. It is clear that labor crews often hired Black men, especially in the canvas crew, which was one of the first parts of the circus to be integrated. For example, one year the Ringling Brothers-Barnum and Bailey Combined Shows employed fifty-nine Black men and twenty white men on the company's big top crew of roustabouts, canvasmen, and razorbacks.[99] The canvas crew grew to as many as 200 men during the era of the biggest circuses.[100] Then, in 1899, there was a paradigm shifting photograph. The 1899 John Robinson route book marks an important moment, as it contains the first known photo of an all-Black crew in a white-owned circus.[101] The "Canvasmen: Colored Brigade" is a first look at Black working men in the circus. There are twenty-eight men in the photograph.[102]

*He Will Come Out on Top*

Canvasmen: Colored Brigade. Used with permission from Illinois State University's Special Collections, Milner Library.

Group Sideshow Canvasmen. Used with permission from Illinois State University's Special Collections, Milner Library.

In another section, the cook house photograph shows an integrated department. Two Black men in the photo are apparently cooks, as they are holding a meat cleaver and a cutting knife. A third photograph, this one of the Group Side Show Canvasmen, shows four white men and five Black men, one of which holds a dog. The photo of the train crew shows it is almost all Black.[103] Some circuses were very open to Black labor: the Sells brothers had many Black workers on their canvas crew. The Ringling Brothers Barnum and Bailey canvas crew was mostly Black by the 1920s. The American Circus Corporation, formed in 1921, kept an integrated canvas department. The ACC sent recruiters to Mississippi every year to recruit as many as 150 Black workers.[104] Both white and Black working men had three-high bunks in the sleepers. As many as 142 men would be crammed into a car.[105] In the Hagenbeck Wallace Show, the majority of waiters, including the head waiter, were African American.

American circuses were socially stratified by race as well as by job category. Segregated circuses kept partitions, often a sheet that divided Blacks and whites, in sleepers and the cookhouses until the early 1950s. In her memoir, Tiny Kline detailed what she called the caste system in the Barnum and Bailey Circus. All aspects of life were segregated by job prestige and by race, from the wardrobe and dressing rooms to the dining tent. As for laborers, they often joined the circus for adventure and romance. They were discouraged, though, when finding out that there were no women in their caste, so no hope of having a romantic interlude. Workers and performers were strictly segregated.[106] African American canvasmen led a completely segregated life. They had their own sleepers and a segregated area in the cookhouse. The typical Black worker would have had very little contact with whites, except his white boss. Ringling Brothers Barnum and Bailey carried a separate Black workingman's cook house in the 1930s.[107]

## Dangers on the Road

Circuses were sometimes notorious for the public unrest that they incited, and people of color were especially vulnerable to violence. Brawls between circus workers and local citizens were common occurrences. Traveling circus life was difficult, and it posed special challenges for African American laborers. Violence from within the circus itself is harder to document due to the private nature of most circus companies. Many general laborers were excluded from unions, often victims of unfair labor practices, and were vulnerable to managerial violence.[108] African American circus workers risked the threat of and actual racial violence ranging from barroom brawls to spectacle lynching. Instances of violence were often fodder for local newspapers to write anticircus diatribes that accused the shows of introducing immorality to otherwise peaceful, God-fearing, small-town audiences. *Billboard* ran a regular column titled "Prudes on the Prowl" that chronicled, in a condescending and sometimes comical way, the fears and anticircus sentiment found in local newspapers across small-town America. However, real-life violence also occurred among circus workers. The *Columbus Dispatch*, for example, reported "Circus Man Murdered," and the alleged murder was said to have grown out of a fight between two longtime employees of the Sells Brothers Circus and the residents of Columbus.[109] Samuel H. Goodwin, described as a "colored" second cook who divided his time between work in the circus and work in restaurants during the offseason, was accused of killing the waiter, George Swinger. The trouble allegedly started between the two men while unloading the cooking utensils. "After some words had been passed" between them, Swinger tried to strike Goodwin with his fist, but failed to hit him. Then Goodwin struck Swinger twice on the head with a tent pin, fracturing his skull. Swinger died from the injury. Goodwin was placed in jail to await his trial.[110]

Violence against workers of color was ubiquitous, originating from both outside and inside of the circus. The Great Pan American Shows route book of 1903 recounted another instance of violence in Picton, Ontario. During the evening performance, a Black canvas man named Ed Clarke, who was known as "Side Show Shorty," stabbed Edward "Yellow" Johnson, another Black workman. Johnson died shortly afterward. Clarke was said to have been drinking heavily during the day and "was very treacherous." Clarke boasted of having stabbed Johnson and threatened to kill more circus people. "The city police, with the assistance of Detective Rogers and several of the circus people, captured and imprisoned Clarke in the local jail. Musicians and cook house employees, from whom Clarke allegedly got the knife, were held as witnesses. At a preliminary hearing, Clarke pleaded not guilty and was held over until October."[111] In an unexpected turn of events, Clarke was found not guilty by the white jury of Picton, a verdict in line with that town's valued image as a haven from industrial urbanization and a crime-free tourist destination. As it turned out, a murder, committed by an outsider with an outsider victim, was not a story the local people on the jury wanted connected to the town's conservative, law-abiding reputation.[112] In another incident in 1901, *Variety* reported that two Black workers with the Ringling Brothers Circus, Frank Benjamin and

Dave Tucker, were sentenced at Laramie, Wyoming, to two or three years in prison upon pleading guilty to having robbed D. K. Pelton and John J. Harigan. Pelton and Harigan claimed that they were invited to ride the circus train but were robbed and thrown from the train by four of the Black workers.[113] The June 12, 1909, edition reported that a Black man on Howe's Great London shot Bert Bower, a labor superintendent. The report claimed that other Black workers attempted to attack him, but local authorities put him in jail. A white mob then broke him out of the jail and lynched him, hanging him from a nearby bridge over the Kentucky River. After the lynching, the governor, like many negligent officials of the era, refused to act in what he called a "local matter."[114] During the 1885 season, the Wallace company scheduled single, morning shows in southern states and claimed that this was a measure taken to avoid the violence against employees typical of evening shows.[115] This strategy helped Wallace avoid a mob of sixteen armed men who aimed to harass circus employees at one southern venue.[116] In 1903, the Great Wallace Show encountered a race riot in Evansville, Indiana, and was not allowed to perform there. The citizens of Linton, Indiana, the next venue, did not allow African American workers into the town, so Wallace left all his Black employees in a nearby city and secretly brought them back just before the trains left that town.[117] One report said that the Great Wallace had experienced no difficulty with Black employees in Indiana, but great care and discretion had been exercised by the management on account of the bitter racial feelings that prevailed in that state.[118]

The racial violence of Jim Crow America was a reality that all people of color were forced to negotiate on a daily basis, and Black circus workers were not exempt from this unfortunate fact. The decades of the 1910s and 1920s saw heightened racial tensions, in part because of white animosities against Black servicemen returning from World War I in uniform and expecting better treatment and civil rights, and in part because of Black migration to northern cities. Nearly one million Black people left the South during and soon after World War I as they filled tens of thousands of positions for unskilled and semiskilled labor in the factories of the North. Chicago's Black population, for example, jumped from 44,000 in 1910 to 111,000 in 1920. Cleveland's Black population jumped from 8,000 to 34,000 over the same period.[119] Increases in Black population all over the North agitated whites, and their openly violent bigotry led to a series of race riots, most notoriously in East St. Louis, Illinois, in 1917, in Chicago in 1919, and Tulsa, Oklahoma, in 1921. Segregation affected circus operations in a variety of ways. Living in Jim Crow America, workers of color faced de jure segregation in the South and de facto segregation in the North and were frequently victims of racial violence. A Melville, Saskatchewan, paper reported on another instance of racially charged violence in the Al G. Barnes Circus on June 17, 1926. It also alluded to what were perhaps common challenges authorities faced when dealing with a circus crime.[120] In this case, a quarrel between a Black man named William Butler and a white man escalated until gunshots were fired. Witnesses claimed that a mob began to viciously beat Butler after they heard gunshots. A local white bystander intervened, but the mob of circus employees beat him for his intrusion. Police arrived before the mob hanged Butler in one of the circus rail cars. The police gave Butler medical attention and ordered the white crowd to disperse and free the man. When the crowd obliged, the police chief prevented the circus train from leaving town so that he could investigate the crime. White employees who had taken part in the riot were questioned and claimed that Butler had fired a gun at an unsuspecting white man. Others said that the white man had fired first. Still others alleged that Butler had made indecent overtures and "improper advances" toward some white women in town, apparently trying to get local people to side with the rioters. The false accusation of molestation of a white woman was most often the cause of anti-Black lynchings during this era. The mob gave a false name for the white man, and Saskatchewan authorities were never able to locate the culprits of the assault.[121]

The most infamous case of racial mob violence occurred in Duluth, Minnesota, in the summer of 1920. A local white woman and her boyfriend claimed that a group of Black men from the John Robinson Circus raped her at gunpoint. Six Black employees of the circus were arrested. The mob broke into the jail the next night and brutally lynched three of the men, Elmer Jackson, Elias Clayton, and Isaac McGhie. After being tortured, they were hanged from a lamp post in the middle of downtown Duluth.[122] The Minnesota National Guard was called out to protect the three surviving men. All the hanged men were described as "show laborers." Later, seven Black men were indicted, and lawyers from the National Association for the Advancement of Colored People (NAACP) defended them. Five had charges against them dismissed, one was found not guilty, and the last, Max Mason, was found guilty and sentenced to seven to thirty years. On appeal, he was released in 1925 with the stipulation that he leave the state. Jerry Mugivan, one of the proprietors of the American Circus Corporation, which owned the John Robinson Circus, wrote a letter to the state parole board on behalf of

Mason in 1922, in which he said, "He had been in our employ for quite a little while and while here was always ready and willing to obey orders, kept his place and his morals and general character and habits about the average. We will appreciate anything that you may do for him to gain his release and will be pleased to re-employ him should he be released from the institution."[123] The Duluth trial and Mugivan's comments in defense of his employee would have been rare, as workers of color (and their white bosses) were the least likely to file legal complaints or go to authorities. Circus managers had a vested interest in keeping up a family friendly image, and reporting violence when they were visiting a town was not to their advantage. Occasionally, *Billboard* reported on drunken brawls or other disturbances. Route books and industry publications give a glimpse into this world. In 1899, the John Robinson route book entry for Cullan, Alabama, said, "No negroes allowed in the town or county."[124] And the Robinson show was heavy on Black working men that year. On one occasion in 1912, the Kit Carson Wild West Show had to pack up because the Ku Klux Klan in Kentucky intimidated its Black employees.[125]

There were occasional events that escalated into what some have called circus race riots. The Sells brothers' route book in 1883 reported that in Concord, North Carolina, there "was the most eventful day of the occasion" because a "coon by the name of J. Campbell" shot and killed a white man named Charles Redmond and also shot another man in the abdomen.[126] The route book goes on to say that the "Nigger Campbell" was taken out of the jail where he had been placed at about two o'clock in the morning and lynched. The blood-thirsty mob went on to shoot and kill other Black people."[127] This was the first circus race riot, according to circus historian Fred Pfening Jr.[128] Reporting on another incident, in 1921, the *Pasadena Star-News* headline read, "Race Fight on Circus Train is Halted Whites and Blacks of Barnes Organization Have Trouble One Negro Shot in Faction War–Whites in Privilege Car fired Upon by Negroes from Outside." In this incident, which began as the Al G. Barnes circus train left San Bernardino for Colton, Thomas "Curly" Madden shot William Owen. Altogether, witnesses said that about one hundred shots were fired. Twelve men were arrested at Colton, and by the time the train reached its next destination at Riverside early the next morning, all was quiet.[129]

Another riot broke out with Christy and His Wonder Show in 1923. George W. Christy remembered that while playing in the mining town of Herrin, Illinois, a Black elephant handler named Sidney Rink got into an altercation with a white miner and hit him with an elephant hook. When other white men heard about this incident, a near riot started, Christy recounted. A mob searched the train cars and started shooting at circus workers as they were in the process of tearing down the tents and loading. Christy went on to tell a harrowing tale:

> When the shooting started we ducked behind wagons and no one was hit. We turned off all the lights so they could not see us. Then I rolled the elephant man in a bunch of canvas and into the canvas wagon with just enough room to breathe. We had many other Black men on the lot. By then the citizens were hungry for any black man. After darkening the lot I sent all the Blacks across a field, advising them to stand along the tracks several miles away by a coal mine. We stopped the train there as we were leaving and picked them up, but nary a colored person came on board. We never knew where they all disappeared to.[130]

This attests to the nasty reality that a private altercation between two men could turn into lynch mob terror if one of the men were African American.

## Conclusion

At first glance, life in the circus seems to be a world apart from the drudgery of agricultural work and intense manual labor that characterized the lives of the majority of African Americans during the late nineteenth and early twentieth centuries. But of course, real life is much more complicated. Look closer and see that although the circus afforded Back workers many novel opportunities, it also reflected and reproduced all of American racial prejudices. For Black performing artists, this meant unstable work contracts from year to year. These artists also relied on work in minstrel shows and other entertainment venues, and some achieved great success. On the labor front, life was a bit more precarious. Although written records leave unclear a Black roustabout's true intentions or motivations, it is possible to imagine that this life on the road was rough but perhaps offered more opportunities than picking cotton, being confined to plantations, or laboring away in the same county year after year. For these laborers, the circus as an industry offered much of the same treatment as other industries at the time: long hours, segregated backbreaking labor, and little stability.

For those who made it, either as a performer or a laborer, the circus industry provided two perks their counterparts in those other industries could not dream of: mobility and broadened possibilities. Mobility in the circus meant that within the confines of the circus schedule, these men could move in and out of the South as they pleased. They could join the show in one city, work their way along the circus route, and leave at any point. Or, they could work all season for pay, very basic accommodations and board, and travel to towns and cities across the United States. The option to remain in a new location, go back home at the end of the season, or even join another entertainment company was a freedom of individual choice that would have been difficult to achieve in other professions. The generations of Black circus workers between 1870 and the 1920s were trailblazers who helped to give reality to African Americans' postbellum desire to travel, change their lives, and eventually change the face of the nation.

CHAPTER FOUR

# But Simply a Man Normal in His Environment
*Indigenous Americans, Wild West Shows, and Taking on the Vanishing Race Narrative*

It was August 1914 and James and Ernest Bucktooth were in trouble. Early in March, circus managers had recruited the Bucktooth brothers and thirteen other men and women from their Onondaga reservation near Syracuse, New York, for a nine-month European tour in the company's Wild West act. The job paid one dollar per day, food, and all travel expenses. The tour went as usual until war broke out and the circus went out of business, leaving performers and animals stranded in Germany. In later interviews, James Bucktooth recounted stories of evading German officers in train stations, feeding the show horses to the lions, being chased by police for attempting to start a parade in a village square, and being temporarily jailed on suspicion of espionage.[1] When they finally returned home with the help of the Society of American Indians and various US ambassadors, the Bucktooth brothers had to face another kind of peril—the disapproval of Native American leaders who aimed to stop Indigenous folks from joining circuses and similar exhibitions that polite society deemed unsavory.

The Bucktooths were prime targets of criticism for some Indigenous thought leaders who believed the brothers were examples of everything that was wrong with the circus and Wild West industries. The laundry list of complaints that Arthur C. Parker, the editor of the *Quarterly Journal of the Society of American Indians*, held against them included degrading tribal habits and customs by fooling everyone into thinking that all Indians dressed in the Lakota war bonnet, left good fields unplowed, succumbed to savagery, and encouraged naked war dances for the enjoyment of white Christians. Moreover, Parker wrote, though it was "a matter of secondary importance," he was not the only victim of "the stranded show Indian" who called on wealthier Native Americans for help buying tickets home from far-off places.[2] The clash between Native American elite leaders and the men and women who joined traveling entertainment communities began in the nineteenth century when Wild West shows and circuses exploded in popularity.

This chapter describes the creation and ideology behind the infamous phenomenon known as the Wild West show. The stealing of Native American

Members of the Society of American Indians on the steps of Engineering Hall, Kansas University, October 1, 1915, from *The Quarterly Journal of the Society of American Indians* 3, no. 4 (1915), plate 14. Edward E. Ayer Collection Newberry Library.

lands and the genocide of Indigenous peoples while building the institution of chattel slavery were the dominant imperial action of the United States in the nineteenth century, and these attitudes informed the ways popular shows exhibited Indigenous artists and performers. Next, exploring the careers of some Indigenous artists and actors in these shows, the chapter considers gendered and racialized dynamics, the social use of such exhibitions to support American white supremacist ideology, modernity, and the need for a "dying race" narrative. Contemporary world's fairs simultaneously appearing across the national landscape helped create false scientific reasoning behind popular racial imagery as educational, while circuses and Wild West shows sent the same racial message as entertainment. Popular portrayals of Indian women, for example, reveal how gender was weaponized to dehumanize all Indigenous peoples. Next, the chapter will explore clashes between Indigenous thought leaders and American Indian policy. The chapter also considers the differences in philosophies between Indigenous leaders, largely middle class, and performers, revealing ways people from both sides of the question understood the role of entertainment and image-making while fighting for sovereignty and basic human rights. Ultimately, key differences in how popular media portrayed Native Americans and African Americans, as well as federal laws governing movement, greatly affected Indigenous people's ability to fully exercise their creativity and freedom of choice. This difference in law and image production led to significant differences in how each group was able to respond to and benefit from the traveling show industry. White Americans viewed Black Americans as crucial cheap labor and as natural musicians and dancers due to African Americans' supposed childlike pursuit of pleasure and closer proximity to base emotions. Both these areas gave Black Americans a place in the country's journey toward modernity. Although their placement in sideshows rather than under circus big tops relegated them to the status of human oddities and freak shows, African Americans' creativity was somewhat protected by sideshow placement. There, they continually innovated music, dance, comedy, and all forms of artistry they touched. Their art and music became staples for American circuses. On the other hand, white Americans used the myth of the disappearing Indian and other imagery to reinforce savage, culturally backward stereotypes that solidified Indigenous people's otherness and explained their exclusion from American citizenship and America's future. Wild West shows centered Indigenous defeat, and white Americans maintained the dominant narratives and symbolism. For that reason, Native Americans did not enjoy the modicum of creative freedom African Americans were able to manipulate into viable careers. However, even these displays are filled with nuance: though Wild West shows perpetuated racist, imperialist representations of Indigenous peoples, Native American performers used these roles to travel, educate, join lecture circuits, and make amounts of money that were otherwise unavailable. In this way, Indigenous performers were important in the creation of a pan-Indian network across the country, as were their middle-class counterparts who questioned their commitments to progress and Indigenous rights.

## The Wild West Show in the American Imagination

Circuses, Wild West shows, and similar exhibitions enabled white Americans to gaze upon people from other cultures and races in controlled, safe spaces. Spectators got up close and familiar with the excitement and danger while feeling safe in the audience. Show managers dressed people from other cultures in fanciful, imagined approximations of their normal dress and placed them into scenes that upheld white fantasies, prejudices, and ignorance. For colonial powers, to exhibit Indigenous peoples became a visible sign of modernity and imperial greatness.[3] These were white supremacist rituals and were part of an Anglo-Saxon celebration of global empire-building.[4] Circuses played an important role in spreading ideas about white superiority and pseudoscientific vocabularies of racial difference. P. T. Barnum was one of many circus impresarios who greatly benefited from a colonial ideology galvanized by popular culture in the form of novels, periodicals, expositions, and human exhibitions. Circus displays, human zoos, and Wild West shows all served to promote and legitimize the violence of colonialism and build mental boundaries between the ever-growing white "civilized" world and the vanishing "savage" Indigenous world.[5] These exhibitions put Indigenous peoples of the world together in one category and pushed the narrative that they were vanishing races and primitive, childlike, warlike, animal-like, and sexually licentious brutes. Native Americans, Africans, and Australian Aboriginal peoples were considered uncivilized remnants of a bygone era that must make room for Western progress, Christianity, and modernity. Hugely popular, these shows included thousands of Indigenous peoples by the turn of the century. Exhibitions came in many sizes and ranged from individual performances to entire villages on display.

World's fairs worked with circuses and Wild West shows ideologically to reinforce the necessity, educational value, and rightness of inhumane displays of Indigenous peoples. Most importantly, world's fairs provided pseudoscientific rationales for racial and social hierarchies. Held all over the United States and Europe primarily (though China, Japan, and Saudi Arabia also hosted these expositions), they showcased the great achievements of the hosting nation. In the United States, the main point of these was to show white American progress beyond Black and Brown and Indigenous peoples' progress. Crowds of spectators—nearly one hundred million between the mid-1870s and 1916, to be specific—visited these exhibitions throughout the country in cities such as Chicago, New York, Saint Louis, Atlanta, San Francisco, and Omaha.[6] They drew upon and reshaped other sources of entertainment including the menagerie, the minstrel show, the circus, and the Wild West show. World's fairs purported to be educational entertainment. Using white supremacist reasoning, they drew upon eugenics and other pseudoscience to explain America's expeditious rise to become a world power and white Americans' dominance within that structure. These international expositions, where science, religion, the arts, and architecture reinforced each other, offered Americans a powerful and highly visible, modern, evolutionary justification for long-standing racial and cultural prejudices.[7] For instance, taking a cue from the Paris Exhibition in 1889, which displayed colonial villages, the Chicago World's Columbian Exposition established living ethnological displays of Native Americans and other nonwhite people from around the world. The treatment of Filipino people at the St. Louis World's Fair in 1904 where a model Filipino village was created is yet another example of how Indigenous peoples were displayed and exploited. Contemporary photographs of the village pictured thatched huts and men in trees sporting loincloths, bows, and arrows. This imagery reinforced imperialist attitudes of the "native other" as uncivilized and backward, just as newspaper advertisements described the Filipinos as savage consumers of dogs, including the occasional unfortunate American pet.

Much like the Zulu craze, the popularity of Wild West shows was catalyzed by wars against Indigenous peoples. There had been a history of violence against the Indigenous West, but when gold was discovered in Montana, white traders, missionaries, prospectors, farmers, and government officials made increased inroads into Lakota territory. By the 1870s, Lakota people had become barriers to the exploitation of natural resources and the spread of white settlement.[8] As violence increased, the Lakota won skirmishes and often eluded American troops. Late in June 1876, Lakota, Arapaho, and Northern Cheyenne forces led by Crazy Horse and Sitting Bull defeated General George Custer and his troops at the Battle of Little Bighorn. This victory over the American army by troops who had much less military technology was crushing, killing 268 American soldiers as well as General Custer himself. After their defeats, the United States poured military might and resources into the Plains campaign. The United States eventually dissolved and reduced Native American homelands, destroyed their military autonomy, attempted to wipe out their cultures, largely toppled their traditional leadership and social structures, and promoted factionalism. Just as Zulus became popular human displays, Lakota had become coveted performers soon after they were confined to reservations by the US Army. Wild West shows told a story of the struggle of white America against a backward and hostile Indigenous power and the American conquest of the lands of the West.

No venue captured the elation of the American land-grabbing ideology and genocide more than the Wild West show. In 1890, the head of the US Census Department announced that the American frontier was closed and that the nation was settled from coast to coast. In 1893, the historian Fredrick Jackson Turner argued that the frontier experience–settler colonial exceptionalism and winning the so-called wilderness to expand US territory is what shaped America's nonviolent, democratic culture and unique ideals such as individualism, egalitarianism, entrepreneurship, and freedom. He

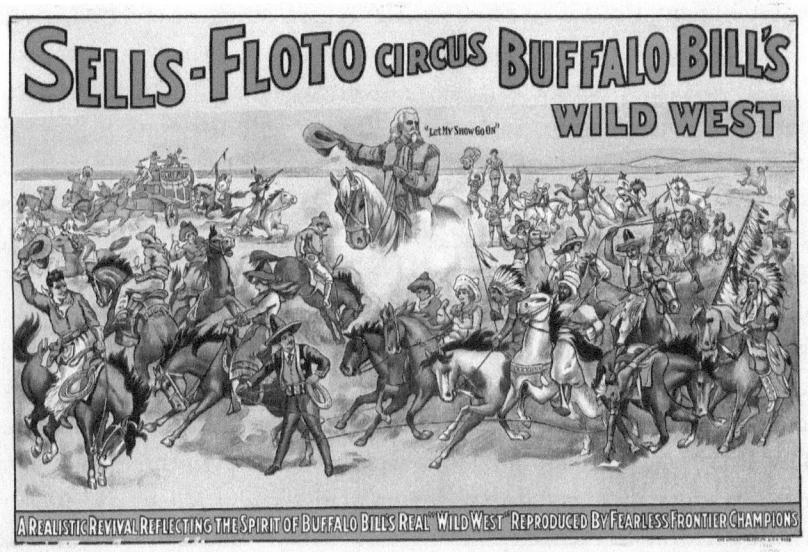

Sells-Floto, 1926. Circus World–Wisconsin Historical Society.

wrote that American democracy gained new strength each time it pushed West and touched a new frontier. Wild West shows celebrated the western frontier and looked back on the good old days of Indian Wars and the expansionist designs of white Americans. They were open air shows from the 1880s to the 1920s that depicted archetypical cowboys and Indians — both real Native Americans and impersonators — who traveled with circuses and as stand-alone shows. Wild West shows were notorious for culturally portraying all Indigenous Americans as western Plains tribes wearing headdresses, homogenizing and deleting hundreds of Indigenous North American cultures while creating the image of the backward savage. The "savage image," Philip Deloria writes, worked in many contexts, for example, the "kill or be killed" hatred of the frontiersmen, the scientific racism of the intellectual, the evangelical demand of the missionary, and so forth.[9]

The mastermind behind the great popularity of Wild West shows was William F. "Buffalo Bill" Cody. Cody fought in the Indian Wars where, to avenge General Custer's defeat at Little Big Horn at the hands of the Lakota, he famously killed and scalped the Cheyenne chief Hay-o-Wei (Yellow Hair). In the middle to late 1870s, Cody was the subject of adventure dime novels, which propelled him to popularity. He garnered the help of two men, one of whom was a former blackface minstrel, to create a new type of entertainment, the Wild West show. The general structure of the show was set when Cody opened *The Drama of Civilization*, a five-part performance. This performance started with Native Americans living among animals and ended with the announcement of civilization with the Pony Express. It eventually included a final scene of Custer's last stand, which concluded with Buffalo Bill arriving at the scene of the so-called massacre.[10] In 1893, the show opened alongside the Chicago World's Fair as the Buffalo Bill Wild West and Congress of Rough Riders of the World and took on the character of an imperial pageant. Buffalo Bill's Wild West Show typically started with the national anthem and included an introduction of Buffalo Bill's Rough Riders, a review of the Sioux and Cheyenne Indians, cowboys, Mexicans, scouts, guides, veteran members of the US cavalry, and cowgirls. Buffalo Bill's show and countless imitators came to last two to three hours and included a grand entry, cowboy demonstrations, and Indian vignettes in which performers reenacted ceremonies, dances, and parts of everyday life. There were historical reenactments, military and ethnic displays, and circus acts that could include large or small animals, acrobats, and other presentations. Shows romanticized the frontier and American expansion, as they praised the civilizing power of the American spirit. In 1889, Buffalo Bill's Wild West played the Paris Universal Exposition, which drew an estimated thirty-two million people. Here the show staged Custer's last stand at Little Bighorn. Having Native Americans in his show authenticated it as educational, much as the "Negro village" or other human zoo attractions.[11] When in Europe, Cody incorporated Zulu men and women. In later shows, he included Filipinos, a sign of the United States' imperial power over its first overseas colony. Cody's show was billed as an authentic representation of the West and succeeded in being a "mobile dream factory capable of producing narratives of heroic conquest for mass audiences numbering in the millions."[12] This conquest mirrored audiences' understanding of the American empire. The Wild West show reflected and encouraged attitudes of American imperialism.

Wild West shows confounded distinctions between reality and representation.[13] Audiences viewed Cody as a real war hero, and Native Americans were seen as savage villains. In fact, Native American performers were encouraged to walk the streets of the towns where they had shows so that they were human advertisements. The most popular Wild West shows scrambled to bring real Native American warriors, law enforcement, and others involved in historic events to act in their shows. The Oklahoma-based 101 Ranch's 1905 show featured Geronimo, the Apache war hero, medicine man, and federal prisoner. Geronimo fought against Mexico and the American empire, spreading to his native lands of northern Mexico, New Mexico, and Arizona from the 1850s to 1886 when he surrendered to the US Army. Though he was a prisoner of war, the government exploited his fame and had him appear in various Wild West shows and other fairs and exhibitions. By the time he appeared at the 101 Ranch show, Geronimo had already been to the 1898 Trans-Mississippi and International Exhibition in Omaha, Nebraska, and the inaugural parade of President Theodore Roosevelt. He was able to make some money at these venues, selling photographs and other knickknacks. Also included in the 1905 101 Ranch program were a buffalo hunt, bronco busting, roping contests, a war dance, and a powwow. Although Geronimo's nation did not hunt buffalo, he was a featured buffalo hunter in the scene. Other acts followed, but the closing feature of the day was the attack of a wagon train by Indians on a hill south of the amphitheater. Spectators were given a chance to feel the excitement of an Indian raid on pioneers from the comfort of their seats. Wagons were set on fire, and show Indians rode fiercely about them, howling and causing a sense of awe over the audience.[14] The reenactment of violence in the form of staged raids, massacres, and famous battles was central to Americans' understanding of Native Americans and themselves. The 101 Ranch, on one occasion, staged a reproduction of the 1875 massacre of the Pat Hennessey party. During this raid, warriors from the Cheyenne tribe killed the Oklahoma travelers. To give the reenactment authenticity, the Ranch asked the US marshal who was called out to investigate the slayings, W. H. Malaley, to be in the production. Both he and Cheyenne chief Bull Bear, who was said to be the author of the massacre, appeared in the reenactment.

## Show Indians

The thousands of Native Americans who performed in over one hundred Wild West shows between 1883 and the 1930s had myriad reasons for joining these largely harmful exhibitions. Much like Black Americans who participated in minstrel shows due to lack of work elsewhere, Native Americans, too, chose to display fact and fictionalized aspects of their cultures to white audiences over facing the dire conditions on the impoverished reservations, and many saw these venues as opportunities.[15] It is impossible to know what every man and woman considered their reasons to join, but Philip Deloria suggests that there are a number of possibilities ranging from escape and adventure to economic need, cultural celebration, and educational outreach.[16] These men and women were savvy and understood that although they performed for the white gaze, the show life could afford them some privileges that reservation life could not. Wild West employment enabled Indigenous performers to experience a degree of freedom as they escaped reservations and traveled, even if just for a season. Shows gave them relatively safe passage through North America, South America, Europe, and locations all over the Pacific and occasionally Africa. Travel was a break from reservation life, but also an act of subversion: performers openly rejected Bureau of Indian Affairs regulations that mandated farming and the segregation of Indigenous people on barren reservations.[17] Although travel had been used to subdue Native Americans, Indigenous performers saw opportunities with the Wild West shows to travel the world.[18] When Red Shirt (Oglala Lakota) was presented to the queen of England, she expressed her pleasure at seeing him. Red Shirt then replied, "I have come many thousand miles to see you; now that I have seen you my heart is glad."[19] Red Shirt, Ghost Dog, Lone Wolf, Standing Bear, Black Elk, and hundreds of other Native men worked for numerous seasons with the Buffalo Bill show. Black Elk was an Oglala Lakota man born in 1863 who survived the 1890 Wounded Knee Massacre. He shared his life's story with John Neihardt who wrote one of the most famous Native American memoirs, *Black Elk Speaks*, in 1932.[20] Black Elk traveled to England in 1887 with Buffalo Bill and performed for Queen Victoria. The following year, he got separated from the show and was left in England. He subsequently joined another Wild West show that afforded him travel to Germany, France, and Italy. In 1889, Buffalo Bill went to Paris where Black Elk connected with him and gained a ticket home to the Pine Ridge Reservation. Black Elk's memoir claimed that this excursion gave him the opportunity to learn about white culture and to speak English better. Luther Standing Bear, a Sicangu and Oglala chief born in 1868, was educated in the Carlisle Indian Industrial School and decided for a time to join Buffalo Bill as well. Standing Bear's tenure with Buffalo Bill was cut short by a fatal train wreck that almost took his life. He recovered, and in later years advised and acted in several Hollywood films alongside movie stars like Tom Mix and Douglas Fairbanks Sr. In all, Native Americans were savvy businessmen and used the demand for Indian actors to their advantage. Wild West shows provided some opportunity for Native Americans to make more money than was typically available to them on many reservations. Native American men in the 1892 season in the Buffalo Bill Wild West Show could earn between $25 and $75 per week (equivalent to $722 to $2,168 in 2021) and had no traveling or living expenses. Many Indigenous men were able to save significant amounts: for example, one Native American performer, Short Bull, saved $600. Another performer, Kicking Bear, said he had saved $750 (around $21,677 in contemporary money) by the end of a season.[21] Native women performers were paid extra for infants and children and supplemented wages by making and selling craftwork.[22]

A third reason shows up in the written reports: Native Americans had a platform and a voice in national and international papers. Native Americans in shows had a platform to express themselves as their counterparts on reservations could not. Through visual and print media—newspaper reports, advertisements, photographs, postcards, show programs, and posters—they expressed reasons why they joined the shows, what they thought about the shows, and how they benefited from the show. Although these outlets were geared toward a white audience, there are many accounts, and what several men thought came through. These experiences were not always positive but not entirely negative. Newspapers across the country reported on "Show Indians," their tribal origins, previous battles, and their views. Overall, Wild West shows promoted a friend-to-foe narrative, putting forth the idea that Native Americans, once mortal enemies of white America, were now in the late nineteenth century not only friendly with whites but open to whites' civilizing influence. Performers expressed their own views, which both supported and challenged prevailing narratives in newspaper reports.[23] In other words, though they routinely spoke of peace and friendship, they also used the press to communicate their opinions about white society, make social and political statements, and give their own interpretations of their experiences in Wild West shows.[24] Native American performers saw varying degrees of success—some saw tragic ends and others died in old age—but all of them left a mark on the written record, communicating their views of white society, their reasons for joining Wild West shows, and sometimes even their hopes and dreams.

Women and children participated in singing and drumming, setting up teepees, Indian vignettes, and everyday activities in the encampment outside the arena. Indigenous women tended to family chores and children, mended clothing and costumes, did beadwork, and made moccasins and other crafts that were sold to encampment visitors. Audiences saw this display of everyday life as a part of the show. Native American women and children were smaller but significant parts of Wild West show life. Indigenous women put their lives on display for spectators, supporting male performers, and sometimes worked on their own skilled performances, craftwork, and various other show events. Newspaper accounts recorded that there were often anywhere from five to fifteen women in a group of eighty to one hundred Native American men.[25] Performers' children and grandchildren were staples of encampments that were open to the public.[26] These performances allowed onlookers a glimpse into what they believed to be the family life of Native Americans, but women and children in the Wild West shows were vastly outnumbered by men; the Buffalo Bill show, for example, had 700 men at its height.

The lives of the Native American families were a frequent topic in white newspapers. They often show up in accounts of visitors to the show encampments. Stories often revolve around marriages, childbirths, physical appearance, and disposition. The *Washington Post* announced the wedding of Mr. High Bear and Miss Holy Blanket of Buffalo Bill's Wild West Show in South Brooklyn on June 11, 1894. Both husband and wife were from the Oglala Lakota tribe. High Bear was reported to be a "wild untutored savage" in the show, but he possessed a "great heart," which, "like the organ of his more civilized brother, beats responsive to the tender sentiments of love."[27] Another event in the camps was the birth and baptism of Native American children. When on tour in England, the show garnered much attention due to the birth of Frances Victoria Alexandra to Good Robe and her husband, Little Chief Ogallala.[28] Alexandra's family had lost a child in London the previous summer. Her baptism was covered as well:

> The baptism of the papoose which was born in the Indian camp . . . took place in the presence of a congregation altogether unique. English ladies and gentlemen, American cowboys, Mexican vaqueros, and Indians assembled for the purpose of witnessing the ceremony. It was indeed a sight worth seeing, and it will long be remembered to all who were privileged to attend. There was no desire or intention on the part of the management that the event should partake at all of a character of a public ceremonial; rather the reverse. . . . "Good Robe," is really a handsome woman—strongly built, intelligent-looking and modest in a high degree. The father and mother are both members of the Episcopalian church, and they naturally desired that their offspring should be baptized according to the faith and ritual of their adoption.[29]

The article went on to say there were seven or eight other Native American women present, one of whom carried a child of her own on her back. The child being baptized, Frances Victoria Alexandra, was said to be the first Native American child to be born in England. Children were also presented to the queen while in England.[30]

Native women performed in acts created to showcase them as well. Indigenous women sometimes rode horses, participated in dances, and took part in traditions around death and mourning. A popular event was relay races pitting women of different races and ethnicities against each other. The 1899 Buffalo Bill Wild West Show held several relay races for women, including one contest between a Native American woman (referred to by the derogatory term, "squaw") and a Filipino woman.[31] This pairing must have made sense to white American audiences who often saw images in American newspapers of Filipino people drawn to look similar to the savage Indians and African warriors they were accustomed to seeing in the media. In fact, since the Spanish-American War and later the American-Philippine War, the United States had harbored imperial ambitions to make the Philippines a colony and perhaps a state in the Union. Filipino people were depicted as just another backward race to be tamed and civilized by Americans. Ringling had Indian women, or imitators of Indian women, perform the green corn dance around the big tent track in the 1890s.[32] Pawnee Bill's Wild West Show carried a "band of Sioux Indians" that showcased Chief Standing Bear, Howling Crow, Big Hawk, Beaver, White Eyes, Swallow, and Black Bull along with women referred to as "Indian Squaws," White Cow, Minnie Ought to Be, Little Woman, and Mrs. Frost. Children and babies, or "papooses," which is another dated and derogatory term, working in the show included White Bird, Sun Woman, and Walking Girl.[33]

## The Marks Family

Charles Marks (1870–1946), a Miami man in the Godfroy village in Indiana, worked on the Hagenbeck-Wallace Circus farm and brought his children to work with him to cut corn.[34] Marks had worked in Mike York's Dog and Pony Show as part of the grounds crew and then began to act as an "Indian villain." He rode in the shows until around 1890.[35] Marks's son LaMoine worked for the circus and related industries for most of his life. The younger Marks was born in 1907 and witnessed the devastating 1913 flood that killed many animals and led Wallace to sell his company.[36] As a young boy, LaMoine Marks learned horse tricks from his father and from the Godfroys. This later helped him to get into circus shows. Marks also stated that he learned trick roping in the quarters from other performers.[37] As a teenager, LaMoine's first independent job was working at a concession stand selling hot dogs, sweets, and ice cream. He helped to build and take down concession stands before and after shows. Marks went on to "candy butchering," managing his own concession stand, and employing two African American teens to work for him in the stand.[38] He later performed in the Western Concert, a pre-circus equestrian showcase.[39] Members of the Marks family found a variety of job opportunities through the circus. Other Miami and white families chose circus professions as well. Gabe Tucker was a Miami man whose family trained elephants. His sister Mary rode elephants during the summer touring season and was a schoolteacher in the winter.[40] His brother-in-law, Cheerful Gardner, was the show's elephant manager at the time and gave Tucker a position as an elephant trainer.[41] Tucker also began a business making bullhooks, an instrument used in training pachyderms. Sarah Tucker Weisenberger sewed outfits for performers, and Susie Tucker Mellinger worked as a cook.[42] Then, when the American Circus Corporation took over management, he continued his professional elephant-training career.[43] These types of small business ventures were common among the Miami people who traveled with the show. In some cases, the company hired them to sell their wares within the circus proper.

## Sitting Bull

Sitting Bull (Hunkpapa Lakota) was a leader against US forces in the West and became perhaps the most famous of the so-called show Indians. Although he only toured with Cody's Wild West show for one season, his legacy lived on in the American imagination decades after he left the show and well after he was shot and killed by Indian agency police on the Standing Rock Indian Reservation. Sitting Bull led his people in resisting the US government policies and westward expansion. In a bold move in 1872, Sitting Bull led an attack on the Northern Pacific Railroad in efforts to stop the further infringement of whites on sacred Indigenous lands and the destructive forces they brought, including their "bison Harvest," which encouraged whites to slaughter bison, the Lakota's food source. Before the Battle of Little Bighorn four years later, Sitting Bull had a vision of victory for the Lakota warriors, which proved true weeks later when the Lakota and Cheyenne killed General Custer and defeated his seventh cavalry. Sitting Bull escaped the US forces by guiding his band to Saskatchewan, Canada, until 1881 when, starving, he surrendered to the United States. Then in 1883, in what seems to be a sadistic request, the Northern Pacific Railway asked Sitting Bull to give a speech celebrating the railroad and white Americans' march westward through Indian country. Expected to give a speech written by a US soldier that celebrated American progress, Sitting Bull instead said in his own language, "I hate all white people. You are thieves and liars. You have taken away our land and made us outcasts."[44] He went on to list white Americans' crimes and offenses in the name of progress. The unsuspecting crowd—including governors of all the states the railroad connected and President Grant—loved having the chance to see an authentic Indian praising them. After this appearance, Sitting Bull was allowed to leave the reservation to go on tour with Buffalo Bill's Wild West Show in 1885.

During his time touring, Sitting Bull was able to use his platform to speak many times about his work, his outlooks, and his views on white society. In fact, he generally welcomed conversations with the press and was able to negotiate a strong contract with Cody. Sitting Bull negotiated a fifty dollar per week contract (equal to over $1,400 in present-day currency) and exclusive rights to sell his photographs and autographed postcards. While on tour, Sitting Bull seemed to have positive things to say about the tour. In one news article dating to a tour in Canada, he said that he was being treated well by Cody and others in the Wild West show.[45] He said that he wanted to make friends with white people and had met thousands on his journeys. In another interview, Sitting Bull said, "I am very much pleased with my trip through the country. I like Canada; those people all treated me well."[46] Sitting Bull's impression of the eastern states was similar: "They treated me very kindly . . . and when I return to my people I shall tell them all about our friends among the white men, and what I have seen. . . . [A]s long as I am all right and my people are all right, I want to travel and see all I can."[47] Many Native Americans echoed the sentiment of wanting to learn, though perhaps not the things that the white public expected them to learn. Vine Deloria writes, "Touring with Buffalo Bill enabled a whole generation of Indians to learn about American society in a relatively non-threatening atmosphere."[48] American Horse, who replaced Sitting Bull as the Native American headliner for the 1886–87 seasons, spoke in an interview on what he thought about his tour of the eastern United States, saying, "I see so much that is wonderful and strange that I feel a wish to go out in the forest and cover my head with a blanket, so that I can see no more and have a chance to think over what I have seen."[49]

Sitting Bull's fame did not shield him from the whims of the American empire. In 1889, a Paiute holy man named Wovoka spread a religious movement from Nevada eastward to the Plains that preached a resurrection of Native American people. Known as the "Ghost Dance Movement," it directed the Indigenous people of all tribes to dance and chant for the rising up of deceased relatives and return of the buffalo. The dance included shirts that were said to stop bullets. When the movement reached the Standing Rock

Reservation, Sitting Bull allowed the dancers to camp on his land. In 1890, the US Indian agent James McLaughlin, believing Sitting Bull to be a major instigator of the dance and that he was planning to leave the reservation with the Ghost Dancers, sent police to arrest him. A gunfight broke out, and Sitting Bull was shot and died from the wounds. Ultimately, the US Army massacred 153 Lakota people at Wounded Knee, mostly women and children.

## Kicking Bear

Engaging Kicking Bear (Lakota) was a major success for William Cody and his Wild West show. Kicking Bear had been not only a warrior; he had fought in the battles of Rosebud, Little Bighorn, and Slim Buttes in 1876 and 1877. He was the nephew of Sitting Bull and the cousin of Crazy Horse and was the band chief among his wife's band of Miniconjou Lakota. Kicking Bear had heard of the Paiute prophet Wovoka and was a delegate in 1889 to travel to Nevada to learn firsthand about the new religion. Kicking Bear met with the prophet, who told him of the future of the world of Native Americans and white people. From there, he became a leader of the Ghost Dance religion among his people. He survived the Wounded Knee massacre but was captured and incarcerated by General Nelson A. Miles in January 1891. Later, Miles suggested to William Cody that he consider hiring the Lakota prisoners for his Wild West show. The commissioner of Indian affairs, Thomas Jefferson Morgan, supported the decision, allowing Cody to take the imprisoned Lakota "restless spirits" on tour. Kicking Bear's response was that he had been a "dead man" but with this, he was "alive again."[50]

## Luther Standing Bear

Luther Standing Bear was a Sicangu and Oglala Lakota actor, author, and educator. In 1902, he went with Buffalo Bill's Wild West Show to Great Britain as the "Chief Interpreter of the Sioux Nation and a manager of the show Indians."[51] Upon telling his wife of the job opportunity, she "was greatly pleased when I told her the news that we were going to have the chance to go abroad."[52] A highlight of the tour for Luther was meeting royalty. He wrote, "I had the honor of being introduced to King Edward the Seventh, the monarch of Great Britain."[53] In another endorsement of the tour, Luther said, "The English people were very good to us. They would invite the Indians to their homes and give them plenty of good things to eat. I recall that one day I visited the house where all the toys were kept with which Queen

Victoria had played as a child, and I was shown where all her jewelry was on display. I also visited Westminster Abbey, one of the most beautiful churches in the world, and a very historic spot."[54] The show stayed in London for three months and, as Luther wrote, "had a royal good time."[55] Altogether, the company was in England for eleven months. While there, the Native Americans made many purchases, needing extra baggage to bring things back to the United States. Luther wrote that Buffalo Bill was a fair employer who encouraged him and stood up for Native Americans' rights. He wrote, proudly, that Cody was "well pleased to note how well the Indians minded me in all their work."[56] In one English town, Luther complained to Cody that the Native Americans were served a dinner of the leftovers that other races had had for breakfast. Infuriated, Cody scolded the manager, demanding that the Native Americans be treated equally. Luther recounted Cody's words: "I want you to understand, sir, that I will not stand for such treatment. My Indians are the principal feature of this show and they are the one people I will not allow to be misused or neglected. Hereafter, see to it that they get just exactly what they want at meal-time. Do you understand me, sir?"[57] Luther and his wife had their baby daughter in Birmingham, England. She was named after the queen of England, and the child's full name was Alexandra Birmingham Cody Standing Bear. Luther agreed that his wife and newborn baby would be displayed in the sideshow. He wrote that it was a great boon to the show, as many patrons brought gifts for the child. Luther commented that before she was twenty-four hours old, she was making more money than he and his wife combined. Later, in 1906, Luther, his brother, and one hundred Pine Ridge Oglalas traveled to New York to appear in an international show. On trips like these outside the confines of the Wild West shows, Indigenous performers came to see that they were part of a national cohort of Indian people working, not just in Wild West shows, but in circuses, traveling medicine shows, urban revues, lecture circuits, and sideshows. Luther's family was a particularly active part of that world.[58]

## Standing Bear

Standing Bear (not to be confused with Luther Standing Bear) was a chief in the Ponca tribe and an important civil rights activist. Standing Bear's successes in the courtroom led to his decision to go on the lecture circuit and eventually join Buffalo Bill's Wild West Show. Standing Bear was born around 1829. About thirty years later, the Ponca tribe sold their homelands in Nebraska to the US government but retained 58,000 acres on Ponca Creek as their own reservation. Then in 1868, the US government established the Great Sioux Reservation and included the Ponca Reserve within that territory. This caused confusion, and the Ponca were left open to Lakota attacks, so the federal government then decided to remove them to Indian territory in Oklahoma. Standing Bear, a tribal leader by now, protested; still, federal troops forced the Ponca to leave. The journey was marked by tragedy: one-third of the travelers died, and the rest were sick or disabled. A tornado ripped through the path as they traversed it. As his dying wish, Standing Bear's son asked to be buried in his homelands, not in the new Indian territory. Standing Bear, wanting to make good on his son's request, left the territory and headed back to his ancestral lands. Because he was labeled a renegade for leaving the reservation without permission, Standing Bear was arrested. Not close to backing down, he brought the case to court: his lawyers filed an application for habeas corpus to test the legality of the detention, basing the case on the Fourteenth Amendment of the US Constitution. The government denied Standing Bear's right to habeas corpus arguing that he was not a "person" in the eyes of the law. The case, *Standing Bear v. Crook*, was seen in the courtroom of Judge Elmer S. Dundy in the US District Court in Omaha. The court ruled in favor of Standing Bear, reasoning that Native Americans were persons under the law and entitled to the rights of any other person in the nation. Standing Bear was entitled to the ability to sever ties with his tribe and live somewhere else. The government appealed, but the Supreme Court refused to hear it, and the decision was upheld.

This case launched Standing Bear's lecture circuit career. During the lead-up to the court hearing, Standing Bear went on a fundraising tour with other Native Americans such as Susette La Flesche, or "Bright Eyes," who was a writer, lecturer, interpreter, and artist of the Omaha Nation. White companions, such as activist and poet Helen Hunt Jackson, also joined him. He attended both private and public receptions at various churches, including a benefit concert put on by the Fisk Jubilee Singers at Berkeley Street Church in Boston.[59] With the court case won, Standing Bear continued his lecture tour, with activist Thomas Henry Tibbles and Susette La Flesche interpreting for him. On one occasion, Standing Bear spoke to a group of laborers saying,

> Your face is white and mine is red, but one God made us both. Why should we not always have been friends and helped each other instead of killing one another? My tribe never killed a white man. There is not one drop of white blood on the hand of any Ponca. The bones of seven

hundred of my young men lie bleaching on the plains of South Dakota, who lost their lives in defending the poor white men of Nebraska who live near the Sioux. I come from that far away country to ask for justice for my people. I knew nothing of your ways, but I see that you are a great people.[60]

In Boston, Standing Bear continued to speak his mind. To a group of activists he said,

> When the white people came to this country, they Indians were turned over to the army. For years the army did what it liked with us and we had war and bloodshed. Then the Indians were turned over to the politicians and they appointed our agents and rulers. That was a hundred times worse and we had continual war. Then your great General who never talked (U. S. Grant) turned us over to the churches and divided us up among them. We still had war and bloodshed. . . . Now I ask you to turn us over once more. Turn us over to the ladies, and they will not murder us or drive us from our lands.[61]

From 1886 to 1887, the three colleagues toured England and Scotland where Standing Bear spoke out about Native American rights. In 1893, he worked for Buffalo Bill Wild West Show. Working in the Chicago Columbian Exposition, Standing Bear rode the Ferris Wheel for the first time wearing a full headdress.[62] Having put his voice to the American public during the groundbreaking court case, Standing Bear may have wanted to stay in the realm of the public, continuing to advocate for Native American rights. When he was done with his own lecture circuit of the eastern United States and Europe, he may have seen the Wild West show as another outlet for his activism.

## Nabor Feliz Netzahualt

Nabor Feliz Netzahualt (1877–1972), like other Indigenous Southwest artists, capitalized on this craze and enjoyed fame as an "Indian sculptor." He displayed work in museums and advocated for the recognition of Native American artistic ability. Netzahualt identified as a Pueblo sculptor, bead worker, historian, interpreter, and storyteller and was an artist relegated to the sideshow tent. He worked in several traveling shows in the late nineteenth through the mid-twentieth centuries. He performed alongside the "Hilton Siamese Twins," a pair of conjoined twins who were musicians

Portrait of Nabor Feliz with some of his sculptures prior to 1950. Unidentified photographer, Southwest region. Nabor Feliz Collection, Autry Museum of the American West.

"Nabor Feliz Speaking to Children, 1923." Unidentified photographer. Nabor Feliz Collection, Autry Museum of the American West.

and dancers, armless man Barney Nelson, and the "elastic skin man," Nels Nelson, at the Mississippi Valley Fair in 1923. Netzahualt's artistry covered a wide range of genres. His sideshow act was to sculpt while telling stories. He used sculptures to illustrate his stories and earned the name "Lightning Sculptor" for the speed with which he changed one figure into another. Between shows, he made silver and turquoise jewelry.[63] However, storytelling, sculpting, and selling jewelry for the circus was not Netzahualt's only occupation. From around 1919 through the 1950s, he maintained relationships with several museums and art societies. In 1919, Netzahualt contacted the Carnegie Institute and donated several pieces of clay sculptures, which he requested be placed in the institute's Pueblo exhibit to demonstrate "that one of his race can, though self-instructed, attain to the standards of modern art." The Carnegie record went on to say, "The model of the grazing buffalo and the eagle are particularly fine."[64] A later report from the Carnegie Institute recorded that Netzahualt had donated several other sculptures that were based on the series that he had created for the American Red Cross. This series was designed as gifts for volunteers at donation centers.

Popular images of Native Americans, whether savage or noble, have had everything to do with white American projections and little to do with Indigenous people themselves. Spurred on by the belief that Indians were a dying people and their cultures would be lost to modernity, American audiences fetishized and commodified Native American cultures, flocking to Wild West shows and other exhibitions that promised to get them up close and personal to the soon-extinct peoples. Contemporary medicine shows, for example, played into stereotypes about Indigenous powers to heal with their knowledge of nature, and some religious sects regarded Native Americans as holy peoples or a Lost Tribe of Israel. The Santa Fe Railroad line that had opened in 1863 increasingly brought in white artists, then crowds of tourists to imbibe Southwest Indian culture. As opposed to Wild West savages, the Indians of the Southwest, including the Pueblo, Hopi, Navajo, and Apache, came to be seen as noble peoples whose art and architecture had mingled with the Catholic Spanish culture before the arrival of Anglo-American settlers. This view was created in large part by white writers and other artists who at times had protested Southwest people's mistreatment, romanticized their cultures, and held them up as primitive, gentle people. Southwestern Indian fetishization took off in places like the Santa Fe and Taos arts communities, where the buying, selling, and displaying of Indian arts and crafts were big attractions for tourists well into the 1940s and beyond. Entrepreneurs such as Fred Harvey, founder of the Fred Harvey Company, capitalized on this sentiment. Harvey formed an "Indian Department" in 1902 to build what he marketed as more authentic displays of the disappearing Indigenous lifestyle. By 1926, he was taking tourists on "Indian Detours," which claimed to give visitors an authentic Native American experience. Hired actors played out made-up narratives that countered the ostentatious Wild West shows, instead showing Indigenous people living sedentary lives, shearing sheep, making blankets, pottery, and other arts and crafts, and overall behaving in a more respectful, if still less civilized, manner.[65] They hid the fact that their employment required them to suppress any appearance that they were familiar with modern American life.[66] In exchange, many Indigenous actors and artists made this trade-off to support their families during a time when their communities suffered from extreme poverty.

The Indian brave character is often the primary focus of Wild West show discussions, but centering Indigenous women laboring in these shows enables a better understanding of how white America dehumanized, alienated, and destroyed Indigenous cultures and people. In the American imagination, there were two kinds of Indian women: the squaw and the princess. Like Pocahontas, the princess typically serves as the colonizers' helpmate by violating the wishes and customs of her own "barbarous" people to save a white man out of love and often out of so-called Christian sympathy.[67] The story of a young, exotic, beautiful "savage" woman who would put her life on the line to save a Christian white man, to later marry a white man and become a proper lady, was long implanted in the European imagination before John Smith's 1624 history of Virginia, which purported to tell the story of Pocahontas. In fact, the caricature and many components of the "Indian Princess" story date back to Scottish ballads and other English texts before 1300, far before European contact with the Americas. For Europeans coming to America, Pocahontas and the Indian Princess myth symbolized their ideal relationship with Indigenous peoples: nurturing, protective, and open to European intrusion.[68] Though reimagined lovingly over many generations of American history, the princess character, just as the squaw characterization, is an intolerable metaphor for the Indian-white experience. The Indian princess was wildly popular and often played by white women, some of whom made great money and found great fame in these roles. Pawnee Bill put Princess Standing Holly in the show's annex or sideshow tent with other "specialties" such as ventriloquists, magicians, tattooed men, fat women, big-footed boys, and others.[69] Several other shows did the same, and whether the "princesses" were actually Indigenous women was up to the show owners. American Indian women were constantly caught between images of a seductive, though saintly, Pocahontas-type Indian princess and the squaw, a dark, fat, and crude woman who is shamed for having sexual relationships with white men. The derogatory term "squaw" was used to connote that Indian women were sexually available to white men and was first recorded in the early seventeenth century. The Algonquian word is based on the Massachusetts words for woman, *squá*, or *ussqua*.[70] Over the years, sexist assumptions brought out other meanings, including a man who sought a wife, male weakness, an effeminate man who did women's work, including homosexuals in European American society, and two-spirited individuals in Indian cultures, or a coward. These uses of the word regularly appeared in fiction, as did the term "squaw man." Squaw also became a verb: to be "squawed" meant for a non-Native man to be married to an Indian woman and degrade himself by living with her people. The "halfbreed" offspring of such unions became villainous or exoticized tropes in poems, dime novels, and melodramas, combining the supposed worst vices of each race or ethnic group. "Squaw" was used to put Indian peoples in their place if they tried to rise too high socially. During the late nineteenth and early twentieth-century reservation period, when tribal nations were plunged into poverty as a result of US policies of containment, "squaw" lost any positive connotation and became a mute, dark-skinned Indian woman with a squat and fat body and an ugly and often toothless face. This trope was depicted in movies, art, theater, music, newspaper cartoons, and fiction.[71] Violence became associated with squaws, especially in the American West, where the imagery was used in rifle competitions as a target representing a figure in a kneeling position. "Squaw" came to imply "vagina," and later it became associated with sexual penetration.[72]

Gendered depictions of Native American men and women went hand in hand with colonialism. Some observers called Native American women "handsome" or compared Indigenous men to women, the writers claiming to be unable to tell the difference between the genders. One paper said that the Native American men were "picturesque American warriors" who were "indistinguishable to the uninitiated eye from women."[73] Another described a man's face as having "an expression of refinement and womanlike tenderness in strong contrast to the rugged and dogged countenance" of some of the other men present.[74] Another writer described the "Indian braves" as "mostly men of powerful physique, with faces full of character and force. The long black hair and the absence of any beard or whiskers give the men a

Wenona—
Champion Indian
Girl Rifle Shot.
Circus World–
Wisconsin
Historical Society.

somewhat feminine look," but that did not change the "dogged and unconquerable courage with which they have met their foes."[75] This feminization of Native American men was both an American and European phenomenon. Travelers from Europe constructed their masculinity as hunters and nature tourists in the West and wrote of the West as an imperial playground.[76] Americans held this attitude as well. Theodore Roosevelt, for example, wanting to be a rugged westerner, passionately sought to project an image of masculinity through his hunting, military, and other exploits. In 1909, Roosevelt went on safari in Africa and remarked that the continent resembled the Dakotas a generation earlier. Using Africa as a substitute for the West, Roosevelt drew comparisons to the West while advocating further colonization in Africa. He was also quick to draw parallels between the

American continental expansion and its overseas imperialism, depicting the former as a prelude to the latter.[77] In the show itself, Native American men, and Native Americans as an entire people, were feminized compared to their white audiences. Audiences took comfort in knowing that although they saw strong warriors in the show, they understood their own social domination, which became apparent as they strolled the camp after the show. Feminized passivity characterized the Indians, and the audience took on a masculine authority derived from ethnographic pretense and the difference in status between the paying customer and the performer.[78]

In this way, Wild West shows were utilized to reassure white audiences that their society was civilized and they possessed complete cultural superiority over American Indigenous people. On the other hand, the tradition of buying and selling Black people and Black work continued in this era as white audiences viewed African American music and dance as another commodity to be bought and sold, enjoyed, and appropriated. This fundamental difference worked against Native American citizenship in ways that African Americans were able to get around due to their growing acceptance as creators of modern music and dance culture. Wild West shows remained under white management, unlike Black bands and troupes who were largely able to manage themselves. Indigenous troupes also worked via contracts created between the white show manager and the Indian agency and reservation. Native American artists were tied to a contract that said they had to be either on the reservation or employed by a white company and in good graces with the white boss. Creatively speaking, many Native American artists and crafters were able to sell their work, but the actual performances were driven by white storytellers, steeped in the myths of manifest destiny and white supremacy. This is in stark contrast to the Black circus musicians who were in the process of creating and evolving totally American forms of music in the forms of ragtime, blues, and jazz. In this way, even manual Black laborers were seen as more "American" than Indigenous people. Though treated as second- or third-class citizens, Black men's presence on work crews reinforced the American idea that Black people were a part of the country to serve white citizens and normalized Blacks being a part of American modernity, though at the bottom rung of society. Portrayals of Indigenous men and women, on the other hand, often depicted as a savage or a brave, as a princess or a squaw, did not afford Native Americans the opportunity of citizenship. Such depictions continually dehumanized them, pushing them out of the labor pool, continuing the legacy of the story that Native American people were too savage to enslave and were thus a vanishing race due to their own cultural backwardness and technological inferiority. So although many Native Americans in Wild West shows used their popularity to create an individual platform for their politics, the legacy of these shows was largely to silence Indigenous people in American history.

### Indigenous Leadership in the Golden Age of the Circus

For many white Americans, the answer to what they called the "Indian problem," much like the "Negro problem," essentially was to "kill the Indian . . . and save the man." Many contemporary white Americans supported this approach, but it was put forth very succinctly in 1892 by Captain Richard H. Pratt, the founder of Carlisle Indian Industrial School in Pennsylvania. Carlisle, like other Indian boarding schools across the country, kidnapped children from their families, forced them by threat of violence to give up their cultures and languages, and instituted English-only education with the stated aim of civilizing them and bringing them into American citizenship. The white agents, religious leaders, and teachers who ran these schools physically, emotionally, and sexually abused Indigenous children for generations, resulting in broken families, severe psychological damage, and hundreds of deaths from malnutrition, neglect, and mistreatment. For his part, Pratt saw the benefits of both African slavery and America's colonization of native lands, even comparing the two. Though the institution of slavery was "horrible," it was ultimately a good thing, as it brought "seven millions of blacks from cannibalism in darkest Africa to citizenship in free and enlightened America."[79] So, too, should this lesson be applied to the Indigenous peoples of America. Pratt said,

> Transfer the savage-born infant to the surroundings of civilization, and he will grow to possess a civilized language and habit. These results have been established over and over again beyond all question; and it is also well established that those advanced in life, even to maturity, of either class, lose already acquired qualities belonging to the side of their birth, and gradually take on those of the side to which they have been transferred. . . . The school at Carlisle is an attempt on the part of the government to do this. Carlisle has always planted treason to the tribe and loyalty to the nation at large.[80]

In this way, Pratt and countless other white reformers justified the murder of Indigenous peoples and defended their attempts at wiping their cultures from the face of the earth.

White reformers saw Wild West shows—as fictitious as they were—as displays of Indian culture and freedom, the very qualities they aimed to exterminate. In his letters to the Pine Ridge community, Superintendent John R. Brennan of Indian Affairs shunned Wild West shows and other such exhibitions. He called attention to a problem that "the better class of Indians from all districts are making complaints" that people in their community were holding disruptive dances in private houses giving any reason "that they might dance all night."[81] On another occasion, Brennan warned, "You are hereby [sic] instructed to notify the Indians of your district that the Indian office is opposed to Indians joining Wild West shows for exhibition purposes. Also notify them that any of them who may hereafter engage their services to show people will do so at their own risk and responsibility, and that this office will refuse to sign contracts or secure bonds to ensure payment of salaries for them unless ordered to do so by the Indian Office."[82] In an "editor's comment," Wild West shows were again condemned, and community members were warned not to participate. The commenter wrote:

> These shows are not doing justice to the Indian. They represent the Indians as being in the same savage state that they were in when this continent was discovered. They make no pretense of showing the present condition of the Indian or the progress that he has made toward civilization. They injure the morals of the participants, they contaminate their physical being and they bring economic ruin. No good has ever come or ever can come to those who take part in such savage display. The racial reputation of the Indian is being greatly injured through this means, for people . . . judge the whole race by the specimens they see in the trappings of savagery and the Indian is accordingly judged to be incapable of progress. . . . No groupe [sic] of people can progress faster than the individual elements that make it up. . . . Let us hope that the time has come when this bar to progress will be effectively removed.[83]

For white reformers, Indian education was a critical component of Indian policy, and music education was a component of the assimilationist agendas of some of the larger boarding schools. Reverence for art and music was limited to classical European forms, considered superior cultural expressions. The Pine Ridge *Oglala Light*, Chilocco's *Indian School Journal*, and the Phoenix *Native American* were monthly school community publications. In articles like "Good Music Is a Character Builder," "Music Education in America," and "Native Indian Art" Native artists encouraged Indian parents to support the arts and for their children to work hard at their musical studies because "good music . . . drives out evil thoughts, making us ashamed of them."[84]

Each year, Buffalo Ranch, Bill Cody's Wild West, the 101 Ranch, the Carl Hagenbeck Circus, the Sells Circuses, and many other Wild West and traveling shows sent agents to recruit Indian workers, both men and women.[85] Indian agents kept track of these numbers and for a while helped with making the contracts between the Indians and the show recruiters.[86] The numbers of men and women leaving every year ranged from 100 to over 300 from one reservation to travel with various shows as they crisscrossed the country and toured overseas.[87] By 1917, Indian agents let it be known that participation in these entertainments was prohibited.[88] So, Indigenous people on reservations were motivated by the idea of making money, getting off the reservation, seeing the world, and escaping the seemingly doomed life of underdeveloped reservations and forced farming. One editor claimed, in an article titled "The Wild West Exodus," that "the Indians that have been going with these wild west outfits from year to year are well known to be the poorest most shiftless and most worthless class of Sioux, and that these habits are developed and encouraged by the wild west craze."[89] Editors and agents complained about and lamented the yearly visits of the Wild West show scouts, who were looking for Indian performers, as well as the sheer number of people interested in the line of work.

Indigenous leaders and middle-class intellectuals responded to both the indignities of the Wild West show and the oppression of the federal government. The Society of American Indians (SAI) was the first pan-Indian national forum for Native American citizenship. Fifty Indigenous men and women from various tribal affiliations established the SAI in Columbus, Ohio, in 1911. They aimed "to encourage Indian leadership, promote self-help, and foster the assimilation of Indians while encouraging them to exhibit pride in their race."[90] To these ends, the SAI addressed various problems facing Native Americans, from health care and education to civil rights and issues with the federal Indian policy. The SAI advocated for the individual absorption of Indian people into American society as patriotic citizens, but it also placed value on and pride in Indian heritage.[91] In other words, education should not make the Indian a white man, but simply a man "normal in their environment."[92] Through conferences, a quarterly journal, and sponsored events, the SAI put forth a message based on hard work and education. Although all SAI leaders advocated for Native American citizenship, there was diversity among the leaders regarding how they would best achieve citizenship and other goals. Charles Eastman (Santee Dakota), for example, was a physician, lecturer, and writer who helped establish several Young Men's Christian Association chapters and the Boy Scouts of America and advocated for education. Another SAI leader, Henry Roe Cloud (Ho-Chunk), was a Presbyterian minister who made education and the opposition of the peyote faith among Native American peoples his main issues. Of the founding members of the SAI, Arthur Parker greatly influenced the journal. Parker, a Seneca anthropologist, was one of the era's most outspoken Native American leaders and advocates for citizenship.[93] He believed that each race or ethnicity lived within a different cultural context, and, therefore, each had a different pathway to American citizenship. He wrote, "In the struggle for better things and for a true adjustment, the Indian must be allowed to feel that he has the principal part. If we would give Indians civilization, we must first awaken his moral energy and provide a clear incentive. It is then for the Indian himself to respond and to reach out for the valuable prizes that belong by right to the man who works and produces by mind and muscle more than he consumes. All this means that race inertia must be overcome. The dormant motor energy again must be applied."[94] Parker wrote that race assimilation was of vital importance to Native Americans.[95] The struggle, he said, was an especially hard one due to the combination of a troubled history between white Americans and Indigenous peoples and contemporary Native Americans' lack of effort to assimilate. In Parker's view, American Indians were capable of assimilating to US culture and becoming American; however, they would achieve this end in different ways than European or Asian immigrants or African Americans.

Performance in Wild West shows, in the view of many educated and middle-class Native American leaders, encouraged the savage Indian stereotype. Native American writers often referred to those who participated in traveling shows as "circus Indians" or "show Indians" and argued that these expositions endangered the progress of Indian people toward civilization, denying them higher social, economic, and political standing in the larger society. The *Quarterly Journal for the Society of American Indians* voiced a vehement hatred of Wild West shows and circus employees. Chauncey Yellow Robe, a Lakota contributor, wrote multiple articles to call attention "to the evil and degrading influence of commercializing the Indian before the world."[96] On one occasion, after listing the ways that white circus owners took advantage of uneducated Native Americans, Parker stated that Indians who would work for circuses should be blamed as much for their inappropriate behavior as white circus owners. He wrote:

And there is something the Indians themselves must consider. There would be no such degenerate antics if the public opinion of the Indians themselves was against it. When white showmen are assailed for recruiting actors "at a dollar a day and feed" the class of Indians who misrepresent their people should likewise be criticized. A bad Indian is no better than a bad white man ordinarily, but an Indian who misrepresents or cheats his people is worse, indeed. The show Indian is not the real Indian any more than the circus white man is the real white man. But just as the ordinary show Indian gets to believing that the circus followers are the best in civilization, so the public gets to thinking that the painted pseudo-Indian of the tan-bark is the typical red-man.[97]

To remedy this situation, Parker argued for closer intervention of the US government in the lives of Native Americans on this matter. His solution was to have the federal government intervene and stop Native Americans from participating in such occupations. He wrote, disapprovingly, "If, then, the circus goers could see the untilled farms, the unhappy wives, the hungry children in the tumble down houses of the Indians who follow shows they would realize who pays the price for traveling around the country. We ask the United States Government to hold back its permission that Indians may be taken from reservations and allowed to travel with shows. It is not a dignified thing for the guardian Government to turn its wards over to circus men. Nor is it conductive of good training on the part of the Indian ward. Away with injurious fakery!"[98] The frequency of articles bemoaning circus Indians, as well as the charges SAI writers laid against them, suggests that this was a contested issue among Indigenous people and that there were alternative opinions on the matter. Opponents of Indian involvement in circuses also voiced a dislike for what they saw as a growing trend among those who were "duped" into running away with a show. Chauncey Yellow Robe warned, "The smooth tempter and corrupter arrives on the reservation at the most opportune season—early spring, when, after the long and dull winter months have passed, the blood in the Indian begins to move, for pleasure, excitement, or work, like sap in the maple,—and falls a ready victim to the briber. The Indian youth is then robbed of the spring and fall months at school, and the adult is taken from his farm or trade at the very time he should be in his field or at his bench in the shop."[99]

The SAI believed circus involvement was disastrous for Indigenous communities, claiming that joining circuses prevented farmers from planting

Masthead of *Wassaja: Freedom's Signal for the Indians*. Publisher Carlos Montezuma, Edward E. Ayer Collection Newberry Library.

crops and children from going to school.[100] Many, they claimed, were being stranded—either due to the season ending with no way home or because of being fired, or simply a show going out of business—and those stranded employees were calling relatives for money to help them back home.[101] Parker implored his readers to not, under any circumstances, have pity on those men and women who were selfish and irresponsible enough to run off with a circus.

Carlos Montezuma (Yavapai-Apache), another physician and writer, became one of the SAI's most vociferous internal critics whom many considered radical. Montezuma called for the immediate abolition of the Bureau of Indian Affairs and instant assimilation of American Indian people as the most effective way to ensure American Indian citizenship, education, and civil rights.[102] When William Cody died, Montezuma, in his newsletter, *Wassaja*, wrote of his friendship with Buffalo Bill and his disapproval of the Wild West show, saying, "He was a friend of the Indians, and again in a higher sense, he was not. . . . So you see we are old friends, but Wassaja never approved his friend's method of showing off the Indian race, off-setting the progress the Indians have made and implanting the wrong idea in the minds of the public—that an Indian was a savage and that was all. As an old friend, Wassaja mourns and extends sympathy to the bereaved."[103] As Montezuma put it, the Wild West shows implanted the wrong idea in the minds of the public of the Indigenous American as a mere savage, which Native American leaders knew would thwart Indigenous people's citizenship efforts. There was much at stake: debates surrounding citizenship at the end of the nineteenth century and beginning of the twentieth century had several implications on class, education, and respectable work. So, too, did those debates affect ideas about equality and the loss of tribal lands, the kidnapping of children, and the appalling practices in boarding schools. For many, citizenship would give people better control over their daily lives, families, and tribal autonomy. It would also give them the tools to fight cultural genocide that white American reformists preached as their solution to the "Indian problem."

It is important to note that the SAI included Indigenous women intellectuals who advocated for political change even before their white female counterparts were able to vote. Women like Angel De Cora (Ho-Chunk) and Marie Louise Bottineau Baldwin (Ojibwa) made waves in policy that reached the federal government. The first woman of color to graduate from Washington College of Law, Marie Louise Bottineau Baldwin, became a lawyer in 1914. She helped found the SAI and served as the group's treasurer in 1915. She also worked for the Office of Indian Affairs for twenty-five years, where she was a fierce advocate for Indigenous people. De Cora was kidnapped from her family when she was twelve and taken to a boarding school. She graduated from Smith College, attended art school, and became a lauded painter. She traveled lecture circuits, teaching art and using it as her entry into activism for Indigenous issues. These women were important intellectuals and crucial to galvanizing the American Indian movement.

Some Indigenous women leaned into the princess stereotype in order to receive media attention and promote their political and social messages. Real-life Indigenous women, such as the Northern Paiute educator, translator, author, and activist Sarah Winnemucca, made decisions to use this Indian princess stereotype when it helped them to gain entrance into circles from which they would have otherwise been banned.[104] Winnemucca was the first Indigenous woman to write a book on the plight of Native Americans and traveled on the lecture circuit. At one event in Boston in 1883 she declared, "I can tell you how few of the Government supplies reach the Indians; how one little blanket was provided to shelter a family of six from the cold . . . how, indeed they often have to buy the very supplies that the Government has promised to give them in exchange for their land. I have asked the agents why they did these wrong things. They have told me

Marie Louise Bottineau Baldwin, 1914. Date created or published later by Bain. Retrieved from the Library of Congress.

Sarah Winnemucca, 1883. National Portrait Gallery, Smithsonian Institution.

Susette La Flesche Tibbles, ca. 1879. National Portrait Gallery, Smithsonian Institution.

it was necessary for them to do so in order to get money enough to send to the Great Father at Washington to keep their position."[105] Winnemucca spoke out about the crimes of Indian agents and said because most Americans knew nothing of Native Americans, she used her lectures to promote cultural and political awareness and to try to persuade the US government to allow the Northern Paiutes to return to the land from which they had been removed. In another lecture, she told audiences, "I want to test the right of the Government to make and break treaties at pleasure. They gave my people that place of land, and I want to ask whether it is legal for them to sell it or not. And in this work I want your help. Will you give me your influence? My work must be done through Congress. Talk for me and help me talk, and all will be well."[106] Winnemucca Hopkins went on to publish her book, *Life among the Piutes: Their Wrongs and Claims*, and met with many influential reformers and politicians. In 1884, she testified before the US House Subcommittee on Indian Affairs. She used her prominent place in the news media to challenge boarding school policies and English-only policies. In all, newspapers printed over 400 news items by or about her between 1864 and her death in 1891.

Before accompanying Kicking Bear, Susette La Flesche had already been the subject of the news media. She was the first Native American woman to become a physician. Although Standing Bear dressed in his chief's regalia, La Flesche always wore modern Anglo-American style clothes. She appeared with prominent male speakers and gave formal lectures. Newspapers framed her sympathetically and as a genteel, "civilized" Indian woman.[107] Like Winnemucca, La Flesche lectured, translated, and wrote on behalf of American Indians. She also understood the power of the news media in shaping representations of American Indians, earning the respect of East Coast reformers and an invitation to testify before a special committee of the US Senate. She wrote an introduction to the book published about the Ponca tour; however, La Flesche represented herself much differently than Winnemucca. La Flesche, a young, mixed-raced unmarried woman (chaperoned by her brother), was called an "Indian maiden," but she rejected the princess label as undemocratic in the British press during her 1887 tour of England.

## Conclusion

Native American efforts during the golden age of the circus unified disparate Indigenous peoples across the nation and helped create a pan-Indian ethos. Whether as middle-class intellectuals or working-class performing artists, Indigenous Americans contributed to this era of growth amid incredible hardship. Although middle-class writers of the SAI may have taken what they believed a more respectable route, performing artists, through their travel, lecture circuits, and press helped foment a national Native American sentiment. Though largely limited to stereotypes and demeaning displays, Native Americans were always a main attraction of Wild West shows, and some effectively used the news media as a platform. The result is a record of their thoughts and opinions about American culture and life and their hopes and dreams for the future of their peoples. Men like Luther Standing Bear and Black Elk went on to write memoirs that although written for a white audience were still very revealing. Native American women were important parts of the shows and the show-life as well. They performed in the Wild West exhibitions and encampments, they tended to children, and they made crafts to sell. The white supremacist ethos of the Gilded Age and Progressive Era that put limits on Indigenous performers persisted, but for many Indigenous artists, participation in the Wild West industry was about having a choice—they could not escape the American power structure, but they could step away from the confines of the reservation, even if only for one season at a time.

CHAPTER FIVE

# Hidden in Plain View
*The Circus Towns of Columbus, Ohio, and Peru, Indiana*

One indicator that a person or family has reached a point of working-class success is the freedom to live like everyone else. For many, attaining this freedom is the essence of the American dream and a building block of self-betterment, community uplift, and the pursuit of happiness. This chapter explores the creation and dismantling of two circus towns, the winter quarters where circus companies stored their equipment and prepared for the coming season. Winter quarters were often small, self-sufficient villages. There were many during the golden age of the circus: from Ohio and Indiana and throughout the Midwest to Connecticut, New York, and down to Florida, circus towns spotted the American landscape. They were responsible for housing the circus as well as a wide variety of jobs related to show operations. Autumn brought the end of the traveling season, and many performing artists returned home or joined theater and vaudeville acts. Laborers who traveled returned to the circus winter quarters where work continued year-round. Columbus, Ohio, the site for the Sells Brothers Circus winter quarters (1873–1908), and Peru, Indiana, the site of the Great Wallace Circus winter quarters (1892–1938), provided working-class and professional occupations for Black and Indigenous peoples and their families. This work enabled them in many ways to hide from the racist interference of neighboring whites in plain sight—to work, raise families, and participate in the American dream. The Sells Brothers Circus winter quarters was a thriving community that employed hundreds of people. African Americans in Sellsville built institutions and created self-supporting networks once they had access to employment. Through nontraditional work in an industry known for its theatricality, Black Americans built a community that embodied many ideals of African American respectability and were recognized for their professionalism, entrepreneurial acumen, and race pride. However, the race history of twentieth-century America is one of great progress and violent backlash. After the Sells Brothers Circus packed up and left town, government intervention fueled by racial politics resulted in the relocation of the Black people of Sellsville. The community was dispersed and has struggled through subsequent generations to find stability. Without circus jobs ranging from menial to skilled labor and performance, the African American community lost its structure, and many residents relocated or were forced to move into segregated low-income housing.

Meanwhile in Indiana, local Indigenous leaders had tough decisions to make. Miami chief Gabriel Godfroy sold a portion of his family land to circus impresario Benjamin Wallace. This enabled Wallace's circus to expand into a mammoth, self-sufficient operation. Godfroy, like his father and other leaders of his community before him, was determined to find or create ways to help his Miami community to remain on their Indiana homelands and find employment opportunities, and at the time, selling land to the circus owner was a way to raise much-needed funds in a time of crisis for the Miami community. The sale of more land, ironically, ensured the survival of the Miami community in their midwestern homelands. For these Indigenous men and women, like many African Americans in the industry, the ability to choose was a key ingredient to feeling a sense of freedom.

## Sellsville: Columbus, Ohio

In 1902, a reporter from *Billboard* visited Sellsville and wrote, "A visit out to Sellsville, the winter quarters of the Sells and Forepaugh Show near Columbus, Ohio, will find a small army of men."[1] One contemporary writer claimed that before the Sells village was established, "A poor farmer was barely able to keep body and soul together. Today there is a village of several hundred inhabitants . . . for employment is found in the various shows of the Sells Brothers and in the different mills and stores."[2] The Sells supported several industries including blacksmiths, railcar builders, carpenters, farmers, animal caretakers, costume makers, and seamstresses.[3] The Columbus Hocking Valley and Toledo Railroad cut through the eastern end of Sellsville, and small service shops and mid-sized manufacturing firms were located along the railroad. Farming and truck gardening were the livelihoods for many Sellsville residents, as were positions in slaughterhouses, saloons, blacksmith shops, greenhouses, and flour mills.[4] Many of the nearby residents were farmers. The Sells often bought produce from local farmers and gardeners for livestock feed. A spur off the railroad provided space for their cars. Car repair and painting were done on-site. Some touring members of the show not employed during the fall and winter worked at Ohio State University, the Excelsior Seat Company, or the Weisheimer Brothers Flour Mill, and some were small-time entrepreneurs.[5] The nonlocal performers arrived a few weeks before the season's opening and stayed both in

Sellsville and at Columbus hotels. The Sells winter quarters, like the show on the road, was a massive operation. At its peak, the Sells company employed hundreds of laborers, main show performers, and sideshow performers.

A successful season demanded a vast number of employees to keep everything from people to animals to equipment in good shape for months at a time. In 1884, The Sells Brothers Fifty Cage Menagerie and Four-Ring Circus employed sixty-eight advance men and around four hundred other employees.[6] Between forty-five and fifty rail cars carried employees, 253 horses and mules, ten elephants, fifty-one cages of animals, and four tents.[7] Moreover, the Sells Brothers Circus had a decent relationship with its African American workers. Recalling one incident from the turn of the century, William H. "Cap" Curtis wrote to George Chindahl that he had been employed by the Sells Brothers in 1891 and had wanted to go to Australia with the show. He was, however, turned away after a fight with a Black man. Because of the Sells brothers' protective stance regarding their Black worker, Curtis went on to say that the Sells show was quite a "negro show them days."[8]

Economic Opportunity

A successful season demanded a vast number of employees to keep everything—from people to animals to equipment—in good shape for months at a time. Around the third season in 1874 or 1875, the Sells brothers, longtime entrepreneurs in Columbus, moved their circus company from Linworth, Ohio, to Clinton Township, near Columbus, where they believed the show would have room to expand.[9] In 1884, the fourteenth season, The Sells Brothers Fifty Cage Menagerie and Four-Ring Circus opened in Columbus in April and closed in New Orleans in December. That season the show covered a total of 11,537 miles by rail, as compared to the 1872 wagon season's 1,741 miles.[10] Between forty-five and fifty rail cars carried employees, 253 horses and mules, ten elephants, fifty-one cages of animals, and four tents.[11]

One result of both the Sells brothers' management style and local peoples' decisions surrounding social and economic institutions was an increased availability of work for African Americans and, to a lesser extent, Native Americans in Clinton Township. These opportunities were unique because they were not limited to menial, unskilled labor, as was the norm in most industries of the era. Instead, the circus and the surrounding community provided a range of employment opportunities that included skilled and unskilled labor, management, and performance careers. As the circus expanded its winter quarters in its first years at Sellsville, local Black families seized opportunities to expand their businesses as well. Before the Sells established their quarters, most African Americans either farmed on their own land or labored on other peoples' farms. For example, in 1900 the Bowens hauled produce for the circus and rented rooms and land to circus employees and tenant farmers. This was a marked expansion of their family farm of the generation before the circus.[12] James Reynolds Hall grew up in the community, and by 1900, his business, Hall's Corners, was one of Sellsville's blacksmith shops.[13] The son of a former enslaved person, Hall began shoeing horses for the Sells Brothers Circus.[14] The expansion of local businesses attracted both skilled and unskilled labor in a range of occupations from the local flour mill to bus drivers for the growing local school.[15] The Weisheimer flour mill provided grain for the circus town and the greater Columbus area for generations. The Weisheimer company also employed many circus men and their families during the offseason.[16] Sellsville enjoyed an emerging professional class that reflected larger trends in the greater Columbus area. African Americans like Reverend George Walker, Laura Walker, and Edward Zimmerman became ministers, teachers, and clerical workers. African Americans also found work with the United States Postal Service.[17] Black families in Sellsville were entrepreneurial and became brick masons, farmers, porters, railroad clerks, teamsters, seamstresses, and cooks.

Though much of the work available to African Americans in the winter quarters involved segregated manual labor for almost four decades, from the mid-1870s to 1904, the integrated Sells Brothers Circus winter quarters and the community that grew up around them were the economic heartbeat for the residents of this community outside of Columbus. With access to relatively stable employment, the people of Sellsville built a self-supporting community, established schools, founded churches, and created a variety of social institutions. The residents of Sellsville, including formerly enslaved people and southerners, built these institutions in large part without the aid of middle-class missionaries, educators, or social workers. This was not an anomaly. African Americans established as many as two hundred towns and communities across the nation during the nineteenth and early twentieth centuries. Black towns, comprised of either mostly or completely African American populations, incorporated communities with autonomous Black city governments and Black-led commercial ventures, and industry often supported surrounding Black farms. They were intentionally created by African Americans with political, social, and economic aims in mind, especially the want to escape the horrors of southern racism and discrimination. Other similar towns such as Nicodemus, Kansas; Boley, Oklahoma; and Mound Bayou, Mississippi, hoped to create thriving urban centers for Black people to succeed in self-government, business, and domestic life.

Sells Brothers' records reveal that African Americans were employed widely and suggest that opportunities became available in Sellsville that were unavailable elsewhere in the state of Ohio. The remarkable integration of the community and the opportunities provided for these and other African Americans by the circus set Sellsville apart from most other midwestern towns and circuses at the turn of the century.[18] The Sells Brothers, and later the combined Sells Forepaugh show, hired African Americans as performers, professional animal trainers, skilled artisans, musicians, and bandleaders, and the enterprise maintained a Black-managed elephant training crew.

## Clinton Township Responds to the Circus

Clinton Township was immediately north of Columbus in Franklin County and had a history of cultural and ethnic diversity dating back to early in the nineteenth century. Residents described the boundaries of Sellsville as west of the Olentangy River and east of Virginia (or Queen) Avenue, running south from Flennekin Pike (or William Chambers Road) through King Avenue to West Fifth Avenue. The river bounded the neighborhood on the east and the Neil Woods on the west. Large farms and woodlands were in the north. Clinton residents that lived in the surrounding farmland often claimed residence in Sellsville, rather than in Clinton Township.[19] In 1896, the quarters doubled in size as a result of a new merger that created the Adam Forepaugh-Sells Brothers Circus, and they came to own over one thousand acres where employees and their families, animals, and equipment lived both seasonally and permanently.[20] Other businesses emerged to support the circus workers, and many circus-related families and businesses remained in the neighborhood year-round.[21]

Although the circus definitely brought diversity to the area, Clinton Township was an ethnically and racially diverse area before the Sells brothers established winter quarters there. This may not have been a coincidence. In addition to Irish, German, Italian, and other white ethnic groups who founded Clinton, Wyandot and Delaware families who resisted the Indian Removal Act and African Americans were among the earliest farmers and laborers of this community.[22] Itinerant communities of laborers and other men called hobo jungles were common along the railroad between King and Fifth Avenues.[23] In the midst of all of its diversity, Clinton Township had a strong Black leadership. Some of its African American families had resided in the area since the early nineteenth century. Joshua Ellsworth Fields was a United States mail clerk and the grandson of Reverend Ezekiel Fields.[24] The Fields's home was south of the Ohio state fairgrounds.[25] By the time the Sells brothers established their winter quarters in Clinton Township, the Bowen family, free people of color, had lived there for nearly a century.[26] Census records reveal that members of the Bowen household included people identified as white, Black, and mulatto.[27] In the late nineteenth century, Benjamin Bowen, whose mother was white and father was Black, lived with his wife, Katie, an African American woman, and their four children: Minni, Della, Lottie, and Leslie. The family primarily farmed and leased land. In 1900, they ran a successful hauling business for the circus. Throughout the circus generation and beyond, members of the Bowen family were active members of the community, involved in church, school, and community leadership.

By the end of the 1870s, families worked with each other to take advantage of the new opportunities provided by the new local industry. The Sells brothers, for their part, seemed supportive of this growth. In this already diverse mixture of people, the Sells constructed a racially integrated winter quarters. Within the Sellsville neighborhood of 1900, Blacks and white residents lived next door to each other, intermarried, and created families and institutions. Of the sixty-nine households in the immediate neighborhood, twenty-three were African American, two were multifamily homes shared by Blacks and whites, three were Native American (whose nation was not specified in the census), and two were multifamily homes shared by Black and white residents.[28] The remaining forty-one households were Euro-American families. These homes were dispersed throughout the neighborhood among the homes and small businesses owned by both Black and white residents. By 1900, many African Americans and white migrants had come to the area surrounding Sellsville, chiefly from North Carolina.[29] Based on census records of the neighborhood in 1880, 1900, and 1910, the neighborhood appeared to be fully racially integrated. Integration also went beyond home placement in some instances. Local members of the circus' all-Black sideshow band often played at integrated community and holiday events and at the local white-owned grocery store.[30]

The Sells family supported some institutions in the quarters, including providing aid in establishing the Antioch Baptist Church, a mixed, but predominantly Black, congregation.³¹ From 1888 to 1893, Clinton Township Christians held Sunday school meetings in various locations around the neighborhood, including the neighborhood school.³² On May 18, 1893, members of the group officially organized the Antioch Baptist Church. Officials from four Columbus-area churches (Bethany Baptist, Second Baptist, Shiloh Baptist, and Union Grove Baptist) met with the eight founders of the Antioch Baptist Church. Reverend Ovie O. Jones of London, Ohio, served as the group moderator.³³ The new church's founding members were Eli Harris, Isaac Howell, Doc Stewart, Lewis Hearns, Cornelius Gilman, Lucy Reed, Clara Thornton, and Prisilla Anderson.³⁴ They formed a deacon board and a trustees' board and welcomed their first pastor, Reverend I. A. Thornton. The first-year members held camp meetings in the nearby Neil Woods. They raised money to purchase two lots for a building site inside of Sellsville. The church was built under Pastor Stewart S. Cochran who laid the cornerstone on October 14, 1894, with Deacon Hezikiah Brandon and Trustee Benjamin Bowen. The Sells family assisted the congregation by loaning tents and seats for the early meetings. Ephraim Sells donated furniture to the congregation.³⁵ The Sells also aided the congregation by renting out the circus cookhouse during the summer while the circus was on tour. This enabled the pastor, George Walker, and his wife, Laura Brown Walker, to live near the church while the parsonage was being built.³⁶

A Clinton Township school was located in the residential section of Sellsville.³⁷ Local residents at the time nicknamed the school "The Polkadot School" because its population was almost equally white and Black during the years of the circus winter quarters.³⁸ In 1900, its two teachers, Katie Martin and Mary Drury, taught Black and white children.³⁹ Of the fifty-seven children attending the school in 1900, twenty-five were recorded as Negro or mulatto.⁴⁰ Benjamin Bowen donated horse-drawn wagons. Two men, mixed-ancestry African American Harley Hughes and Euro-American Richard Cradic, used the wagons to take schoolchildren from around the neighborhood to and from school.⁴¹

There are other instances of institution building by African Americans that were likely catalyzed by the presence of the circus in Clinton Township. Local members of P. G. Lowery's sideshow band formed a neighborhood band called the Sellsville Clippers, which practiced in the local white-owned Neiderlander Grocery Store in the 1880s. The Neiderlanders hosted holiday parties at which the sideshow band regularly played during the offseason. Les Bowen was a member of the band and another Black Sellsville neighborhood institution, The Sellsville Sluggers.⁴² The Sellsville Sluggers was an all-Black

The Polkadot School from Sellsville, ca. 1900. Courtesy of the
Ohio History Connection.

baseball team that formed just as the circus was coming under new management and leaving the area. The Sluggers formed in 1909, and several Sellsville men joined the team.[43]

## The Decline of Circus Opportunity in Sellsville

Just after the turn of the twentieth century, the Sells brothers began to sell off their circus properties in Ohio. One of the buyers, James Bailey, told the *Columbus Evening Dispatch* in 1905 that he would keep the winter quarters in Sellsville, enlarge it, and allow the former employees to continue in their current jobs.[44] In 1905, Bailey created a winter zoo for Columbus citizens to visit circus animals.[45] The circus left Sellsville for the last time to tour in the 1906–7 season. After James Bailey's death in 1906, Ringling bought the Barnum and Bailey show in 1907 and on April 20, 1907, the Sells-Forepaugh Circus permanently closed. Many residents of Sellsville had grown to depend heavily on circus employment. The area became a low-income neighborhood full of unemployed African Americans, unskilled laborers, and itinerant and unwanted people considered Gypsies and hobos. African American former employees faced pressures from the white community and the Black middle class.

On April 21, 1907, the *Ohio State Journal* wrote that Lewis Sells, owner of the remaining grounds, planned to immediately begin the process of "cleaning up and beautifying the land. All buildings and everything used in connection with wintering the shows are to be taken away." The area was up for immediate platting for building lots. "The removal of the winter quarters will take away from one of the most beautiful parts of Columbus that which has always been an objection and detriment to the real estate there. In order to open up the locality better there is a movement on foot to have constructed a streetcar line past what was the show grounds and on the Scioto River storage dam."[46] Ephraim Sells had already begun the process of suburban development in the area. In 1905 he purchased about a hundred acres for development.[47] On May 12, 1907, the *Ohio State Journal* announced that all buildings in Sellsville, except one, would be demolished by June 1, at which time lots would be sold, and houses erected.

The closing of the Clinton Township Polkadot School was another blow to the African American community. This once multiracial school closed just after the turn of the century and was demolished in 1913, around the time of municipal redistricting.[48] The Sellsville Polkadot School stands out among Columbus schools, which were plagued with anti-Black policies throughout the nineteenth and early twentieth centuries. At stake, according to white Columbians, was not that Blacks could not be educated; rather, they just did not believe it appropriate for white children to be forced to mix with them. The majority of white Columbians favored separate schools for Black children. However, most schools for Black children were becoming or were already so desperately inferior to white schools that many Black people chose private or homeschooling. This was the order of the day. With the 1896 Supreme Court decision *Plessy v. Ferguson*, white supremacy and Jim Crow segregation laws dominated social relations in the South. Northern states also limited Black people's livelihoods through a culture of de facto racial segregation and outright racist laws. Across the country, racial discrimination severely limited economic opportunities for African Americans, who were restricted to agricultural and unskilled labor.

With the demolition of Sellsville, Black residents scattered. Those who were able had already moved into more affluent neighborhoods of Columbus. Musicians, for instance, had a valuable skill. They played in bands and taught music lessons to Columbus' Black middle-class children. Other African American residents, like artist Aminah Robinson's family, moved to the Black Berry Patch neighborhood.[49] From about 1900 to the late 1930s, the Blackberry Patch was a working poor African American community. Then in 1939, it was demolished to create Poindexter Village. Poindexter Village was one of the first federally funded housing projects. President Franklin Roosevelt showed his support for the project with visits at the groundbreaking ceremony in 1939 and the dedication ceremony on Columbus Day in 1940.[50] From the viewpoint of city officials, the removal of former circus employees and other "undesirable" people from the old Sellsville quarters enabled a large land development project that turned thousands of acres of Clinton Township into a new, predominantly white suburb. In 1940, a developer obtained a government loan to erect the University View subdivision, housing for defense workers on the former site of Sellsville. The subdivision consisted of about 250 single-family homes. For the first five years, the homes were rental units and were later sold to many of the original renters. In 1948, the local residents association formed and planned recreation for area children. A 1957 *Columbus Citizen* article described it as a pleasant "community of families with two cars, two children and two dogs" in the southwest corner of Clinton Township.[51]

## The Wallace Quarters: Peru, Indiana

By the 1820s, the Miami and the Potawatomi were the last tribes in northern Indiana. Though American officials were successful in shrinking the Miami population and landholdings in Indiana, removal was not at all straightforward. A long history of interracial interaction and adaptability enabled Miami to devise resistance strategies to remain in the county long after official government removal and the aggressive efforts of whites to steal Indian land and remove Indigenous people. In 1830, up to six thousand Miami lived on about four million acres. By 1840, Miami landholdings shrank to around eight hundred people holding thirty thousand acres. Though it would shrink even more in the coming decades, generations of Miami-white relations impeded the total removal of Native American people and culture. Working with the Wallace Circus Company became one adaptation in a generations-long struggle to remain in Miami County, Indiana. Another strategy was to rely on white people or those who appeared to be white to speak for them at treaty negotiations. This tactic proved successful, but it also resulted in the obscuring of Native Americans in official records. Since the eighteenth century, missionaries and government officials obsessed with racial hierarchies had expressed difficulty ascertaining the lineage of members of the Miami villages of north-central Indiana. Some asserted that the entire tribe consisted of people of mixed ancestry.[52] In the multicultural landscape of the nineteenth century, interracial relationships were necessary for survival. Miami people fluidly combined traditional tribal values, European ideas, and shrewd decision-making skills to remain on their lands.[53] The

Gabriel Godfroy and family. Courtesy of the Miami County Historical Society, Inc. 2001.049.001.

Miami had effectively created not two distinct worlds but rather one drawing from Indigenous and European ideologies and lifestyles.

A long history of interracial interaction and adaptability enabled the Miami to devise resistance strategies to remain in the county long after official government removal. Rather than relocating with others of their tribe to comply with an 1840 treaty, a small group of Miami of mixed heritage asserted their whiteness, gained leverage, and succeeded in gaining exemption.[54] Among these groups was the family of Francis Godfroy. The treaty included several exemptions for select Miami families; however, these lands were to be individually rather than tribally owned. The leaders of the families negotiated to secure personal land allotments, knowing that the majority of their tribe would be removed to Kansas territory in 1846. Indian rolls, however, reveal that they not only insured their own families' places in Miami County but took in dozens of families who returned from Kansas after removal.[55] As far as the federal government was concerned, the remaining 148 people would meld into white American society, and true Miami leadership now resided in Oklahoma. However, the remaining families continued to govern themselves through the Mississinewa Council, a body representative of all of the Miami groups and that traced its roots back to late eighteenth-century leaders. The remaining heads of the family acted as village chiefs representing the people on their private reserves. In the generation after removal, the Indiana Miami had unified around this group of village leaders and met as a tribal council. The remaining Miami families formed a cluster of individual reserves between the Wabash and Mississinewa Rivers east of Peru, the Miami County seat. These reserves were within walking distance of each other along old paths and were also located along riverways for easy boat access.[56] Reserve holders used their lands as sanctuaries and enabled Miami families and neighbors to remain or return to the county. By 1850, the remaining Miami population combined with returning families was over 250.[57] Recognized as official tribal land or not, the area in Butler Township that Miami men and women owned became a haven for remaining and returning Miami people. Miami people remained in Butler Township, and prominent men held leadership roles.

Francis Godfroy's land formed one of the major private Miami reserves in Butler Township just outside Peru. Godfroy's farm was located at the confluence of the Wabash and Mississinewa Rivers near the markets of Peru. The lands surrounding his village, Nan-Matches-Sin-A-Wa, became his personal reservation that he titled in his Christian name to ensure legal protection for its inhabitants. Godfroy's reserve near Peru gathered the largest collection of refugees. He built cabins around his former trading house to accommodate nearly sixty people who had returned from Kansas.[58] Because of the addition of returning families from Kansas, the Godfroy group represented about half of the remaining tribe. At his death, Francis Godfroy bequeathed his land to his son Gabriel, who, by the mid-1850s, began to assert himself as the family leader.

Like his father, Gabriel built a reputation among local Miami and nearby white residents in Peru as a strong, dedicated, and generous leader.[59] Indeed, the Godfroys in general were known for always lending a helping hand in their community. One resident of the Godfroy village remembered that "they always said that they don't turn nobody away from their home. They'd [visitors] come there—a good time to get there would be in the evening because you're going to get fed night and morning and stay all night."[60] Like his father, Gabriel provided for several Miami people. Many had returned from Oklahoma and lived in cabins that the Godfroys had built on their property for that very reason.[61] Charlie Underwood, a Black man who had formerly been enslaved, also lived in Godfroy's village cabins.[62] Godfroy worked to maintain the Miami people's ability to remain together and continued his father's legacy of urging Miami people to farm, learn new agricultural skills, and look

*Hidden in Plain View* 139

The Hagenbeck-Wallace Quarters, ca. 1920. Circus World–Wisconsin Historical Society.

for a diverse range of jobs that would enable them to remain economically stable in Miami County. In 1855, he won a lawsuit to have a white squatter evicted from his family land. Later, he would win restitution of 185 acres of land from a prominent local white family due to a fraudulent sale contract. In 1889, Gabriel became one of the leaders of the Indiana Miami.[63] Chief Gabriel Godfroy encouraged Indian men on his land to farm and encouraged women to do more traditionally Euro-American women's work. He hired Miami and white farm laborers to cultivate his land and by 1870, was one of the most important farming teachers and advocates in the community.[64] Gabriel Godfroy's sale of a large portion of this land to Wallace led to a new dynamic among all the people of the county.

Wallace's 1891 purchase of Godfroy's 220-acre farm was big news in the neighboring town of Peru and in the circus world. Local papers boasted about how Peru's own "noted showman," Benjamin Wallace, had had his eye on the property for a number of years.[65] One community historian claimed that it was "perhaps one of the most beautifully situated farms in the state."[66] Another paper wrote, "The location is, naturally, one of the prettiest in all the country. There is no reason why it should not be, but every reason in the world why it should be. The original owner of the land, Francis

140 CHAPTER FIVE

Godfroy, when he was chief of the great Miami tribe, had the pick and choice of ten miles square of the very garden spot of America."[67] Locating the Wallace Circus winter quarters near Peru was a tremendous benefit to this small Indiana town, as it ensured jobs and agricultural training for the surrounding community. The circus' ability to provide a variety of jobs, some leading to careers and the possibility of economic growth in the Miami community, reflected the aims of both Chief Francis Godfroy and Gabriel Godfroy. This outcome could not have been a surprise to Godfroy. Since the 1860s when the Chesapeake and Ohio, Nickel Plate, and Wabash railroad lines were built through the town, a variety of traveling circuses, menageries, dog and pony shows, and other traveling entertainment had come to Miami County. Many of the shows stopped in Peru to rest and resupply.[68] Godfroy must have been somewhat familiar with job opportunities as well as the labor and skill needs of these types of traveling companies.

In the twenty-nine-year span that Wallace owned and ran the circus town in Miami County, the circus became a major industry, critical to the life of the county and its seat, Peru. During the touring season from April to October, The Great Wallace Show employed around six hundred people.[69] The "off-season," too, was a major industry for the county and extended many circus-related jobs throughout the year. The winter quarters included nineteen functioning farms in Miami County, encompassing an area of more than two thousand acres. The labor forces of the Hagenbeck-Wallace Circus grew to an estimated 150 laborers and performers in the quarters and traveling show and consistently employed an estimated six hundred people from the surrounding community.[70] This number did not reflect the employees' nonworking family members or the many local people who lived outside of the quarters and commuted to work. Around one hundred employees at any given time were roustabouts, pole men, canvasback men, farmhands, and ground maintenance workers. The quarters' commissary and livestock ration departments placed continuing demands upon the agricultural resources of the county. In 1907, Wallace formed a partnership with Jerry Mugivan and John Talbott to purchase the liquidated Carl Hagenbeck Trained Wild Animal Show. This merger established Wallace's Circus as one of the most well-known traveling shows and it became one of the largest, taking up forty-five or more rail cars.[71]

The circus helped create and support an emerging industrial economy. One Peruvian contemporary boasted, "The mere quartering of his extensive shows in the county has had distinctive value in the supporting and furthering of various industrial and commercial enterprises, and thus in fostering the civic prosperity of the community."[72] He went on to say that "from the time the show comes into winter quarters in the fall, until it leaves again in the spring, all Peru is busy getting ready for the spring opening. This is one reason why every citizen in Peru, boasts of his city as the home of the Wallace Shows."[73] The circus relied on a wide range of industries to keep it going. Wallace employed Miami County's wagon builders, upholsterers, seamstresses, painters, carpet makers, printers, carpenters, and many other skilled laborers to get the circus ready each season. Wallace gained the favor of Peru's industries by keeping as much work inside the city and county as possible. Another contemporary wrote that out at the circus farm, "One finds thousands of dollars invested in the large buildings, which taken collectively would almost make a good-sized village by themselves."[74] By 1881, the tribal population had shown rapid growth, and by 1895, the circus had dramatically impacted the Indiana Miami community. The population increased from 318 to 440, or 38 percent in fourteen years. The median age of children fell from nineteen on the 1881 roll to fifteen on the 1895 roll. This suggests that family formation increased along with the birth rate. Families became larger, with thirteen of seventy families having five or more children compared to only ten families having four or more children on the 1881 census. The proportion of men to women was 47 percent to 53 percent, an almost equal ratio. The increase in the population suggests that a majority of Miami people experienced better circumstances after 1880 and that some who had previously moved to Kansas or Oklahoma returned.[75] Despite lower agricultural prices and a drop in local land base from 2,200 acres in 1880 to about 1,800 acres in 1890, Miami people fared relatively well due to the jobs in Wallace's circus.[76] Circus work paid relatively well and employed an ethnically mixed collection of outsiders, some of whom began to marry into the Miami community. The circus also provided opportunities for intertribal interactions, as Indians from across the country passed through the transportation hub of Peru, and more Miami people ventured out from Indiana to perform across the country.

One resident of Peru boasted about the Wallace show that "the mere quartering of his extensive shows in the county has had distinctive value in the supporting and furthering of various industrial and commercial enterprises, and thus in fostering the civic prosperity of the community."[77] Wallace gained the favor of Peru's industries by keeping as much work inside the city and county as possible. For people of the Miami tribe in and around Peru, Indiana, circus work was often a family affair. The Wallace Show and later the Hagenbeck-Wallace Circus would quarter from November to April before going on the road each season. Benjamin Wallace hired Miami people for various jobs, which they took advantage of to survive during otherwise hard economic times, especially in the 1880s through a period of lowered agricultural prices.[78] Circus employment was generally seasonal, but some positions were consistent because they continued in the winter quarters. Around one hundred to one hundred and fifty people worked in the quarters year-round on the circus farms, fed and handled animals, and performed in preshow concerts, equestrian shows, Wild West shows, and more.[79] Men who worked as animal feeders and farmhands brought their sons to work with them. Many Miami farmers, like the Bruell family, kept horses and were skilled in riding, driving, and caring for them.[80] The Bruell family, members of which joined labor and farm crews for the circus, also had family members drive horses as circus teamsters.[81] Miami man Alex Ralston was also a driver who worked with teamster Andy Bruell.[82]

Circus towns employed a cosmopolitan mix of people from various backgrounds, races, and ethnicities, and employment opportunities for African American and Native American workers were prevalent. The mix of people working in and around the Wallace Circus included Germans, Irish, African American, Miami, Cherokee, Delaware, Dutch, and Lakota.[83] LaMoine Marks, a longtime Native American circus worker from the Miami tribe in Peru, Indiana, remembered the circus as a positive part of his community, just after the turn of the century. He said, "They were good to them. They were a good thing for a town."[84] There was a constant flow of people from a variety of places around the country and the world who socialized outside of the quarters in the town of Peru. Marks remembered, "You could walk down the street on a Saturday night in Peru, because it was a Saturday night town, and you could hear French language, Italian, Greek, German, and many others. They even had a Russian group, Cossack riders."[85] Miami children grew up with ethnic and national diversity, exotic animals, artistic diversity, and circus culture in their backyards.[86] Miami who worked with the area circuses also occasionally worked with some of America's top entertainers. Marks, for example, worked with famed lion tamer Clyde Beatty and cowboy Tom Mix.[87] Lakota performers from Montana made seasonal trips to Miami County to participate in the circuses' equestrian shows.[88] African Americans and other southerners came for seasonal employment in the circuses.[89] European circus laborers and performers stopped in Peru for

*Hidden in Plain View* 143

extended stays, allowing those Miami who worked in the circus further opportunities to meet and connect to more and more people and cultures from around the world.[90]

Miami County was by no means a utopian community free of the racism that plagued the rest of the nation. In the circus quarters, Wallace employed a large mixture of people, but they remained largely segregated on several levels. The Wallace circus maintained a hierarchical structure that included race and occupation-based segregation. Management segregated laborers into Black and white work teams. Miami men often worked together or with either white or Black laborers. African American porters and tent raisers, for example, had Black foremen who worked with white managers.[91] Class status based on a person's occupation also divided circus employees. Laborers, management, and performers kept strict divisions and did not mix with each other. In the dining hall, for example, laborers, of any race, did not eat with employees of higher status in management or performance roles. In some cases, racially mixed groups of laborers came together in social situations. They held card games and amateur boxing tournaments in Peru and shared a gymnasium facility.[92] The availability of work also enabled African Americans to build stable communities adjacent to Miami and white neighborhoods. Marks remembered a very intentional way of separating laborers, performers, and management in the Hagenbeck Wallace show:

> The circus was made up of people who were your group, and you didn't mix with the other groups. . . . Now if you were a performer, you never mixed with a worker . . . they had a divided tent. The cook tent was divided right in the middle. On the right side, the one that we ate in, was, it started off the lowest class in there, the sideshow people and the ushers, and our group, which was the commissary, "candy butchers" was what they called them. And they had the performers in an area of their own, all close to each other. Now you speak and talk to any of them people, that was all right, but you didn't mix with the workers on the other side. But the workers, bosses ate on their side.[93]

Miami people working for the Wallace circus in Indiana aspired for careers beyond menial labor and created avenues to performance-oriented roles, travel, and networking with a diverse mixture of people from across the country and around the world. Many of these opportunities through the circus may have otherwise been unavailable to them. Miami laborers who initially had found jobs caring for horses, for instance, joined equestrian shows.

Others began a local trade of more exotic animals from outside the Midwest. Eventually, Wallace's Circus gained Miami County the reputation of Indiana's circus center. Peru eventually surpassed several other Indiana-based show towns and others such as Macon, Georgia, and Sarasota, Florida, to hold the industry title of "America's Circus City."

After a devastating flood in 1913, Benjamin Wallace's Circus came under the ownership of Jerry Mugivan, Ed Ballard, and Bert Bowers. They formed the American Circus Corporation in 1921 in Peru. Between 1921 and 1929, the American Circus Corporation owned and managed several circuses including Hagenbeck-Wallace, Howes Great London Shows, Robinson's Famous Shows, Sells-Floto, Sparks Circus, and the Al G. Barnes Circus. By the 1929 season, the American Circus Corporation sent out five circuses on 145 rail cars. Their major competitor, the combined Ringling Brothers and Barnum and Bailey show, sent out ninety rail cars. In about one generation, the circus industry changed from several companies with varying management styles to basically two large outfits that dominated the industry. Through all of those changes, Miami County remained the center of much circus industry and activity. Circus employment opportunities lasted from the late nineteenth century into the twentieth century. Generations of Miami people took advantage of stable local employment. After Wallace sold his company, the American Circus Corporation employed Miami people into the twentieth century, through the Great Depression, and into the 1940s and 1950s. Unlike the residents of Sellsville in neighboring Ohio, the people of Miami County kept their jobs in circus-related industries and maintained their community.

## Conclusion

During the span of his circus career, Peter Sells and his brothers helped usher in the golden age of the circus. During that time, between the closing decades of the nineteenth century and the first two decades of the twentieth century, the American circus industry reached its highest number of touring companies, boasted the largest number and variety of acts, and made the industry's most significant number of advancements in technology and management.[94] The Sells saw their company grow from a relatively small-scale wagon company to one of the largest railroad circuses in the country.[95] The Sells brothers broke the overwhelming trend in the circus industry of excluding all but Euro-American males to senior workmen positions by employing scores of African Americans in the 1880s.[96] The Sells hired more Black laborers and performers than contemporary white-owned traveling shows, but they still limited opportunities for Black men and women compared to opportunities open to white employees. They located their company town in an area that was already populated by a racially mixed group of farmers and low-skilled laborers. What was unique about the Sells Brothers Circus was its winter quarters and what the people who lived there were able to do in an era of violent racial hostility and decreasing civil rights. However, the Sells provided low-skill, steady employment for local African Americans. Once they obtained stable employment, Black Americans built churches, invested in education, and created new economic opportunities. With stable employment, not social uplift programs, residents of Sellsville created their own self-supporting community for three decades.

The legacy of Sellsville did not end with the circus. Residents of Poindexter benefited from some community services in the middle of the twentieth century, such as GED training, literacy programs, home-buyer education programs, Head Start, and several programs aimed at the working poor.[97] However, in 2009, the Columbus Metropolitan Housing Authority cited high crime and homicide rates combined with the physical decay of the structures as reasons to demolish Poindexter Village. Community activists decried the city's plan to demolish what they believed was an important part of Columbus' African American history. Residents organized festivals, created blogs, and attempted to organize support for village improvement rather than demolition.[98] Despite the outcry, the Columbus Housing Authority went ahead with plans, claiming that they would be sure to include community leaders, churches, and other groups in their plans to raze and rebuild the project.[99] Much of the community was demolished by 2013 when an expert committee was appointed and presented a report that recommended that several of the remaining buildings be saved.[100] The artist Aminah Robinson captured feelings of loss of history and community in her 2010 piece, *The Razing and Demolition of Historic Poindexter Village Would Empty Between Sept 2011 and 2013*. It pictures a displaced family on a crowded boat in a river, off the coast of a tangled landscape. Robinson, whose grandparents were pushed from Sellsville and whose parents were pushed from the Blackberry Patch, prepared to witness the community at Poindexter Village being pushed from their homes. Through years of government neglect, Poindexter Village fell into disrepair, and all but two buildings were demolished by 2013. The Ohio History Connection purchased the remaining structures with the help of the James Preston Poindexter Foundation and plans to establish a museum and cultural center there. The foundation aims to highlight the many stories of Columbus's Black community that have been lost over the years. African Americans in circuses have been largely invisible for generations, as have the many contributions to the industry and American society at large. The Ohio History Connection and the Poindexter Foundation hope that this center will help to add those voices back into American history.

Although existential debates raged across the nation over every aspect of Native American life, Indigenous artists and local leaders had difficult decisions to make if they wanted to practice their skills and if they wanted to remain on their lands. For some Indigenous artists, travel with circuses and Wild West shows enabled them to practice their arts and make much-needed money for survival. In the case of Chief Godfroy and his village outside Peru, Indiana, a strategic sale of a portion of his land enabled his Miami people to continue to hide in plain sight, assimilating some ways of white Americans while retaining important aspects of culture and lifestyle. Here, Miami people used a number of strategies to remain on their lands in Indiana over several generations.[101] In addition to utilizing circus employment, some families played down their Indigenous identities to thwart removal, enabling generations of Miami to hide in plain view.[102] Over the last century, the Miami population has fluctuated, but the tribe has maintained its efforts at regaining federal recognition. In 2011, Senate Bill 0311 was introduced as an attempt to provide state recognition to the Miami Nation of Indiana, but the bill was never brought to a vote. Currently, the Miami Nation of Indians of Indiana records over six thousand members in the region.[103] This is a testament to the perseverance and savvy of many determined generations.

The Great Wallace Circus and the later expanded Hagenbeck-Wallace Circus changed owners several times, and the Peru winter quarters remained functional and housed many circuses throughout the twentieth century. For its part, the Hagenbeck-Wallace Circus went bust in California in 1938. This was the fate of many railroad circuses in the United States in the 1930s, and circus families began to leave Peru at this time.[104] After experiencing several ups and downs in the industry, retired circus professionals in Peru founded the Circus City Festival Incorporated in 1959 to preserve the city's rich history. Additionally, the Peru winter quarters is now home to the International Circus Hall of Fame. Every July, the Circus City Festival puts on performances throughout the winter quarters and parades throughout the city. The festival, the museum, and the research center all stand as testaments to the rich history of the city and continue to introduce the circus to new generations. The Miami Nation of Indians of the State of Indiana maintains its headquarters across town and serves as a government and cultural center. It holds powwows and other cultural and educational events throughout the year, grants scholarships, and supports fellowship among the Miami who remain in Indiana.

CONCLUSION
# The Big Black Boom
*Black Art on an International Stage*

Charles Hicks was happy. In 1889, he wrote to the *Indianapolis Freeman*, saying, "The 'Big Black Boom' has struck 'Maori Land' and what is more, with much success!"[1] On a subsequent tour, Charles Pope, one of the performers in Hicks's troupe, wrote to the *Indianapolis Freeman* in 1902 to share his preference to remain in New Zealand:

> I am yet in Antipodes, doing nicely and were it not for business reasons, I would remain in this country a few years longer. There are so many advantages to be considered that I am convinced that the progressive Negro performer makes no mistake in choosing a field where his talent is appreciated and in demand. . . . The Negro performer is welcomed and appreciated in foreign countries and it is to this fact I base my conclusion. I am touring New Zealand with Dix's Gaiety Co. and at the conclusion of my present twelve month's contract I propose to come to America for the purpose of settling up my affairs, and as a matter of fact will come back to fill a new contract of fifty-two weeks.[2]

Other performers favored living and performing environments in Western Europe. In 1905, African American performer Billy McClain wrote to the *Indianapolis Freeman* that he was on his way to Paris from England and was having the "biggest joy" he had ever had in his life.[3] He went on to say that France was "bounding with colored acts at the present and all going well. I had the pleasure of seeing Harry Brown and Tom Brown." McClain also expressed a fondness for life abroad but longed for the right conditions to return to America. He wrote, "I would come back to America tomorrow and fight for my people if they would only stick together. I have everything I want, motor car, big fine house, servants, valet, etc., but I am not satisfied. I have a home in America as well. But above it all I have a mission on earth to perform. I want to be teaching my own people. I hope the day will come."[4] Several other African American performers found temporary or permanent careers abroad and wrote back to notify the *Indianapolis Freeman* of their decisions. In each instance, performers expressed race pride at Black people's accomplishments abroad mixed with the regret of not finding that ideal in America. Historians have written a good amount about Black American travel to Western Europe. Though many circus artists made the journey from San Francisco to Hawai'i, Asia, and the Antipodes, there is a surprisingly small amount of information on Black travel in the Pacific.[5] However, African American artists repeatedly reported to Black newspapers such as the *Indianapolis Freeman* that life in the Pacific was tolerable and sometimes preferable to life in the United States. In fact, several Black performers extended their tours and relocated to locations throughout the Pacific between the 1870s and 1920s. Newspapers, traveling show trade journals, and show route books provide a view into the experiences and significance of African Americans in the Pacific. A number of Black artists found great satisfaction and success on the Pacific circuit—going from California to Hawai'i to New Zealand to Australia to Japan and the Philippines— during the last quarter of the nineteenth century. As their tours stretched across the Pacific, artists gained wider perspectives on race and formed new relationships, both collaborative and contentious.

On the other side of the world, circus artist extraordinaire Eph Thompson crossed the Atlantic and found his greatest successes touring Europe and Russia. Thompson's story is amazing, not just for an African American at the turn of the twentieth century but for any American in that era. Born around 1860 in Colchester, Ontario, to African American immigrants from Kentucky, Eph began life in a community where Black people owned their own farmland, worked for themselves, and welcomed the formerly enslaved.[6] By the 1870s, the family settled in Ypsilanti, Michigan, a town outside of Detroit. In 1873, when Thompson was twelve or thirteen years old, the Adam Forepaugh Circus passed through Detroit and young Eph joined, running away with P. T. Barnum's main competitor.[7] Thompson quickly fell in love with elephants, spending every spare moment with them between his chores, cookhouse duties, and roustabout work. Soon, Addie Forepaugh, the son of Adam, took Thompson on as his assistant elephant trainer and, showing great talent and skill, Thompson was granted permission to create his own acts.[8] Thompson worked successfully with Bolivar and other elephants many trainers had deemed dangerous and unmanageable. He quickly rose to stardom in the Forepaugh Circus and developed a crowd-pleaser with his boxing elephant act. In this act, he sparred with an elephant he named after the contemporary white boxer John L. Sullivan. The boxing act propelled Thompson to stardom, but the circus industry and racial climate in America were limiting, so in 1885, Thompson went into business for himself. For the remainder of the 1880s and 1890s, he found great success touring his elephant show throughout Europe. He married, divorced, and married again, the second time to Jessie Amelia Kelly Leopold, an Irish acrobat. England, France, and Germany were all particular draws to African Americans who saw Europe as more racially egalitarian, and Thompson and his "Somersaulting Elephants" were hugely popular. In 1908, he was reported to be worth $250,000, virtually all of his wealth earned in European circus lots and variety show halls.[9] During these years, Thompson developed unique and very difficult acts in which elephants did barber shop routines, boxed, played baseball, lit matches to light candles, and played drums. Observers—both audiences and fellow animal trainers—respected Thompson as the best, and perhaps the flashiest, in his field. He exuded confidence, covered his elaborate costumes with diamonds, and refused to dress in blackface.

These men's overseas successes bring up several topics concerning the dissemination of African American culture at the turn of the twentieth century. First, their testimonies place African Americans on international stages, landing in Europe and the Pacific only a generation after the end of slavery. Black artists in circuses of the Gilded Age and Progressive Era were some of the earliest African Americans to regularly traverse the globe. Second, the men's testimonies point to a difference in racial atmosphere. This was the height of European nations' colonizing, terrorizing, genocidal campaigns in Africa, accompanied by their growing practice of exhibiting Africans and Asians in zoos and fairs and other exhibitions around the globe. Yet Black American performers often felt great differences in the way they were welcomed and treated overseas, where they could shake off feelings of defeat and live in places with no cultural expectations of them.[10] Third, the men's comments point to economic advancement. Paris, for example, was hugely popular for Black artists of all sorts as it provided a vibrant, cosmopolitan space for Black artists and intellectuals to gather, network, and create. Unlike the United States, Paris allowed boundary crossing and was a place friendly to collaborations that were available nowhere else to the same degree.[11]

In an era when African American leaders fought racial discrimination and searched for venues through which to assert their voices, Black traveling show entertainers broke racial barriers as they built careers that spanned the country and the globe. International forms of employment were a type of transformative experience for African Americans and inspired pride and excitement when Black artists were known to achieve international success. Robin D. G. Kelley argues that there are a variety of ways to express Black nationalism and pride beyond Pan-Africanism.[12] Black globetrotting entertainers bringing African American culture to the world must be added to international movements such as socialism or religion. Black circus artists inspired racial pride through their national fame and international connections. Performers provided access to Blacks and Indians across the country that otherwise would not have had access to the wider Black and Indian populations of the United States. Black performers who worked and relocated to Europe, Africa, and the Pacific experienced a pride and sense of identity that were unavailable to them in the United States. They became part of independent communities of African Americans who felt that they had greater choice in determining the direction of their careers and their lives. Newspapers included letters from performers on tour in Europe, Africa, and the Pacific region, and whenever possible added reviews and eyewitness accounts of audience reactions to African American shows.

Although Black and Indigenous artists working during the golden age of the circus understood their successes in part as a mark of their potential to raise their social, political, and economic possibilities, other parties outside of their adoring fan bases were also taking note. The financial success of African American artists and musicians overseas, as well as the popularity of the dying race narrative, reiterated in Wild West shows, revealed to American businessmen and politicians another strong way to promote ideas of American exceptionalism and America's racist and colonial agendas: cultural imperialism. Previously, American businesses and governments labeled racist, pseudo-scientific propaganda as fact, which shaped race and ethnic relations around the globe starting in the antebellum period. Business-government collaborations marketed human zoos as educational exhibits at world's fairs, and tented sideshows enabled white Christians to see what life was like for the maladapted, backward peoples of the world. The ostensible advancements of industrial and technological inventions were also tools of propaganda, as they explained the great differences between the industrialized, civilized nations and the peculiar, uncivilized non-white peoples of the world. The sign of industry made a distinction between those who deserved land because they knew how to put it to use for capitalism and those who were understood to not be properly exploiting the land, and, therefore, deserved to have it taken away. So, too, Black cultural forms and the engineered story of the dying Wild West became tools American business and government used to promote white American exceptionalism, racism, and colonization. Golden Age traveling entertainment companies modeled for the US government a way to use Black and Indigenous art, culture, and false narratives to reach broader audiences than even pseudo-educational exhibits and technological advancements. The idea stuck, and US government-corporate interests combined to promote American influence around the globe in subsequent generations.

Golden age tented companies showed how culture could be monetized and used for imperial purposes, and cultural imperialism became a major tool in subsequent generations. There was not one institution that solely orchestrated American global ambition; rather, multiple actors shaped US domination, including the US Pentagon and State Department and corporations. For example, politicians put Progressive Era trade restrictions in place with the explicit intention of providing US industries with a competitive global advantage. American military bases throughout the Pacific were one of the major vehicles for the circulation of rock 'n' roll music, Coca-Cola, and a wide variety of US-American culture.[13] Postwar governmental funding of films and Disney cartoons aided in shaping US relations with Mexico and Latin America, as US officials believed that cartoons were highly effective ways of communicating.[14] Interests coincided during World War II when Coca-Cola's ambition to dominate the world soft-drink market in conjunction with American insistence on controlling access to resources, the US Army gave the Coca-Cola Corporation privileged access to war and occupation zones. Later, musicals such as *South Pacific* and *The King and I*, as well as magazines, films, and novels, promoted a global vision of economic and racial integration where "undeveloped" peoples could be integrated into the world order on American terms.[15] In the immediate aftermath of World War II, the United States and the Soviet Union engaged in Cold War competition over the political allegiances and resources of peoples emerging from decades of colonialism, as well as a culture war. Between 1945 and 1960, forty new nation-states emerged, and as the Soviet Union sent classical orchestras and ballet companies around the world, the United States responded with jazz, dance, and a dazzling array of other cultural forms. The United States produced and distributed films, radio programs, and vast numbers of pamphlets and news releases aimed at showing the world the superiority of the American way of life and American democracy.[16] The US government distributed transistor radios so that audiences around the world would have access to American programs.

The federal government sponsored world tours of African American artists and musicians, including Louis Armstrong, Duke Ellington, Dizzy

Gillespie, and dancer and choreographer Alvin Ailey.[17] In the case of jazz and the cultural programs, state sponsorship brought performing artists to places that would not have been logistically viable or commercially profitable. Yet, just as performing artists of the golden age generations before them, these efforts had unintended consequences. Musicians brought their own agendas, which included promoting civil rights and challenging US State Department priorities, as well as their desire to learn new musical styles and collaborate with musicians in other countries, thereby destabilizing the purported distinctiveness of national cultures promoted by governments of the era.

Histories of the Black Atlantic and the Black Pacific together reveal Black cultural influence and Black self-determination reaching to every corner of the world. Paul Gilroy's *Black Atlantic* stands at the center of an expanding literature about the transnational dynamics of African American culture. Gilroy suggests that the experience of musicians abroad was representative of the ways in which Black music was incorporated into the "popular-cultural industries," demonstrating "distinctive patterns of cross-cultural circulation" within the context of the late nineteenth-century Atlantic world.[18] Black people's music during the golden age of the American circus was innately political. The postbellum/pre-Harlem generation's artistic endeavors—like Harlem in the 1920s and '30s, the Black Arts movement in the 1960s and '70s, and hip hop in the 1970s and '80s—were inseparable from its political and social aspirations. Well-known Black entertainers like those with the Georgia Minstrels and the Fisk Jubilee Singers often moved between the worlds of the Atlantic and the Pacific and seeded the waters for the burgeoning Jazz Age. African American traveling artists carved out new audiences in diverse racial systems and colonial contexts other than the United States or Britain. Illuminating these other realms of Black intellectual, artistic, and cultural activity has the potential to create deeply nuanced histories beautifully descriptive of the diverse geniuses of the era, which are effectively corrective and replace whitewashed memories; they are prescriptive and point to the potential strength and unity among Black Americans and the entire African diaspora.

# Notes

## Introduction

1. *Indianapolis Freeman*, 10 December 1904.
2. Abbott and Seroff, *Ragged but Right*, 248–68.
3. "Along the Color Line Jim Crow," *Crisis: A Record of the Darker Races*, February 1911, 6.
4. Abbott and Seroff, *Ragged but Right*, 248–68.
5. Dray, *At the Hands of Persons Unknown*; Jenkins, *Climbing Up to Glory*; Litwack, *Trouble in Mind*.
6. Equal Justice Initiative, "Reconstruction in America: Racial Violence after the Civil War, 1865–1876," accessed 13 May 2024, https://eji.org/report/reconstruction-in-america/.
7. See Prucha, *Great Father*.
8. See Troutman, *Indian Blues*, 6.
9. See also Prucha, *Great Father*; Hoxie, *Final Promise*; Deloria and Lytle, *American Indians, American Justice*; Holm, *Great Confusion in Indian Affairs*.
10. Abbott and Seroff, *Ragged but Right*, 158.
11. Ronald G. Shafer, "Hattie McDaniel Was the First Black Oscar Winner, It Didn't Help Her Career," *Washington Post*, 27 March 2022.
12. Davis, *Circus Age*, 10.
13. Deloria, "Indians," 56–58.
14. Deloria, *Indians in Unexpected Places*, 14.
15. Kasson, *Buffalo Bill's Wild West*, 171.
16. Chindahl, *History of the Circus*, 106; Pfening, "Sells Brothers," 1. The brothers were Ephraim (1834–98), William "Ad" Allen (1836–94), Lewis (1841–1907), and Peter (1845–1904).
17. *Ohio State Journal*, 8 March 1872.
18. "The City," *Ohio State Journal*, 25 April 1872.
19. "The City," *Ohio State Journal*, 25 April 1872.
20. *Official Route Book of the Sells Brothers Circus*, 1881, 1882, 1883. The bandleaders for 1881–82 were R. N. Thompson and conductor T. S. Roadman. See Sells Brothers file, Robert L. Parkinson Library and Research Center, Circus World Museum Records.
21. Perry George Lowery file, Robert L. Parkinson Library and Research Center, Circus World Museum Records.
22. "Big Circus Has Passed Its Last Winter in the Long-Used Quarters. New Location in or Near Columbus—Old Site to Be Sold in Lots," *Ohio State Journal*, 21 April 1907.
23. Graham, *Wait for the Muncie Boys*, 135–36.
24. Reeder, *No Performances Today*, 10.

25. Graham, *Wait for the Muncie Boys*, 20. In addition to banking and his burgeoning circus business, Wallace also invested in real estate, built the Wallace Theatre Building and Colonial Apartments in downtown Peru, and held a one-third interest in the Senger Dry Goods Company, which he helped organize in 1906.

26. Sampson, *Ghost Walks*, 127.

27. "Notes from the Great Wallace Show," *New York Clipper*, 11 March 1893. This short entry documented that the Wallace Show sideshow included "C. W. Jones' colored band, ten pieces; Prince Mungo, Morean chieftain; Princess Julia, snake charmer; Zamora, triple jointed wonder," among other sideshow acts that season.

28. Abbott and Seroff, *Ragged but Right*, 158.

29. See "Al G. Barnes' Greatest Wild Animal Circus," *Indianapolis Freeman*, 13 March 1920; "Walter L. Main's Shows," *Indianapolis Freeman*, 31 July 1920; "Circus Friends Meet," *Indianapolis Freeman*, 17 July 1920.

## Chapter One

1. Posey, "Magnificent Entrees," 68.
2. Davis, *Circus Age*, 3.
3. Davis, *Circus Age*, 5.
4. Wittmann, *Circus and the City*, 63.
5. Wittmann, *Circus and the City*, 63.
6. "Here and There Among the Folks," *Billboard*, 1 April 1922, 45.
7. Lavers, "Horses," 141.
8. Lavers, "Horses," 141.
9. *The Federal Gazette* and *Philadelphia Daily Advertiser*, 17 May 1793, as cited in Moy, "Entertainments," 200.
10. Thayer, *Annals of the American Circus*, 24.
11. Thayer, *Annals of the American Circus*, 24–26.
12. Thayer, *Annals of the American Circus*, 24–26.
13. Thayer, *Annals of the American Circus*, 37.
14. Thayer, "Steamboat," 11.
15. Davis, *Circus Age*, 19.
16. See *Official Route Book of the Sells Brothers Circus*, 1873.
17. *Official Route Book of the Sells Brothers Circus*, 1891, Milner Library, Illinois State University.
18. Southern, *Music of Black Americans*, 244.
19. Rydell, *All the World's a Fair*.
20. Abbott and Seroff, *Ragged but Right*, 211.
21. Chude-Sokei, *Last Darky*, 6. The italics are in the original text.
22. Chude-Sokei, *Last Darky*, 8.
23. See also Davis, *Circus Age*, 50. Circusgoers often paid an extra fee, around twenty-five cents, to attend the aftershow, or concert performance. The concert often included the Black sideshow band or an equestrian show and provided an opportunity to watch as canvasmen took down and packed away tents.

24. Thayer, "Out-Side Shows"; see also "Plantation Darkey at the Circus," 113–14; and Renoff, *Big Tent*, 98–100.

25. Thayer, "Out-Side Shows."

26. Thayer, "Out-Side Shows."

27. "Plantation Darkey at the Circus," 113–14.

28. Thayer, "Out-Side Shows."

29. Renoff, *Big Tent*, 5.

30. Renoff, *Big Tent*, 99.

31. "The Circus Enthusiasts: Redmen Unrivaled in Their Love for the Show, Mexicans, Negroes, and Chinese Little Less Eager in their Admiration, Says an Old Employee," *New York Times*, 28 April 1901.

32. Sylvester Russell, "Chicago Weekly Review," *Indianapolis Freeman*, 22 July 1911.

33. Calhoun, *Medicine Show*, 3.

34. McNenly, *Native Performers*, 39.

35. McNenly, *Native Performers*, 54–55.

36. McNenly, *Native Performers*, 60–61.

37. "Notes of the J. H. Harris Band and Minstrel Company with Gollmer Brothers Shows," *Indianapolis Freeman*, 6 June 1914.

38. Davis, *Circus Age*, 184.

39. "Under the Tents," *New York Clipper*, 22 February 1902.

40. "Under the Tents," *New York Clipper*, 22 February 1902.

41. Rydell and Kroes, *Buffalo Bill in Bologna*, 33.

## Chapter Two

1. "The Parrot in the Theater Loft," *Indianapolis Freeman*, 14 May 1910.

2. "Lowery's Band, Orchestra, Minstrel Show and Other Attractions with The Wallace and Hagenbeck Show," *Indianapolis Freeman*, 14 June 1913.

3. Abbott and Seroff, *Ragged but Right*, 158.

4. See "Al G. Barnes' Greatest Wild Animal Circus," *Indianapolis Freeman*, 13 March 1920; "Walter L. Main's Shows," *Indianapolis Freeman*, 31 July 1920; "Circus Friends Meet," *Indianapolis Freeman*, 17 July 1920.

5. Peretti, *Lift Every Voice*, 57.

6. Peretti, *Lift Every Voice*, 40.

7. Peretti, *Lift Every Voice*, 47.

8. Southern, *Music of Black Americans*, 249.

9. Peretti, *Lift Every Voice*, 58.

10. Peretti, *Lift Every Voice*, 76.

11. Peretti, *Lift Every Voice*, 76.

12. Peretti, *Lift Every Voice*, 47.

13. Southern, *Music of Black Americans*, 244.

14. Southern, *Music of Black Americans*, 244.

15. Sampson, *Ghost Walks*, 39.

16. Abbott and Seroff, *Ragged but Right*, 211.

17. Chude-Sokei, *Last Darky*, 2.

18. *Indianapolis Freeman*, 9 May 1891.

19. Watkins, *Showman*, 7.

20. "With the Circuses: Origin of Band and Minstrel Annex—Prof. P.G. Lowery Blazes the Way Four Hundred Musicians Now Employed—A Greater and Grander Season Promised for 1911," *Indianapolis Freeman*, 28 January 1911.

21. Watkins, *Showman*, 92.

22. "P. G. Lowery, Originator," *Indianapolis Freeman*, 9 July 1910.

23. "P. G. Lowery, Originator," *Indianapolis Freeman*, 9 July 1910.

24. *Hagenbeck-Wallace Official Route Book 1913*, 28.

25. "Harrisburg, Pa., Lowery's Minstrels, the Best Under Canvas," *Indianapolis Freeman*, 31 May 1913.

26. "Stage," *Indianapolis Freeman*, 25 March 1916.

27. *Eureka Herald*, 22 August 1912.

28. *Eureka Herald*, 17 September 1914.

29. *Indianapolis Freeman*, 10 June 1905.

30. *Indianapolis Freeman*, 9 November 1901.

31. *Indianapolis Freeman*, 28 December 1907.

32. "P. G. Lowery Returns to the Circus Field," *Indianapolis Freeman*, 25 March 1916.

33. See Abbott and Seroff, *Ragged but Right*, 199.

34. Watkins, *Showman*, 99.

35. "Notes from R. Roy Pope's Band, Ringling Brothers Band, Ringling Brothers Circus," *Indianapolis Freeman*, 4 September 1915.

36. *Indianapolis Freeman*, 17 April 1920; see also Watkins, *Showman*, 114.

37. Chillicothe, Missouri, December 1885, sheet 3, Sanborn maps of Missouri.

38. *New York Clipper*, 28 April 1894, 117.

39. "Wolfscale's Band," *New York Age*, 11 April 1912; "Jas. Wolfscale's Band and Vaudeville Company: With Barnum and Bailey's Circus at Madison Square Garden," *Indianapolis Freeman*, 20 April 1912.

40. "Prof. Wolfscale's Company: With Barnum and Bailey's Greatest Show on Earth," *Indianapolis Freeman*, 31 May 1913.

41. "Notes from Wolfscale's Band with Barnum & Bailey," *Indianapolis Freeman*, 24 October 1914.

42. Abbott and Seroff, *Ragged but Right*, 167.

43. *Indianapolis Freeman*, 19 July 1913, 6; 21 November 1914, 6; 3 June 1916, 6; *Billboard*, 9 April 1921, 43.

44. "Prof. Wolfscale Cancels Engagement with Barnum and Bailey after Sixteen Years with Big Circus Will Spend Summer in Chicago," *Indianapolis Freeman*, 6 March 1915.

45. *Indianapolis Freeman*, 7 June 1913, 6.

46. *Kansas City Sun*, 13 September 1919, 8.

47. Abbott and Seroff, *Ragged but Right*, 170–72.

48. Abbott and Seroff, *Ragged but Right*, 171.

49. "R. Roy Pope Spends Sunday in the City," *Indianapolis Freeman*, 17 July 1909.

50. "R. Roy Pope Spends Sunday in the City," *Indianapolis Freeman*, 17 July 1909.

51. "Successful Career of a Great Musician: How R. Roy Pope Reached the Top Round as Band Master," *Indianapolis Freeman*, 25 December 1909.

52. "R. Roy Pope Spends Sunday in the City," *Indianapolis Freeman*, 17 July 1909.
53. *New York Age*, 7 April 1910.
54. "Negro Concert Band with Ringling Bros.' Circus," *Indianapolis Freeman*, 21 January 1911.
55. *Indianapolis Freeman*, 21 November 1914.
56. Abbott and Seroff, *Ragged but Right*, 135.
57. Abbott and Seroff, *Ragged but Right*, 166–70.
58. Allen and Rust, *King Joe Oliver*, 8.
59. Shapiro and Hentoff, *Hear Me Talkin' to Ya*, 77.
60. Bushell, *Jazz from the Beginning*, 11–12.
61. Bushell, *Jazz from the Beginning*, 13.
62. See also Lewis, "Untamed Music."
63. Jones, *Blues People*, 93.
64. Davis, *Blues Legacies*, 3.
65. Davis, *Blues Legacies*, 3.
66. Davis, *Blues Legacies*, 94.
67. Davis, *Blues Legacies*, 4.
68. Jones, *Blues People*, 91.
69. Davis, *Blues Legacies*, 11.
70. Harrison, *Black Pearls*, 34–35.
71. Harrison, *Black Pearls*, 35.
72. Harrison, *Black Pearls*, 52.
73. Southern, *Music of Black Americans*, 372.
74. "Ida Cox Hits Comeback Road," *Washington Tribune*, 13 January 1940.
75. *Inter-State Tattler*, 13 July 1928.
76. "Backstage With Stagestruck," *Inter-State Tattler*, 2 November 1928.
77. "An Interview With Ida Cox," *Plaindealer*, 22 July 1932.
78. "1940 Edition of 'Spirituals to Swing' Ready," *Listener News*, 23 December 1939.
79. *Inter-State Tattler*, 6 September 1929; *Los Angeles Tribune*, 17 October 1958.
80. *Los Angeles Tribune*, 17 October 1958; Abbott and Seroff, *Ragged but Right*, 178.
81. Abbott and Seroff, *Ragged but Right*, 179.
82. Abbott and Seroff, *Ragged but Right*, 182.
83. *Billboard*, 30 September 1922.
84. *Negro World*, 4 August 1923.
85. *Negro World*, 4 August 1923.
86. *Cleveland Gazette*, 17 November 1923.
87. *Inter-State Tattler*, 28 September 1924.
88. "Cabaret News," *New York Age*, 20 September 1924.
89. "Miss Lizzie Miles, Creole Songbird, Plans Foreign Trip," *New York Age*, 8 November 1924.
90. "Miss Lizzie Miles, Creole Songbird, Plans Foreign Trip," *New York Age*, 8 November 1924.
91. "Miss Lizzie Miles, The Creole Songbird, Writes Her Impressions of Paris," *New York Age*, 27 December 1924.

92. "Miss Lizzie Miles, The Creole Songbird, Writes Her Impressions of Paris," *New York Age*, 27 December 1924.

93. "Miss Lizzie Miles Is Mont Martre's Smart Entertainer," *New York Age*, 21 March 1925.

94. "At the Capitol Club," *Inter-State Tattler*, 18 September 1925.

95. *Inter-State Tattler*, 18 September 1925.

96. "Harlem Night Life," *Inter-State Tattler*, 6 September 1929.

97. "Theatrical Jottings," *New York Age*, 3 September 1932.

98. "New York Is My Beat," *New York Age Defender*, 22 August 1953.

99. "Capitol's "History of Jazz," *Billboard*, 1 July 1957.

100. *Billboard*, 24 January 1958.

101. "Lizzie Miles on 'Stars of Jazz' Monday," *Los Angeles Tribune*, 17 October 1958.

102. Almena Lomax, "Television Review," *Los Angeles Tribune*, 24 October 1958.

103. Almena Lomax, "Television Review," *Los Angeles Tribune*, 24 October 1958.

104. "Lizzie Miles Dies in New Orleans," *Billboard*, 30 March 1963.

105. "Lizzie Miles Dies in New Orleans," *Billboard*, 30 March 1963.

106. Chude-Sokei, *Last Darky*, 6.

107. Lott, *Love and Theft*, 15.

108. Huggins, *Harlem Renaissance*, 540.

109. *Indianapolis Freeman*, 21 November 1914.

110. Gaines, *Uplifting the Race*, 67.

111. Schmalenberger, "Shaping Uplift through Music," 59.

112. Higginbotham, *Righteous Discontent*, 195–96.

113. Hine, "Black Women in the Middle West," 60.

114. Terrell, "Duty of the National Association," in Higginbotham, *Righteous Discontent*, 206–7.

115. Smith, *Photography on the Color Line*, 2.

116. Smith, *Photography on the Color Line*, 9.

117. Smith, *Photography on the Color Line*, 75.

118. Penn, *Afro-American Press*.

119. Penn, *Afro-American Press*.

120. Penn, *Afro-American Press*, 330.

121. Penn, *Afro-American Press*, 336.

122. *National Leader*, quoted in Penn, *Afro-American Press*, 336–37.

123. Abbott and Seroff, *Out of Sight*, xii.

124. Schmalenberger, "Shaping Uplift through Music," 59.

125. Schmalenberger, "Shaping Uplift through Music," 57.

126. Schenbeck, "Music, Gender, and 'Uplift,'" 344.

127. "Notes from Wolfscale's Band with Barnum & Bailey," *Indianapolis Freeman*, 24 October 1914.

128. "Prof. Bismark Ferris: Satisfied Musical Enterprise with Two Bills," *Indianapolis Freeman*, 27 May 1911.

129. "Prof. Bismark Ferris and His Satisfied Boys," *Indianapolis Freeman*, 3 August 1912.

130. *Chicago Defender*, 19 January 1924.
131. *Billboard*, 19 May 1923.
132. *Chicago Defender*, 16 September 1922 and 26 January 1924.
133. *Chicago Defender*, 23 September 1922.
134. *Chicago Defender*, 10 October 1925.
135. *Chicago Defender*, 2 January 1928 and 19 November 1927.
136. *Chicago Defender*, 19 September 1925.
137. *Chicago Defender*, 8 October 1927.
138. See, for example, *Chicago Defender*, 9 June 1928 and 8 October 1927.
139. *Chicago Defender*, 24 June 1921 and 9 August 1924; *Chicago Defender*, 20 September 1924.
140. *Chicago Defender*, 2 February 1924 and 20 January 1923.
141. *Chicago Defender*, 26 August 1922.
142. *Chicago Defender*, 26 August 1922.
143. *Chicago Defender*, 13 September 1924.
144. *Chicago Defender*, 20 September 1924.
145. Abbott and Seroff, *Ragged but Right*, 158.
146. Abbott and Seroff, *Ragged but Right*, 77.

## Chapter Three

1. "The Stage," *Indianapolis Freeman*, 23 May 1908; Abbott and Seroff, *Out of Sight*, 309–10; "J. A. Jackson's Page: Our Losses," *Billboard*, 9 December 1921.
2. Hoh and Rough, *Step Right Up*, 68.
3. Hoh and Rough, *Step Right Up*, 68.
4. "J. A. Jackson's Page," *Billboard*, 27 August 1921.
5. "Here and There Among the Folks," *Billboard*, 29 April 1922.
6. *Cleveland Gazette*, 28 January 1893, 1.
7. Rubin Haysede Green, "Under the Marquee," *Billboard*, 28 August 1915, 18.
8. "J. A. Jackson's Page: Our Losses," *Billboard*, 9 December 1921.
9. Schwalm, *Emancipation's Diaspora*, 10.
10. Schwalm, *Hard Fight for We*, 142.
11. *Indianapolis World*, 14 July 1894.
12. Al Wells, "Negro Novelty Acts," *Indianapolis Freeman*, 26 August 1916.
13. Sampson, *Ghost Walks*, 531–32; Al Wells, "Negro Novelty Acts," *Indianapolis Freeman*, 26 August 1916.
14. Sampson, *Ghost Walks*, 531–32.
15. Lahti, *American West*, 101–2.
16. Lahti, *American West*, 102.
17. Vinson and Edgar, "Zulus Abroad," 45.
18. Vinson and Edgar, "Zulus Abroad," 49.
19. Mitchell, *Monsters*, 118.
20. Anderson, "Red Coat," 13.
21. Anderson, "Red Coat," 13.
22. Asim, *N Word*, 151.

23. Asim, *N Word*, 151.
24. Lindfors, "Ethnological Show Business," 216.
25. Lahti, *American West*, 173.
26. Lahti, *American West*, 173.
27. Robinson, *Old Wagon Show Days*, 95.
28. Vinson and Edgar, "Zulus Abroad," 48.
29. Vinson and Edgar, "Zulus Abroad," 48.
30. Middleton, "Circus Memoirs," 216.
31. Lahti, *American West*, 174.
32. Vinson and Edgar, "Zulus Abroad," 48; Pfening, "Black Workingman Notes."
33. Vinson and Edgar, "Zulus Abroad," 54.
34. Smith, "'Things You'd Imagine,'" 26; Vinson and Edgar, "Zulus Abroad," 54.
35. See Pulley Hudson, *Real Native Genius*.
36. "Here and There Among the Folks," *Billboard*, 12 February 1925, announced that Oskazuma would celebrate his sixtieth birthday on 5 March 1925.
37. "Here and There Among the Folks," *Billboard*, 21 February 1925.
38. "Fine Performances of Superior Shows Attract Large Crowds," *Indianapolis Freeman*, 18 August 1917.
39. Abbott and Seroff, *Ragged but Right*, 190.
40. "Prince Azkazuma Visits the Buffalo Bill Show," *Indianapolis Freeman*, 28 July 1917.
41. "Minstrel and Tent Show Talk," *Billboard*, 26 January 1924.
42. "J. A. Jackson's Page," *Billboard*, 21 April 1923 and 15 November 1924.
43. "J. A. Jackson's Page," *Billboard*, 21 April 1923 and 15 November 1924.
44. "William H. Reed's [sic] Band," *Indianapolis Freeman*, September 27, 1913; "Seeing Young Buffalo Bill's Show," *Indianapolis Freeman*, 25 July 1914.
45. "Here and There Among the Folks," *Billboard*, 6 December 1924.
46. "Prince Askazuma: Sends an Interesting Letter from Porto Rico," *Billboard*, 15 October 1921.
47. Childress, "Life Beyond," 177.
48. Childress, "Life Beyond," 177.
49. Childress, "Life Beyond," 178.
50. Slout, *Olympians*, 330.
51. Slout, *Olympians*, 330.
52. Robinson, *Old Wagon Show Days*, 42.
53. Robinson, *Old Wagon Show Days*, 42.
54. Turner, *Victorian Arena*, 91.
55. Turner, *Victorian Arena*, 91, in Pfening, "Black Performer Notes."
56. Slout, "Olympians," 210; Slout, *Royal Coupling*, 84.
57. Thornton interview with Chang Reynolds, 9 May 1964, in Pfening, "Black Performer Notes."
58. Slout, *Olympians*, 301.
59. Thurman, *Singing Like Germans*, 56.
60. Edwards, *Practice of Diaspora*, 4.

61. "Eph Sells His Elephants," *Variety*, 26 June 1908. Thompson was worth $250,000.
62. Davis, *Circus Queen*, 131, 330.
63. Coup, *Sawdust*, 48.
64. Coup, *Sawdust*, 48–49.
65. Coup, *Sawdust*, 48. Pfening believed that Coup was possibly referring to Aaron Moore, a very tall Black man from North Carolina called "The Colored Giant."
66. Pfening, "Black Side Show Performers."
67. Davis, *Circus Age*, 86.
68. Davis, *Circus Age*, 83.
69. Childress, "Life Beyond," 188.
70. Childress, "Life Beyond," 177.
71. Mitchell, *Monster*, 44.
72. Allen, *Horrible Prettiness*, 225.
73. Allen, *Horrible Prettiness*, 227–28.
74. "J. A. Jackson's Page: A Colored Burlesque Show story," *Billboard*, 4 June 1921.
75. "J. A. Jackson's Page," *Billboard*, 9 December 1922.
76. "J. A. Jackson's Page," *Billboard*, 9 December 1922.
77. "Coy Cogitates," *Chicago Defender*, 23 September 1922.
78. "Coy Cogitates," *Chicago Defender*, 23 September 1922.
79. "Coy Cogitates," *Chicago Defender*, 20 January 1923.
80. "Coy Cogitates," *Chicago Defender*, 13 January 1923 and 19 January 1924, Ethel Waters.
81. *Billboard*, 29 March 1924 and 22 March 1924.
82. "Coy Cogitates," *Chicago Defender*, 19 October 1927.
83. "Coy Cogitates," *Chicago Defender*, 13 September 1924.
84. "Coy Cogitates," *Chicago Defender*, 27 October 1928.
85. Mitchell, *Monsters*, 56.
86. Barclay, *Mark of Slavery*, 27.
87. "Princess Wee-Wee," *Billboard*, 9 April 1921.
88. Mitchell, *Monsters*, 49.
89. Barclay, *Mark of Slavery*, 14.
90. Thompson, *On the Road*, 51.
91. Pfening, "Black Workingman Notes."
92. "Behind the Scenes: The Life of a Circus Employee as Seen by a Herald Reporter," *The Carroll Herald*, 15 July 1885.
93. North and Hatch, *Circus Kings*, 190–91.
94. North and Hatch, *Circus Kings*, 190–91.
95. Pfening, "Black Workingman Notes."
96. Childress, "Life Beyond," 194.
97. Bill "Cap" Curtis to George Chindahl, 10 October 1950, George Chindahl Papers, 70.
98. "Too Much Prosperity Hurts the Big Circus," *Washington Times*, 8 November 1903, in Davis, *Circus Age*, 70.

99. George Werner Papers file; Blacks in Shows file, Robert L. Parkinson Library and Research Center, Circus World Museum Records.

100. Pfening, "Black Workingman Notes."

101. Route Books were published by major circuses each year. In addition to listing types of acts, performers, workers, and staff people, these industry publications chronicled day-to-day schedules from city to city, notable events on the road, challenges, advertisements, and other interesting information.

102. *Route Book of the John Robinson's 10 Big Shows*, 76.

103. *Route Book of the John Robinson's 10 Big Shows*, 99.

104. McKennon, *Logistics*, 43.

105. McKennon, *Logistics*, 45.

106. Davis, *Circus Queen*, 129. For an account of life in the traveling show, see "Behind the Scenes: The Life of a Circus Employee as Seen by a Herald Reporter," *The Carroll Herald*, 15 July 1885.

107. McKennon, *Logistics*, 45.

108. Janet Davis, *Circus Age*, 79.

109. "Circus Man Murdered," *Columbus Dispatch*, 26 June 1891.

110. "Circus Man Murdered," *Columbus Dispatch*, 26 June 1891.

111. *Great Pan American Shows 1903 Route Book*, 35.

112. Strange and Loo, "Spectacular Circus," 181.

113. "Three Years for Robbery," *Variety*, 14 August 1909.

114. "Circus News: Circus Laborer Lynched," *Variety*, 12 June 1909.

115. Condon, "B. E. Wallace," 4.

116. Condon, "B. E. Wallace," 4.

117. Condon, "B. E. Wallace," 4.

118. "Circus Gossip," *Billboard*, 1 August 1903.

119. Meier and Rudwick, *Along*, 235, 238.

120. "Intervention of Police Saves Negro's Life in Circus Employees' Riot: William Butler, Colored, With Al G. Barnes Circus, Severely Mauled by Enraged White Men of 'The Lot' at Melville," *The Leader* (Saskatchewan), 18 June; the exact year on this article is unknown, however, the Al G. Barnes Circus toured from 1895 to 1929.

121. "Intervention of Police Saves."

122. "Under the Marquee," *Billboard*, 26 June 1920.

123. Max Mason, Case no. 6785, letter from Jerry Mugivan to Frank A. Whittier, 13 July 1922, Minnesota Historical Society, https://www.mnhs.org/duluthlynchings/documents/max-mason-case-no-6785-interview-max-mason-august-26-1922.

124. *Route Book of the John Robinson's 10 Big Shows*, 70.

125. Hinkle, "Kit Carson," 20.

126. *Official Route Book of the Sells Brothers Circus*, 1883.

127. *Official Route Book of the Sells Brothers Circus*, 1883, 18.

128. Pfening, "Black Workingman Notes."

129. "Race Fight on Circus Train Is Halted Whites and Blacks of Barnes Organization Have Trouble One Negro Shot in Faction War–Whites in Privilege Car Fired Upon by Negroes from Outside," *Pasadena Star-News*, 11 November 1921.

130. Pfening, "Christy and His Wonder Show," *Bandwagon* (May–June 1996): 20.

Chapter Four

1. "Onondaga Indians Were Stranded in Germany," *Quarterly Journal of the Society of American Indians* 2, no. 3 (1914): 239–41.
2. Parker, "Editorial Viewpoint" (1914), 174–76
3. Lahti, *American West*, 168.
4. Vinson and Edgar, "Zulus Abroad," 44.
5. Lahti, *American West*, 167.
6. Rydell, *All the World's a Fair*.
7. Rydell, *All the World's a Fair*, 6.
8. Lahti, *American West*, 101–2.
9. Deloria, *Indians in Unexpected Places*, 8.
10. Rydell and Kroes, *Buffalo Bill in Bologna*, 31–32.
11. Lahti, *American West*, 171.
12. Rydell and Kroes, *Buffalo Bill in Bologna*, 31.
13. Kasson, *Buffalo Bill's Wild West*, 162.
14. Wallis, *Real Wild West*, 251.
15. McNenly, *Native American Performers*, 39.
16. Deloria, *Indians in Unexpected Places*, 56.
17. McNenly, *Native American Performers*, 69.
18. Deloria, "Indians," 56.
19. "The Queen and the American Exhibition," *Hampshire Advertiser*, 14 May 1887; "'Wild West' Show a Success: Queen Victoria Gives the Show a Special Audience and Seems Pleased," *Columbus Journal*, 1 June 1887.
20. Neihardt, *Black Elk Speaks*.
21. "Our Sioux Swells," *The Daily Inter Ocean*, 21 March 1892.
22. Heppler and Seefeldt, "Buffalo Bill's Wild West."
23. McNenly, "Foe, Friend, or Critic," 144.
24. McNenly, "Foe, Friend, or Critic," 145.
25. *The Western Daily Press* recognized "four squaws who travel with the troupe" (The Wild West in Bristol, 28 September 1891), and *The Courier* mentioned at least eight or nine women (Buffalo Bill's Wild West, 16 February 1888).
26. "Wild West Ladies, How they Entertain Visitors," *News of the World*, 21 August 1892; Boorn, *Oskate Wicasa*, 164.
27. "Cowboys and Mexicans Danced, Mr. High Bear and Miss Holy Blanket Married in South Brooklyn," *Washington Post*, 11 June 1894.
28. "The Luck of Cody's Camp," *Sunday Chronicle*, 12 February 1888; "Birth at the Wild West Camp," *Evening News*, 9 February 1888; "Buffalo Bill's Wild West," *Evening Mail*, 8 February 1888.
29. "Buffalo Bill's Wild West," *The Courier*, 16 February 1888; "The Wild West Show," *Manchester Times*, 18 February 1888.
30. "The Queen and the American Exhibition," *Hampshire Advertiser*, 14 May 1887.
31. *Route Book: Buffalo Bill's Wild West Season*, 1900, 24.
32. *Official Route Book of Ringling Brothers*, 1892, 88.
33. *Official Route Book of the Pawnee Bill*, 1899, 30.

34. Rafert, *Miami Indians of Indiana*, 45; Marks, interview by Rafert, 12 May 1993, "Hunting, boxing."

35. Marks, interview by Rafert, 4 November 1980, "Hunting, fishing, taxidermy."

36. "Social Security Death Index," no. 306-26-3905, Indiana State.

37. Marks, interview by Rafert, 11 October 1991, "Circus/elephants."

38. Marks, interview by Rafert, 11 May 1993, "Circus"; Marks, interview by Rafert, 12 May 1993, "Hunting, boxing."

39. Marks, interview by Rafert, 11 October 1991, "Circus/elephants."

40. The 1910 federal census recorded Mary as Indian and born circa 1904. Her mother and siblings were also Indian, and her father was recorded as white on the 1910 census. See Census Place, *Butler, Miami, Indiana*; roll T624_370, page 4A, Enumeration District 0112, image 937, FHL number 1374383. Their residence in 1910 was in Butler Township. On the 1920 census, Mary's father, Daniel, had been reported as deceased, and the family was living in Erie, Indiana. All household members were recorded as white on the 1920 census. See Census Place, *Erie, Miami, Indiana*, roll T625_441, page 2B, Enumeration District 138, image 31. Mary married Cheerful Gardner, a man twenty-two years her senior, and worked with him in his elaborate elephant acts.

41. Marks, interview by Rafert, 11 May 1993, "Circus." See also Cheerful Gardner's obituary in *Bandwagon* 7, no. 3 (March 1952): 8.

42. Sarah Tucker married George Weisenberger. See *Miami County, Index to Marriage Record, 1850–1920*, book C-11, p. 421. The 1900 federal census recorded Sarah as Indian, but later records classify her as white. Her sister Susie married James Mellinger. Susie is recorded as Indian in the 1910 federal census and white in later records. *Original Record Located County Clerk's Office, Peru*; book C-22, p. 571.

43. See *Miami County, Index to Marriage Record*.

44. Hiltzik, *Iron Empires*, 261.

45. "The Wild West Show: Buffalo Bill and His Band of Indians" [Montreal, 1885?], Nate Salisbury scrapbooks, microfilm 18, reel 1, vol. 1, Denver Public Library; in McNenly, "Foe, Friend, or Critic."

46. "Sitting Bull in Camp, Interview with One of General Custer's Murderers," *Evening Journal*, 5 September 1885.

47. "A BBQ at Beacon Park: Eating Roast Ox with Sharp Sticks as Guests of Sitting Bull," *Boston Daily Globe*, 31 July 1885. Nate Salisbury scrapbooks, microfilm 18, reel 1, vol. 1, Denver Public Library; in McNenly, "Foe, Friend, or Critic," 156.

48. Deloria, *Indians*, 54.

49. Moses, *Wild West Shows*, 33.

50. Moses, *Wild West Shows*, 109–10; see also Landrum, "Kicking Bear," 193.

51. Luther Standing Bear, *My People the Sioux*, 198.

52. Luther Standing Bear, *My People the Sioux*, 194.

53. Luther Standing Bear, *My People the Sioux*, 200.

54. Luther Standing Bear, *My People the Sioux*, 201.

55. Luther Standing Bear, *My People the Sioux*, 202.

56. Luther Standing Bear, *My People the Sioux*, 198.

57. Luther Standing Bear, *My People the Sioux*, 202–3.

58. Deloria, *Indians in Unexpected Places*, 75.
59. Mathes, "Helen Hunt Jackson," 47.
60. La Flesche, "Bright Eyes," 25.
61. La Flesche, "Bright Eyes," 27.
62. Larson, *Devil in the White City*, 284–85.
63. Erny Karoly, "Circus Historical Society," accessed 20 September 2011, https://circushistory.org.
64. "The Carnegie Institute Annual Reports of the Officers, Committees, and Departments for the Fiscal Year Ending March 31, 1919," vols. 22–26 (Pittsburgh, 1919).
65. Murphy, "Antidance Rhetoric," 81.
66. Bokovoy, *San Diego World's Fairs*, 128.
67. Sorisio, "Playing the Indian Princess?," 10.
68. Green, "Pocahontas Perplex," 703.
69. *Official Route Book of the Pawnee Bill, 1898*, 26.
70. Parezo and Jones, "What's in a Name?", 373.
71. Parezo and Jones, "What's in a Name?", 378–79.
72. Parezo and Jones, "What's in a Name?", 378–79.
73. "'The Wild West' in Bristol," *Western Daily Press*, 28 September 1891.
74. "The Death of Eagle Star in Sheffield," *Sheffield and Rotherham Independent*, 26 August 1891.
75. "The Wild West in Sheffield," *Sheffield and Rotherham Independent*, 10 August 1891.
76. Lahti, *American West*, 153–54.
77. Lahti, *American West*, 158.
78. Vine and Lytle, *American Indians, American Justice*, 65.
79. "'Kill the Indian, and Save the Man': Capt. Richard H. Pratt on the Education of Native Americans," History Matters, George Mason University, accessed 29 March 2023, https://historymatters.gmu.edu/d/4929/.
80. "'Kill the Indian, and Save the Man.'"
81. John R. Brennen, *The Oglala Light*, 5 March 1917.
82. John R. Brennen, *The Oglala Light*, 8 March 1917.
83. *The Oglala Light*, 8 March 1917.
84. "Good Music Is a Character Builder," *The Indian School Journal* 7, no. 9 (September 1907).
85. "News Items and Rumors of Pine Ridge," *The Oglala Light*, 1 March 1913, 27.
86. *The Oglala Light*, 1 March 1913.
87. "The Above Picture," *The Oglala Light*, 1 March 1913.
88. Superintendent John R. Brennen, *The Oglala Light*, 8 March 1917, 12.
89. "The Wild West Exodus," *The Oglala Light*, 1 April 1911.
90. Wilkins, *American Indian Politics*, 190.
91. Porter, *To Be Indian*, 92.
92. Parker, "The Editor's Viewpoint" (1916), 104–7.
93. Hertzberg, "Nationality, Anthropology," 47. Parker was the great-nephew of Ely S. Parker, Seneca chief.
94. Parker, "Problems of Race Assimilation," 285–304.

95. Parker, "Problems of Race Assimilation," 285.
96. Parker, "Editorial Comment" (1914), 175.
97. Parker, "Editorial Comment" (1914), 175.
98. Parker, "Editorial Comment" 1914, 174–76.
99. Yellow Robe, "Indian and the Wild," 39–40; Yellow Robe, "Menace of the Wild West Show," 224–25.
100. Yellow Robe, "Indian and the Wild," 39–40; Yellow Robe, "Menace of the Wild West Show," 175.
101. Gohl, "Effect of Wild Westing," 174–76.
102. Parker, "Editorial Comment" (1914), 95.
103. Montezuma, "Buffalo Bill."
104. Sorisio, "Playing the Indian Princess?," 1–2.
105. Sorisio, "Sarah Winnemucca, Translation, and US Colonialism," 35–60.
106. Sorisio, "Playing the Indian Princess?," 2.
107. Sorisio, "Playing the Indian Princess?," 6.

## Chapter Five

1. A. Gilder, "Circus at Home: A Visit to the Winter Quarters of the Sells-Forepaugh Show," *Billboard*, 25 January 1902.
2. "Sells-Forepaugh Shows," *Billboard*, 15 December 1900, 20.
3. "Sells-Forepaugh Shows," *Billboard*, 15 December 1900, 20.
4. Weisheimer, "Sellsville ca. 1900 [1971]," 7.
5. "Sells-Forepaugh Shows," *Billboard*, 15 December 1900, 20.
6. *Official Route Book of the Sells Brothers Circus*, 1884.
7. St. Leon, *Circus in Australia*, 273.
8. Letter from William H. "Cap" Curtis to George Chindahl, 10 October 1950, Circus World Museum, George Chindahl Papers, box 3, folder 6.
9. During its first two to three seasons, the Sells Brothers Circus wintered near Dublin in Linworth, Ohio, where they had a large barn. They also stored supplies and equipment on Main Street in Columbus.
10. *Official Route Book of the Sells Brothers Circus*, 1844.
11. St. Leon, *Circus in Australia*, 273.
12. Weisheimer, "Sellsville ca. 1900 [1971]," 68.
13. Weisheimer, "Sellsville ca. 1900 [1971]," 61.
14. Weisheimer, "Sellsville ca. 1900 [1971]," 64.
15. Weisheimer, "Sellsville ca. 1900 [1971]," 53.
16. The Weisheimer flour mill building is the last standing building from the era of Sellsville.
17. Weisheimer, "Sellsville ca. 1900 [1971]," 53. The postal clerks in 1900 were Joshua Ellsworth Fields and James Scurry.
18. Richardson, *Death of Reconstruction*; Schwalm, *Emancipation's Diaspora*.
19. Weisheimer, "Sellsville ca. 1900 [1971]," 6. Several army draft cards turn up with Sellsville as the soldiers' hometown, and when crosschecked in the United States Census, the soldiers' addresses are found in Clinton Township.

20. Pfening, "Sells Brothers," 7.
21. Pfening, "Sells Brothers," 2.
22. Weisheimer, "Sellsville ca. 1900 [1971]," 7.
23. Weisheimer, "Sellsville ca. 1900 [1971]," 35.
24. Weisheimer, "Sellsville ca. 1900 [1971]," 59.
25. Weisheimer, "Sellsville ca. 1900 [1971]," 59–60. Fields Avenue is named for Reverend Ezekiel Fields.
26. Weisheimer, "Sellsville ca. 1900 [1971]," 59–60.
27. Weisheimer, "Sellsville ca. 1900 [1971]," 63.
28. Weisheimer, "Sellsville ca. 1900 [1971]," 4.
29. Himes, "Forty Years of Negro Life," 134.
30. *Official Route Book of the Sells Brothers Circus*, 1900; Weisheimer, "Sellsville ca. 1900 [1971]," 53.
31. A fire destroyed the original history of the Antioch Baptist Church in 1968. The church was rebuilt in 1969. Church historians since the fire have gathered information from Minnie Hughes, who attended organizational Council Meetings in the 1890s with her parents. Carl Weisheimer's account places Hughes at the meetings with her parents when she was nine years old; see Weisheimer, "Sellsville ca. 1900 [1971]," 68. Weisheimer interviewed his neighbors who were members during the circus era including John (Minnie) Bowen Hughes. The church bulletin also mentions Nettie Lewis, Della Bowen, and Descrette Lenear, and other parishioners with firsthand knowledge of the founding years who also provided information contained in the current church history. Today, it remains the only predominantly African American church in its area of Columbus.
32. *Antioch Baptist Church History, 1893-2001*, 8; Weisheimer, "Sellsville ca. 1900 [1971]," 68.
33. *Antioch Baptist Church History, 1893-2001*, 8.
34. *Antioch Baptist Church History, 1893-2001*, 8.
35. *Antioch Baptist Church History, 1893-2001*, 8.
36. Weisheimer, "Sellsville ca. 1900 [1971]," 46; *Antioch Baptist Church History, 1893-2001*, 9.
37. Though no records indicating when the school was built could be found, some evidence suggests that it may have been built in the late 1870s or early 1880s. See Wayne Carlson, "History of the Schools in Grandview Heights and Marble Cliff," Grandview Heights and Marble Cliff Historical Society, 2001, accessed 27 May 2024, https://ghmchs2.org/schools.html.
38. Weisheimer, "Sellsville ca. 1900 [1971]," 50.
39. Weisheimer, "Sellsville ca. 1900 [1971]," 50.
40. Weisheimer, "Sellsville ca. 1900 [1971],"50.
41. Weisheimer, "Sellsville ca. 1900 [1971]," 50.
42. Weisheimer, "Sellsville ca. 1900 [1971]," 52. Several members of the sideshow band lived in Sellsville in the offseason when they were not employed in other musical troupes or minstrel shows. They also found work in and around Columbus, an added benefit of living in a circus town in close proximity to a large urban area.
43. "Sellsville ca. 1900 [1971]," 61.

44. *Columbus Evening Dispatch*, 10 January 1905.
45. *Columbus Evening Dispatch*, 7 April 1905.
46. *Ohio State Journal*, 21 April 1907.
47. *The Columbus Dispatch*, 8 October 1905.
48. Himes, "Forty Years of Negro Life," 130.
49. Himes, "Forty Years of Negro Life," 149. Aminah Robinson's family were initially residents of Sellsville, then her parents moved to Poindexter Village, what many local people still called the Blackberry Patch, in 1940. Poindexter Village was one of the first federally funded housing projects. She alternated living with her grandparents in the former Sellsville and with her parents in Poindexter Village. Poindexter Village was named after the late Reverend James Poindexter, a prominent religious and political leader for Black Columbians.
50. Himes, "Forty Years of Negro Life," 149.
51. *Columbus Citizen*, 24 March 1957.
52. Birzer, "Jean Baptiste Richardville," 94–95.
53. Sleeper-Smith, "Resistance to Removal," 109–10; Buss, "'They Found and Left Her an Indian,'" 6.
54. Sleeper-Smith, "Resistance to Removal," 113; Rafert, *Miami Indians of Indiana*, 77–114.
55. Sleeper-Smith, "Resistance to Removal," 113; Rafert, *Miami Indians of Indiana*, 77–114.
56. Tanner, *Atlas of Great Lakes*, 97.
57. Sleeper-Smith, *Indian Women*, 139.
58. Sleeper-Smith, *Indian Women*, 120.
59. For a biographical account of a white family's impressions of the Godfroys, see Hundley, *Squawtown*.
60. Marks, interview by Rafert, 11 July 1989, p. 10.
61. Marks, interview by Rafert, 11 July 1989, p. 10.
62. Marks, interview by Rafert, 11 July 1989, p. 10.
63. Marks, interview by Rafert, 11 July 1989, p. 10.
64. Rafert, *Miami Indians of Indiana*, 162.
65. "Ben Wallace Buys Godfroy Farm on the Mississinewa Banks," *Peru Republican*, 27 November 1891.
66. Beasley, *Twentieth Century Peru*, 49.
67. *Miami County Sentinel*, 6 April 1893.
68. Several advertisements for such shows may be found in Peru and other Miami County newspapers. See also Rafert, *Miami Indians of Indiana*, 165.
69. Bodurtha, *History of Miami County*, 787. This number is from the year 1903, but the circus maintained approximately this amount from the time of the Hagenbeck merger until 1913.
70. Bodurtha, *History of Miami County*, 787.
71. Graham, *Pioneer History*, 23. Hagenbeck was a German animal trainer who had met success in the United States. When he decided to return to Germany, he hired liquidators to sell his animals and equipment. The American partners sold the menagerie to Wallace, but Hagenbeck sued to take back the rights to using his

name, claiming that he had never agreed to sell it. Wallace won the case and opened the 1907 season as the Hagenbeck-Wallace Circus or The Carl Hagenbeck and Great Wallace Circus.

72. Bodurtha, *History of Miami County*, 787.
73. Bodurtha, *History of Miami County*, 787.
74. Beasley, *Twentieth Century Peru*, 49.
75. Rafert, *The Miami Indians of Indiana*, 166. According to the Tenth and Thirteenth Census of the United States, 1880 and 1910, Miami County's overall population increased from 24,083 in 1880 to 29,350 in 1910, marking a 21.8 percent increase.
76. Rafert, *Miami Indians of Indiana*, 166.
77. Bodurtha, *History of Miami County*, 787.
78. Rafert, *Hidden Community*, 164. This is compared to both previous periods in Miami County and to neighboring Native communities during the same period.
79. Marks, interview by Rafert, 11 October 1991.
80. Marks, interview by Rafert, 1 July 1986.
81. Marks, interview by Rafert, 4 November 1980. Pete Bruell also worked on the Wabash Railroad line.
82. Marks, interview by Rafert, 11 May 1993.
83. Bodurtha, *History of Miami County*, 787.
84. Marks, interview by Rafert, 11 October 1991.
85. Marks, interview by Rafert, 11 October 1991.
86. Marks, interview by Rafert, 11 October 1991.
87. Rafert, *The Miami Indians of Indiana*, 211; Marks, interview by Rafert, 11 October 1991.
88. Marks, interview by Rafert, 11 October 1991.
89. Marks, interview by Rafert, 11 October 1991.
90. Marks, interview by Rafert, 11 October 1991.
91. Marks, interview by Rafert, 11 May 1993, p. 25.
92. Marks, interview by Rafert, 11 May 1993, p. 25; Marks, interview by Rafert, 10 October 1991, p. 76.
93. Marks, interview by Rafert, 11 May 1993; Marks, interview by Rafert, 10 October 1991, p. 76.
94. Chindahl, *History of the Circus*, 118.
95. Peter Sells, *Bandwagon*, 30 November 1901, 4. The Sells advanced in other areas as well. In the advertising department, they grew from using woodblock printing, the typical nineteenth-century mass production method, to lithographs, a method that enabled detailed artwork drawn by chosen artists, then produced en masse. This printing innovation, as well as others in animal training, architecture, and transportation, caused great excitement in the industry and in the general public throughout the era.
96. Davis, *Circus Age*, 70.
97. See US Department of Housing and Urban Development Office of Public and Indian Housing: PHA Plans, 5 Year Plan for Fiscal Years 2009–2013 and Annual Plan for Fiscal Year 2009, Appendix E: Resident Advisory Board Comments, and Appendix F: Community Service and Self Sufficiency Programs, accessed 12 January 2012, https://www

.huduser.gov/portal/publications/The-Indian-Housing-Program-Program-Briefing-and-Statistical-Summary.html.

98. See "Justice for Poindexter Village," accessed 13 May 2024, https://housingjustice.wordpress.com/; "Poindexter's Last Stand," accessed 13 May 2024, https://www.columbusmonthly.com/story/lifestyle/2016/05/17/poindexter-s-last-stand/22806104007/.

99. *US Department of Housing and Urban Development Office of Public and Indian Housing*, accessed 12 January 2012, http://www.cmhanet.com/pdf/oh001v01.pdf.

100. See Chris Gaitten, "The Second Life of Poindexter Village," *Columbus Monthly*, June 18, 2021, https://www.columbusmonthly.com/story/lifestyle/around-town/2021/06/18/second-life-poindexter-village/7743562002/.

101. See Sleeper-Smith, *Indian Women*, 116, and Sleeper-Smith, "Resistance to Removal," 109, 120. Invisibility led to persistence but ultimately to the federal government administratively terminating its recognition of the Miami Nation of Indiana in 1897. The United States no longer considered the Indiana Miami "Indians."

102. Rafert, *The Miami Indians of Indiana*, 190.

103. "About Us," Miami Indians, accessed 9 August 2022, http://www.miamiindians.org/new-page-2.

104. Adkins, *Peru*, 117.

## Conclusion

1. The Georgia Minstrels, led by African American manager Charles Hicks, made several tours through Hawai'i, Australia, and New Zealand starting in 1877 (and continued for three years). Hicks and several others from his troupe found the Pacific—and New Zealand in particular—so appealing that they spent the remainder of their lives abroad. For these artists, New Zealand proved particularly attractive and afforded Black artists a degree of commercial and artistic autonomy that was largely denied to them in the United States.

2. *Indianapolis Freeman*, 27 October 1905.

3. *Indianapolis Freeman*, 27 October 1905.

4. *Indianapolis Freeman*, 27 October 1905.

5. Just as railroads in the United States opened new avenues for travel, a transpacific telegram system completed in the 1870s integrated much of the Pacific into an emerging global communication network (a trans-Tasman cable in 1876 integrated New Zealand), and international steamship routes opened greater possibilities of promotion and world travel for these men and women.

6. Canadian Census, 1861 (Canada East, Canada West, Prince Edward Island, New Brunswick, and Nova Scotia) for Image No.: 4107404_00202.

7. "Sullivan the Slugger," *Chicago Inter-Ocean*, 6 June 1885; George Ridenour, "Eph Thompson—Elephant Trainer," *Ypsilanti Gleanings* (Spring 2010), accessed 27 May 2024, https://ypsihistory.org/wp-content/uploads/2021/11/spring2010Gleanings.pdf.

8. "Sullivan the Slugger," *Chicago Inter-Ocean*, 6 June 1885; Adam Forepaugh's Circus Route Book, 1880, Milner Library; Zapff, *Jumbo auf dem Drahtseil*; "A Natural Trainer," *Cincinnati Enquirer*, 27 September 1906.

9. *Variety*, 26 June 1908, 13.
10. Thurman, *Singing Like Germans*, 56.
11. Edwards, *Practice of Diaspora*, 4.
12. Kelley, "How the West Was One," 137.
13. Von Eschen, "Globalizing Popular Culture," 56–63.
14. Fein, "Everyday Forms of Transnational Collaboration."
15. Klein, *Cold War Orientalism*.
16. Dudziak, *Cold War Civil Rights*.
17. Von Eschen, *Satchmo Blows Up the World*.
18. Gilroy, *Black Atlantic*, 56.

# Bibliography

## Censuses

Census of Miami Indians in Indiana and Elsewhere. Prepared by Thad Butler. Department of the Interior, 10 September 1881. Miami County Historical Society.

Miami County, Indiana, Miami Indian Census, 1850, 1860, and 1870. Miami County Historical Society.

United States Bureau of the Census. *Negro Population, 1790–1915.*

United States Bureau of the Census. *Negroes in the United States.* Bulletin 8, 1904.

United States Census Schedules for Franklin County, Ohio, 1800, 1830, 1870, 1880, and 1900–20.

United States Census Schedules for Miami County, Indiana, 1830, 1850, 1860, 1870, 1880, and 1900–20.

## Archival Sources

*Columbus Metropolitan Library, Columbus, OH*

Bill Moose file, local history
Columbus Business and Professional Negro Directory
Columbus City Directories
The Columbus Illustrated Negro Directory
Sells Brothers Circus file, local history

*Indiana Historical Society Records, Indianapolis, IN*

Butler, Amos W. (1860–1937) Papers
    Daniel R. Bearss Collection
Daniel R. Bearss Miami Indiana Claims
LaMoine Marks. Interviews by Stewart Rafert. 4 November 1980. Transcript.

*Miami County Historical Society*

African American file
Annuity Pay-Roll Miami Indians of Indiana
Box Car Town/Peru Steel Works file
Francis Godfroy Collection
Miami County Churches file
Miscellaneous Indian file
*Stony Point School: The School with Many Names and an Historic Past.* Pamphlet, 1986.

*Milner Library Circus Route Books Collection, Illinois State University, Normal, IL*

Adam Forepaugh's Circus Route Books

*Miscellaneous Papers of the Continental Congress, 1774–89*

Records of the Continental and Confederation Congresses and the Constitutional Convention. Record Group 360. National Archives, Washington, DC, 1988.

*Newberry Library, Chicago, IL*

American Circus Collection. Irving Kane Pond Collection. Box 1, folder 8. Hagenbeck-Wallace file

"Why Indians are now to be permitted to vote under certain conditions . . ." Edgerton, a letter from Richardville to Me-she-kun-nogh-quoh. Little Turtle-Great Chief . . . Vault box, Ayer MS 710.

*Robert L. Parkinson Library and Research Center, Baraboo, WI*

Adam Forepaugh and Sells Bros. Circus Papers
African Americans in the Circus file
Baraboo, George Werner Papers file
Blacks in Shows file
Eph Williams file
Great Wallace Winter Quarters file
Miscellaneous Indian file
Perry George Lowery file
Sells Brothers Shows file

*Tippecanoe County Historical Association, Lafayette, IN*

George Winter Manuscript Collection

Newspapers

*Bandwagon*
*Billboard*
*The Carlisle (PA) Arrow*
*The Carlisle (PA) School News*
*The Carroll (IA) Herald*
*The Chicago Defender*
*Chicago Inter-Ocean*
*Cincinnati Enquirer*
*Crisis: A Record of the Darker Places* (New York)
*Eureka (KS) Herald*
*Evening Journal* (Detroit)
*Indianapolis Freeman*
*Indianapolis Recorder*
*Indianapolis World*
*The Indian School Journal* (Chilocco Indian Agricultural School, OK)
*Inter-state Tattler* (New York)
*The Leader* (Saskatchewan)
*The Listener News* (New York)
*The Los Angeles Tribune*
*The Miami County (IN) Sentinel*
*The National Leader* (DC)
*The Native American* (The Phoenix Indian School, AZ)
*The New York Age*

The New York Age
   Defender
The New York Clipper
The New York Times
The North Star
   (Rochester, NY)
The Oglala Light (Oglala
   Indian Training
   School, SD)
Ohio State Journal
   (Columbus, OH)
Pasadena Star-News (CA)

The Peru (IN) Republican
The Peru (IN) Tribune
Plaindealer (Kansas
   City, KS)
Quarterly Journal of the
   Society of American
   Indians
Queensland (Australia)
   Times
The Redman (Carlisle
   Indian Industrial
   School, PA)

The Short North
   (Columbus, OH)
The Southern Workman
   (The Hampton Normal
   Agricultural Institute,
   VA)
The Washington Tribune
   (DC)
Wassaja (Columbus,
   OH)

## Primary Sources

*Antioch Baptist Church History, 1893-2001*. Columbus, OH, n.p., 2001.

Barnes, Al G. *Master Showman*. London: Jonathan Cape, 1938.

Barnum, P. T. "The Adventures of an Adventurer, Being Some Passages in The Life of Barnaby Diddleum," *New York Atlas*. Weekly or biweekly series, 11 April 1841–June 1841.

Barrett, Edward, David Alan Hole, J. B. Edmonson, Charles W. Shannon, A. W. Magnum, N. P. Neill, Herbert W. Marean, et al. *The Thirty-Sixth Annual Report of Department of Geology and Natural Resources*. Indiana Department of Geology and Natural Resources. Indianapolis: Wm. B. Burford, 1911.

Beasley, Al. D. *Twentieth Century Peru*. Peru, IN: n.p., 1901.

Bert, Joseph Griswold, and Samuel R. Taylor. *The Pictorial History of Fort Wayne, Indiana: A Review of Two Centuries of Occupation of the Region About the Head of the Maumee River*. Chicago: Robert O. Law, 1917.

Bill "Cap" Curtis to George Chindahl, 10 October, 1950. Box 2, folder 6. George Chindahl Papers, Robert L. Parkinson Library and Research Center, Baraboo, WI.

*Biographical and Genealogical History of Cass, Miami, Howard, and Tipton Counties, Indiana*. Vol. 1. Chicago: Lewis Publishing, 1898.

Black Elk, and John G. Neihardt. *Black Elk Speaks: Being the Life Story of a Holy Man of the Oglala Sioux, as told through John G. Neihardt*. New York: State University of New York Press, 2008.

Bodurtha, Arthur L. *History of Miami County: A Narrative Account of Its Historical Progress, Its People, and Its Principal Interests*. Vol. 1. Chicago: Lewis Publishing, 1914.

Brown, Robert M. "The Ohio River Floods of 1913." *Bulletin of the American Geographical Society* 45, no. 7 (1913): 500–509.

"Circus Alive Abroad." *The Washington Post*, 22 July 1956.

*City Directory of Peru, 1886-1887*. Logansport, IN: Hall and O'Donald, 1887.

*Combination Atlas Map of Miami County, Indiana*. Chicago: The Kingman Brothers, 1877.

Coup, W. C. *Sawdust and Spangles: Stories and Secrets of the Circus*. Chicago: Herbert S. Stone, 1901.

Dillon, John Brown. *A History of Indiana from Its Earliest Exploration by Europeans*. Indianapolis, IN: Bingham and Doughty, 1859.

*Directory to the Iron and Steel Works of The United States. Embracing a Full Description of the Blast Furnaces, Rolling Mills, Steel Works, Tinplate and Terne Plate Works, and Forges and Bloomaries in the United States; also Classified Lists of the Wire Rod Mills, the Structural Mills, Plate, Sheet, and Skelp Mills, Black Plate Mills, Rail Mills, Steel Casting Works, Besssemer Steel Works, Open Hearth Steel Works, and Crucible Steel Works*. 16th ed. Philadelphia: The American Iron and Steel Association, 1904.

Dresser, Paul. *On the Banks of the Wabash, Far Away*. New York: Howley, Haviland and Co., 1897.

Dryer, Charles Redway. "The Maumee-Wabash Waterway." *Annals of the Association of American Geographers* 9 (1919): 41–51.

Field, Al G. *Watch Yourself Go By*. Columbus, OH: n.p., 1912.

Finley, James Bradley. *History of the Wyandot Mission at Upper Sandusky under the Direction of the Methodist Episcopal Church*. Cincinnati: J. F. Wright and L. Swormstedt, 1840.

Gates, Henry Louis, Jr., and Gene Andrew Jarrett, eds. *The New Negro: Readings on Race, Representation, and African American Culture, 1892–1938*. Princeton, NJ: Princeton University Press, 2007.

Godfroy, Chief Clarence. *Miami Indian Stories*. Winona Lake, IN: Light and Life Press, 1961.

Gohl, E. H. "The Effect of Wild Westing." *Quarterly Journal of the Society of American Indians* 2, no. 3 (July–September 1914): 174–76.

Graham, John. *Pioneer History of Peru and Miami County*. Peru, IN: Peru Republican Printing Office, 1877.

Herschler, Dale. "Highlander Staff Reporter Interviews 'Indian Bill.'" In *The Highlander 1930*, 58–59. Columbus, OH: Grandview Heights High School, 1930.

*History of Columbus Franklin County, Ohio: Pictorial and Biographical*. New York: S. J. Clarke Publishing, 1909.

*History of Miami County Indiana*. Chicago: Brant and Fuller, 1887.

Hodge, Frederick Webb, ed. *Handbook of American Indians North of Mexico*. Bureau of American Ethnology Bulletin 30. Washington, DC: Smithsonian Institution, 1907.

Holman, Omer. *Here We Live over the Last Fifty Years*. Peru, IN: Peru Republican Printing Office, 1935.

———. *Peru Pictures Past and Present*. Peru, IN: Peru Republican Printing Office, 1909.

Hundley, Will M. *Squawtown: My Boyhood Among the Last Miami Indians*. Caldwell, ID: Caxton Printers, 1939.

Kappler, Charles J. *United States Indian Affairs: Laws and Treaties*. Vol. 2. Washington DC: Government Printing Office, 1904.

Kettleborough, Charles. *Drainage and Reclamation of Swamp and Overflowed Lands: Indiana Bureau of Legislative Information*. Bulletin no. 2. Indianapolis: State of Indiana, 1914.

La Flesche, Susette. (Bright Eyes). "Law Is Liberty." Unpublished manuscript, compiled and edited by Anna C. Smith Pabst, 1958. Thomas H. Tibbles Papers, Smithsonian Institution, National Museum of the American Indian Archives. https://sova.si.edu/record/nmai.ac.066.

Lazenby, W. R. "Plants Introduced at Sellsville, Near Columbus." *Bulletin of the Torrey Botanical Club* 18, no. 10 (October 1891): 301–2.

Martin, George W. *Collections of the Kansas State Historical Society*. Vol. 12. Topeka, KS: State Printing Office, 1912.

Martin, William T. *Martin's History of Franklin County Ohio to 1858*. Columbus, OH: Follett, Foster, 1858.

McClurg, Martha Una, ed. *Miami Indian Stories*. Winona Lake, IN: Light and Life Press, 1961.

Miami County Recorder. Plat of Mill Lots at Peru. Book 1, 1851, p. 584.

Montezuma, Carlos. "Buffalo Bill." *Wassaja* 1, no. 10 (January 1917).

Parker, Arthur C. "Editorial Comment." *Quarterly Journal of the Society of American Indians* 2, no. 3 (July–September 1914): 174–76.

———. "Editorial Comment." *Quarterly Journal of the Society of American Indians* 1, no. 2 (April–June 1916): 96–98.

———. "Problems of Race Assimilation in America with Special Reference to the American Indian." *Quarterly Journal for the Society of American Indians* 4, no. 4 (October–December 1916): 285–304.

Perry, George W. *Buckskin Mose; or, Life from the Lakes to the Pacific, as Actor, Circus-Rider, Detective, Ranger, Gold-Digger, Indian Scout, and Guide*. New York: H. L. Hinton, 1873.

"Pioneer Negro Citizens of Peru, Indiana and Negroes in Miami County." In *Encyclopedia of Miami County*. The Genealogy Collection, Indiana State Library, Indianapolis, IN.

"The Plantation Darkey at the Circus: How He Enjoys It, Getting to Town, Incidents on the Lot, The Snack Stands." In *The Official Route Book of Ringling Brothers World's Greatest Railroad Show Season*, 1895–96, 110–14.

Puckett, Niles Newbell. *Folk Beliefs of the Southern Negro*. Montclair, NJ: Patterson Smith Publishing, 1926.

Sampson, Henry. *The Ghost Walks: A Chronological History of Blacks in Show Business, 1865–1910*. Metuchen, NJ: Scarecrow, 1988.

Scott, Margaret, and Medrith Mollenkamp. *Index and Genealogical Notes to "Sellsville, ca 1900" Headquarters of the Sells Brothers Circus Columbus, Ohio*. Columbus, OH: Franklin County Genealogical Society, 1986.

Selby, Aug. D. "Notes for Columbus, Ohio." *Botanical Gazette* 16, no. 5 (May 1891): 148–49.

Sernett, Milton C. *African American Religious History: A Documentary Witness*. Durham, NC: Duke University Press, 1999.

Standing Bear, Luther. *My People the Sioux*. 1928. Reprint, Lincoln: University of Nebraska Press, 1975.

Stephens, John H. *History of Miami County: Illustrated*. Peru, IN: John H. Stephens Publishing House, 1896.

*Struggles and Triumphs, or, Forty Years' Recollections of P. T. Barnum*. Buffalo: Warren, Johnson, 1873.

Tanner, Helen Hornbeck, Erminie Wheeler-Voegelin, and United States Indian Claims Commission. *The Greenville Treaty, 1795*. New York: Garland Publishers, 1975.

Thompson, W. C. *On the Road with a Circus*. New York: New Amsterdam Book Company, 1903.

US Bureau of Labor. "Condition of the Negro in Various Cities." *Bulletin of the United States Bureau of Labor* 2, no. 10 (May 1897): 25–137. https://fraser.stlouisfed.org/title/3943/item/477562/toc/498120.

Weaver, Clarence E. *A Description of the City of Peru, Miami County, Indiana*. Peru, IN: The Indiana Advancement Company, 1897.

Weisheimer, Carl. "Sellsville ca. 1900 [1971]." Self-published book. Special Collections, Ohio Historical Society, Columbus, OH.

Wheeler-Voegelin, Erminie. *Miami Wea, and Eel River Indians of Southern Indiana*. New York: Garland, 1974.

Wheeler-Voegelin, Erminie, Helen Hornbeck Tanner, and United States Indian Claims Commission. *Indians of Northern Ohio and Southeastern Michigan: An Ethnohistorical Report*. New York: Garland Publishers, 1974.

Whiting, Allen. "The Organization of the Modern Circus." *Cosmopolitan Magazine* (1902): 370–77.

Yellow Robe, Chauncey. "The Indian and the Wild West Show." *Quarterly Journal of the Society of American Indians* 2, no. 1 (January–March 1914): 39–40.

———. "The Menace of the Wild West Show." *Quarterly Journal of Society for American Indians* 2, no. 3 (July–September 1914): 224–25.

Young, Andrew W. *History of Wayne County, Indiana: From Its First Settlement to the Present Time*. Cincinnati: Robert Clarke & Company, 1872.

Young, Rosa. "What Induced Me to Build a School in the Rural District." In *African American Religious History: A Documentary Witness*, edited by Milton C. Sernett. Durham, NC: Duke University Press, 1999.

Route Books

*Adam Forepaugh's Circus Route Book*, 1880.
*Great Pan American Shows Route Book*, 1903.
*Great Wallace Circus Official Route Book*, 1892, 1900, 1899, 1898, and 1897.
*Hagenbeck-Wallace Official Route Book*, 1913. Hagenbeck Wallace Combined Show file. Circus World Museum, Baraboo, WI.
*Official Route Book of the Pawnee Bill Wild West Show Presenting a Complete Chronicle of Interesting Events, Happenings, and Valuable Data for the Season 1898*.
*Official Route Book of the Pawnee Bill Wild West Show Presenting a Complete Chronicle of Interesting Events, Happenings, and Valuable Data for the Season 1899*.
*The Official Route Book of Ringling Brothers World's Greatest Railroad Show*, 1892, 1895–1896.
*The Official Route Book of the Sells Brothers Circus*, 1873, 1881, 1882, 1883, 1899, 1898, 1891, 1897, and 1900.

*Route Book: Buffalo Bill's Wild West Season*, 1900.
*Route Book of the John Robinson's 10 Big Shows Combined Seasons*, 1899.
*Sells Brothers' Route for the Season of 1884: Places, Distance, Events, Etc.* Houston: Franklin Publishing House, 1884.

Secondary Literature

Abbott, Lynn, and Doug Seroff. *Out of Sight: The Rise of African American Popular Music, 1889–1895.* Jackson: University Press of Mississippi, 2002.

———. *Ragged but Right: Black Traveling Shows, "Coon Songs," and the Dark Pathway to Blues and Jazz.* Jackson: University Press of Mississippi, 2007.

Abrahams, Roger D. *Singing the Master: The Emergence of African-American Culture in the Plantation South.* New York: Pantheon Books, 1992.

Adams, Bluford. *E Pluribus Barnum: The Great Showman and the Making of U.S. Popular Culture.* Minneapolis: University of Minnesota Press, 1997.

Adams, Francis D., and Barry Sanders. *Alienable Rights: The Exclusion of African Americans in a White Man's Land, 1619–2000.* New York: HarperCollins, 2003.

Adams, Judith A. "The American Dream Actualized: The Glistening 'White City' and the Lurking Shadows of the World's Columbian Exposition." In *The World's Columbian Exhibition: A Centennial Bibliographic Guide,* edited by David J. Bertuca, Donald K. Hartman, and Susan Neumeister, xix–xxix. Westport, CT: Greenwood, 1996.

Adkins, Kreig A. *Peru: Circus Capital of the World.* San Francisco: Arcadia, 2009.

Agnew, Jeremy. *Entertainment in the Old West: Theater, Music, Circuses, Medicine Shows, Prizefighting and Other Popular Amusements.* Jefferson, NC: McFarland, 2011.

Ahern, Wilbert H. "An Experiment Aborted: Returned Indian Students in the Indian School Service, 1881–1908." *Ethnohistory* 44, no. 2 (Spring 1997): 263–304. https://doi.org/10.2307/483370.

Alcorn, Richard S. "Leadership and Stability in Mid-Nineteenth-Century America: A Case Study of an Illinois Town." *Journal of American History* 61, no. 3 (December 1974): 685–702. https://doi.org/10.2307/1899927.

Allen, Robert C. *Horrible Prettiness: Burlesque and American Culture.* Chapel Hill: University of North Carolina Press, 1991.

Allen, Walter C., and Brian Rust. *King Joe Oliver.* London: Sidgwick and Jackson, 1958.

Anderson, Catherine E. "Red Coat and Black Shields: Race and Masculinity in British Representations of the Anglo-Zulu War." *Critical Survey* 20, no. 3 (2008): 6–28. https://www.jstor.org/stable/41556281.

Arnett, Benjamin W. "The New Black Laws." In *The African-American Archive: The History of the Black Experience through Documents,* edited by Kai Wright. New York: Black Dog and Leventhal, 2001.

Asad, Talal. "Agency, Subject, and the Body." Paper presented at the conference "The Body: A Retrospective," University of Manchester, Manchester, England, June 1998.

Asim, Jabari. *The N Word: Who Can Say It, Who Shouldn't, and Why*. New York: Houghton Mifflin Harcourt, 2007.

Badger, Reid R. *The Great American Fair: The World's Columbian Exposition and American Culture*. Chicago: Nelson-Hall, 1993.

Barclay, Jenifer L. *The Mark of Slavery: Disability, Race, and Gender in Antebellum America*. Urbana: University of Illinois Press, 2021.

Bean, Annmarie, James V. Hatch, and Brooks McNamara, eds. *Inside the Minstrel Mask: Readings in Nineteenth-Century Blackface Minstrelsy*. Hanover, NH: Wesleyan University Press, 1996.

Benes, Peter. "Itinerant Entertainers in New England and New York, 1687–1830." In *Itinerancy in New England and New York: The Dublin Seminar for New England Folklife Annual Proceedings 1984*, edited by Peter Benes and Jane Montague Benes. Concord, MA: Boston University, 1986.

Bennett, Tony. "The Exhibitionary Complex." In *Culture, Power, History: A Reader in Contemporary Social Theory*, edited by Nicholas B. Dirks, Geoff Eley, and Sherry B. Ortner, 123–54. Princeton, NJ: Princeton University Press, 1994.

Berkhofer, Robert F. Jr., "Americans versus Indians: The Northwest Ordinance, Territory Making, and Native Americans." *Indiana Magazine of History* 84, no. 1 (March 1988): 90–108.

Berlin, Ira. *The Making of African America: The Four Great Migrations*. New York: Penguin Books, 2010.

———. *Many Thousands Gone: The First Two Centuries of Slavery in North America*. Cambridge, MA: Belknap Press of Harvard University Press, 1998.

———. *Slaves without Masters: The Free Negro in the Antebellum South*. New York: Vintage Books, 1971.

Bernhard, Virginia, Betty Brandon, Elizabeth Fox-Genovese, and Theda Perdue, eds. *Southern Women: Histories and Identities*. Columbia: University of Missouri Press, 1992.

Berwanger, Eugene H. *The Frontier Against Slavery: Western Anti-Negro Prejudice and the Slavery Extension Controversy*. Urbana: University of Illinois Press, 1967.

———. "Western Anti-Negro Sentiment and Laws, 1846–1860: A Factor in the Slavery Extension Controversy." PhD diss., Illinois State University, 1965.

Bhabha, Homi. "Remembering Fanon: Self, Psyche and the Colonial Condition." Foreword to *Black Skin, White Masks*, by Frantz Fanon, vii–xxv. Translated by Charles Lam Markmann. London: Pluto, 1986.

Birzer, Bradley J. "Jean Baptiste Richardville: Miami Metis." In *Enduring Nations: Native Americans in the Midwest*, edited by R. David Edmunds, 94–108. Urbana: University of Illinois Press, 2008.

Blassingame, John W. *The Slave Community: Plantation Life in the Antebellum South*. New York: Oxford University Press, 1972.

———, ed. *Slave Testimony: Two Centuries of Letters, Speeches, Interviews, and Autobiographies*. Baton Rouge: Louisiana State University Press, 1977.

Bleser, Carol, ed. *In Joy and in Sorrow: Women, Family, and Marriage in the Victorian South, 1830–1900*. New York: Oxford University Press, 1991.

Blight, David W. *Race and Reunion: The Civil War in American Memory*. Cambridge, MA: Belknap Press of Harvard University Press, 2001.

Block, Sharon. *Rape and Sexual Power in Early America*. Chapel Hill: University of North Carolina Press, 2006.

Bodurtha, Arthur Lawrence. *History of Miami County, Indiana: A Narrative Account of Its Historical Progress, Its People and Its Principal Interests*. Chicago: Lewis Publishing, 1914.

Bogdan, Robert. *Freak Show: Presenting Human Oddities for Amusement and Profit*. Chicago: University of Chicago Press, 1989.

Bokovoy, Matthew. *The San Diego World's Fairs and Southwestern Memory, 1880–1940*. Albuquerque: University of New Mexico Press, 2005.

Boorn, Alida S. *Osksate Wicasa*. Warrensburg: Central Missouri State University, 2005.

Bouissac, Paul. *Circus and Culture: A Semiotic Approach*. Lanham, MD: University Press of America, 1985.

Braunberger, Christine. "Revolting Bodies: The Monster Beauty of Tattooed Women." *NWSA Journal* 12, no. 2 (Summer 2000): 1–23.

Brooks, Tim. *Lost Sounds: Blacks and the Birth of the Recording Industry, 1890–1919*. Urbana: University of Illinois Press, 2005.

Brown, Kathleen M. *Good Wives, Nasty Wenches, and Anxious Patriarchs: Gender, Race, and Power in Colonial Virginia*. Chapel Hill: University of North Carolina Press, 1996.

Brown, Laura. "Spectacles of Cultural Contact: The Fable of the Native Prince." In *Fables of Modernity: Literature and Culture in the English Eighteenth Century*, 177–220. Ithaca, NY: Cornell University Press, 2001.

Bushell, Garvin, and Mark Tucker. *Jazz from the Beginning*. Ann Arbor: University of Michigan Press, 1988.

Buss, James J. "'They Found and Left Her an Indian': Gender, Race, and the Whitening of Young Bear." *Frontiers: A Journal of Women's Studies* 29, no. 2/3 (2008): 1–35.

Calhoun, Mary. *Medicine Show: Conning People and Making Them Like It*. New York: Harper and Row, 1976.

Carney, Judith A. *Black Rice: The African Origins of Rice Cultivation in the Americas*. Cambridge, MA: Harvard University Press, 2001.

Cayton, Andrew R. L., and Peter S. Onuf. *The Midwest and the Nation: Rethinking the History of an American Region*. Bloomington: Indiana University Press, 1990.

Chaffee, Don L. *Indiana's Big Top*. Grand Rapids, MI: Foremost Press, 1969.

Cha-Jua, Sundiata Keita. *America's First Black Town: Brooklyn, Illinois, 1830–1915*. Urbana: University of Illinois Press, 2000.

Chang, David A. Y. O. "From Indian Territory to White Man's Country: Race, Nation, and the Politics of Land Ownership in Eastern Oklahoma, 1889–1940." PhD diss., University of Wisconsin-Madison, 2002.

———. "Where Will the Nation Be at Home? Race, Nationalisms, and Emigration Movements." In *Crossing Waters, Crossing Worlds: The African Diaspora in Indian

*Country*, edited by Tiya Miles and Sharon P. Holland, 80-100. Durham, NC: Duke University Press, 2006.

Cheng, Anne Anlin. *Second Skin: Josephine Baker and the Modern Surface*. New York: Oxford University Press, 2011.

Child, Brenda J. *Boarding School Seasons: American Indian Families, 1900-1940*. Lincoln: University of Nebraska Press, 1998.

Childress, Micah. "Life beyond the Big Top: African American and Female Circusfolk, 1860-1920." *The Journal of the Gilded Age and Progressive Era* 15, no. 2 (2016): 176-96.

Chindahl, George L. *A History of the Circus in America*. Caldwell, ID: Caxton Printers, 1959.

Chude-Sokei, Louis. *The Last Darky: Bert Williams, Black-on-Black Minstrelsy, and the African Diaspora*. Durham, NC: Duke University Press, 2006.

Cody, William F. *An Autobiography of Buffalo Bill (Colonel W. F. Cody)*. New York: Farrar and Rinehart, 1920.

Cohen, William. *At Freedom's Edge: Black Mobility and the Southern White Quest for Racial Control, 1861-1915*. Baton Rouge: Louisiana State University Press, 1991.

Collings, Ellsworth, and Alma Miller England. *The 101 Ranch*. Norman: University of Oklahoma Press, 1937.

Columbus Museum of Art. Aminah's World. http://www.aminahsworld.org.

Condon, Chalmer. "B. E. Wallace." *Bandwagon* 8, no. 4 (July-August 1964): 3-6.

Conzen, Katherine. "Pi-ing the Type: Jane Grey Swisshelm and the Contest of Midwest Regionality." In *The American Midwest: Essays on Regional History*, edited by Andrew R. L. Cayton and Susan E. Gray, 91-110. Bloomington: Indiana University Press, 2001.

Coup, W. C. *Sawdust and Spangles; Stories and Secrets of the Circus*. Chicago: Herbert S. Stone, 1901.

Cox, Anna-Lisa. "Nineteenth-Century: African Americans." In *The American Midwest: An Interpretive Encyclopedia*, edited by Richard Sisson, Christian Zacher, and Andrew Cayton, 199-200. Bloomington: Indiana University Press, 2005.

———. *A Stronger Kinship: One Town's Extraordinary Story of Hope and Faith*. New York: Little, Brown, 2006.

Curry, Leonard P. *The Free Black in Urban America, 1800-1850: The Shadow of the Dream*. Chicago: University of Chicago Press, 1981.

Daniel, G. Reginald. *More Than Black? Multiracial Identity and the New Racial Order*. Philadelphia: Temple University Press, 2002.

Davis, Angela Y. *Blues Legacies and Black Feminism: Gertrude "Ma" Rainey, Bessie Smith, and Billie Holiday*. New York: Vintage Books, 1998.

Davis, Janet. *The Circus Age: Culture and Society under the American Big Top*. Chapel Hill: University of North Carolina Press, 2002.

———, ed. *Circus Queen and Tinker Bell: The Memoir of Tiny Kline*. Urbana: University of Illinois Press, 2008.

Day, Cathy. *The Circus in Winter*. Orlando, FL: Houghton Mifflin Harcourt, 2004.

Deloria, Philip J. *Indians in Unexpected Places*. Lawrence: University Press of Kansas, 2004.

———. *Playing Indian*. New Haven, CT: Yale University Press, 1998.
Deloria, Vine, Jr. "The Indians." In *Buffalo Bill and the Wild West*, edited by Leslie A. Fiedler, 45–56. Brooklyn, NY: The Brooklyn Museum, 1981.
Deloria, Vine, Jr., and Clifford M. Lytle. *American Indians, American Justice*. Austin: University of Texas Press, 1983.
DeVries, James. *Race and Kinship in a Midwestern Town: The Black Experience in Monroe, Michigan, 1900–1915*. Urbana: University of Illinois Press, 1984.
DeWall, Beth Barclay. "Edward Sheriff Curtis: A New Perspective on 'The North American Indian.'" *History of Photography* 6, no. 3 (1982): 223–39. https://doi.org/10.1080/03087298.1982.10443044.
Drake, St. Clair, and Horace R. Cayton. *Black Metropolis: A Study of Negro Life in a Northern City*. Chicago: University of Chicago Press, 1945.
Dray, Philip. *At the Hands of Persons Unknown: The Lynching of Black America*. New York: Modern Library, 2002.
Du Bois, W. E. Burghardt. "The Negro Farmer." In *Department of Commerce and Labor Bureau of the Census Special Reports Supplementary Analysis and Derivative Tables, Twelfth Census of the United States, 1900*. Washington, DC: Government Printing Office, 1906.
———. *The Souls of Black Folk*. New York: Signet Classic, 1995.
Dudziak, Mary L. *Cold War Civil Rights: Race and the Image of American Democracy*. Princeton, NJ: Princeton University Press, 2002.
During, Simon. *Modern Enchantments: The Cultural Power of Secular Magic*. Cambridge, MA: Harvard University Press, 2002.
Dykstra, Robert. *Bright Radical Star: Black Freedom and White Supremacy on the Hawkeye Frontier*. Cambridge, MA: Harvard University Press, 1993.
Edwards, Brent Hayes. *The Practice of Diaspora: Literature, Translation, and the Rise of Black Internationalism*. Cambridge, MA: Harvard University Press, 2003.
Elsner, John, and Roger Cardinal. *The Cultures of Collecting*. Cambridge, MA: Harvard University Press, 1994.
Feest, Christian F., ed. *Indians and Europe: An Interdisciplinary Collection of Essays*. Lincoln: University of Nebraska Press, 1989.
Fein, Seth. "Everyday Forms of Transnational Collaboration: U.S. Film Propaganda in Cold War Mexico." In *Close Encounters of Empire: Writing the Cultural History of U.S.-Latin American Relations*, edited by Gilbert M. Joseph, Catherine C. LeGrand, and Ricardo D. Salvatore, 400–450. Durham, NC: Duke University Press, 1998.
Foner, Eric. *Reconstruction: America's Unfinished Revolution, 1863–1877*. New York: Harper and Row, 1988.
———. "Slavery, the Civil War, and Reconstruction." In *The New American History*, 85–106. Philadelphia: Temple University Press, 1997.
Forbes, Jack D. "Mulattoes and People of Color in Anglo-North America: Implications for Black-Indian Relations." *Journal of Ethnic Studies* 12, no. 2 (1984): 17–61.
Foreman, Carolyn Thomas. *Indians Abroad, 1493–1938*. Norman: University of Oklahoma Press, 1943.
Formisano, Ronald. "The Edge of Caste: Colored Suffrage in Michigan, 1827–1861." *Michigan History* 56, no. 1 (Spring 1972): 19–41.

Fox, Charles Philip. *The Circus in America*. Waukesha, WI: Country Beautiful, 1969.

Franklin, John Hope, and Alfred A. Moss Jr. *From Slavery to Freedom: A History of African Americans*. 7th ed. New York: Knopf, 1994.

Freeman, Larry. *The Medicine Showman*. Watkins Glen, NY: Century House, 1949.

Gaines, Kevin. "Assimilationist Minstrelsy as Racial Uplift Ideology: James D. Corrothers's Literary Quest for Black Leadership." *American Quarterly* 45, no. 3 (September 1993): 341–69.

———. *Uplifting the Race: Black Leadership, Politics, and Culture in the Twentieth Century*. Chapel Hill: University of North Carolina Press, 1996.

Gaitten, Chris. "The Second Life of Poindexter Village." *Columbus Monthly*, June 18, 2021. https://www.columbusmonthly.com/story/lifestyle/around-town/2021/06/18/second-life-poindexter-village/7743562002/.

Garroutte, Eva Marie. "The Racial Formation of American Indians: Negotiating Legitimate Identities within Tribal and Federal Law." *American Indian Quarterly* 25, no. 2 (Spring 2001): 224–39.

Gates, Henry Louis, Jr., and Gene Andrew Jarrett, eds. *The New Negro: Readings on Race, Representation, and African American Culture, 1892–1938*. Princeton, NJ: Princeton University Press, 2007.

Genovese, Eugene D. *Roll, Jordan, Roll: The World the Slaves Made*. New York: Vintage, 1972.

Genser, Wallace Vincent. "'A Rigid Government over Ourselves': Transformations in Ethnic, Gender, and Race Consciousness on the Northern Borderlands, Michigan, 1805–1865." PhD diss., University of Michigan, 1998.

Gerber, David A. *Black Ohio and the Color Line: 1860–1915*. Urbana: University of Illinois Press, 1976.

———. "The 'Careers' of People Exhibited in Freak Shows: The Problem of Volition and Valorization." In *Freakery: Cultural Spectacles of the Extraordinary Body*, edited by Rosmarie Garland Thompson, 38–54. New York: New York University Press, 1996.

Gilroy, Paul. *The Black Atlantic: Modernity and Double Consciousness*. London: Verso, 1993.

Gjerde, Jon. *The Minds of the West: Ethnocultural Evolution in the Rural Middle West, 1830–1917*. Chapel Hill: University of North Carolina Press, 1997.

Graham, Frederick H. *Wait for the Muncie Boys: Indiana's Early Circuses*. Indianapolis: Guild Press of Indiana, 1995.

Graham, Lawrence Otis. *Our Kind of People: Inside America's Black Upper Class*. New York: HarperCollins, 1999.

Gray, Susan E. *The Yankee West: Community Life on the Michigan Frontier*. Chapel Hill: University of North Carolina Press, 1996.

Green, Rayna. "The Pocahontas Perplex: The Image of Indian Women in American Culture." *The Massachusetts Review* 16, no. 4 (Autumn 1975): 698–714.

———. *Women in American Indian Society: Indians of North America*. New York: Chelsea House, 1992.

Grimsted, David. *Melodrama Unveiled: American Theater and Culture, 1800–1850*. Chicago: University of Chicago Press, 1968.

Gruen, Sara. *Water for Elephants*. Chapel Hill, NC: Algonquin Books, 2007.
Gustafson, Donna. "Images from the World Between: The Circus in Twentieth-Century American Art." In *Images from the World Between: The Circus in Twentieth-Century American Art*, edited by Donna Gustafson, 9–84. Cambridge, MA: MIT Press, 2001.
Haney Lopez, Ian F. *White by Law: The Legal Construction of Race*. New York: New York University Press, 1996.
Harrison, Daphne Duval. *Black Pearls: Blues Queens of the 1920s*. New Brunswick, NJ: Rutgers University Press, 1988.
Heinegg, Paul. "Free African Americans of Virginia, North Carolina, South Carolina, Maryland and Delaware." Book. Accessed 13 May 2024. http://www.freeafricanamericans.com.
Heppler, Jason A., and Douglas Seefeldt. "Buffalo Bill's Wild West and the Progressive Image of American Indians." The Buffalo Bill Project, University of Nebraska-Lincoln. http://buffalobillproject.unl.edu/research/showindians/.
Herskovits, Melville J. *The Myth of the Negro Past*. Boston: Beacon Press, 1990.
Hertzberg, Hazel Whitman. "Nationality, Anthropology, and Pan-Indianism in the Life of Arthur C. Parker (Seneca)." *Proceedings of the American Philosophical Society* 123, no. 1 (February 1979): 47–72.
Herzog, Don. *Happy Slaves: A Critique of Consent Theory*. Chicago: University of Chicago Press, 1989.
Hesslink, George K. *Black Neighbors: Negroes in a Northern Rural Community*. New York: Bobbs-Merrill, 1968.
Higginbotham, Evelyn Brooks. *Righteous Discontent: The Women's Movement in the Black Baptist Church, 1880–1920*. Cambridge, MA: Harvard University Press, 1993.
Hiltzik, Michael. *Iron Empires: Robber Barons, Railroads, and the Making of Modern America*. Boston: Houghton Mifflin Harcourt, 2020.
Himes, J. S. "Forty Years of Negro Life in Columbus, Ohio." *The Journal of Negro History* 27, no. 2 (April 1942): 133–55.
Hine, Darlene Clark. "Black Women in the Middle West: The Michigan Experience (Clarence M. Burton Memorial Lecture, Kalamazoo, Oct. 14, 1988)." In *Hine Sight: Black Women and the Re-Construction of American History*, 59–87. Bloomington: Indiana University Press, 1994.
———. *Hine Sight: Black Women and the Re-Construction of American History*. Bloomington: Indiana University Press, 1994.
Hine, Darlene Clark, and Kathleen Thompson. *A Shining Thread of Hope: The History of Black Women in America*. New York: Broadway Books, 1998.
Hinkle, Milton David. "Kit Carson Wild West." *Bandwagon* 7, no. 6 (November–December 1963): 17–21.
Hippisley Coxe, Anthony D. "Equestrian Drama and the Circus." In *Performance and Politics in Popular Drama: Aspects of Popular Entertainment in Theatre, Film and Television, 1800–1976*, edited by David Bradby, Louis James, and Bernard Sharratt, 109–18. New York: Cambridge University Press, 1980.
Hodes, Martha. *White Women, Black Men: Illicit Sex in the Nineteenth-Century South*. New Haven, CT: Yale University Press, 1997.

Hoh, LaVahn G., and William H. Rough. *Step Right Up! The Adventure of Circus in America*. White Hall, VA: Betterway Publications, 1990.

Holm, Tom. *The Great Confusion in Indian Affairs: Native Americans and Whites in the Progressive Era*. Austin: University of Texas Press, 2005.

Holton, Woody. *Forced Founders: Indians, Debtors, Slaves, and the Making of the American Revolution*. Chapel Hill: University of North Carolina Press, 1999.

Horton, James, and Lois Horton. *In Hope of Liberty: Culture, Community, and Protest among Northern Free Blacks*. New York: Oxford University Press, 1997.

Hoxie, Frederick E. *Final Promise: The Campaign to Assimilate the Indians, 1880–1920*. Lincoln: University of Nebraska Press, 1984.

Hudson, Lynn M. *The Making of "Mammy Pleasant": A Black Entrepreneur in Nineteenth-Century San Francisco*. Urbana: University of Illinois Press, 2003.

Huggins, Nathan Irvin. *Harlem Renaissance*. Updated ed. New York: Oxford University Press, 2007.

Hunter, Tera W. *To 'Joy My Freedom: Southern Black Women's Lives and Labors after the Civil War*. Cambridge, MA: Harvard University Press, 1997.

Jackson, Bruce, ed. *The Negro and His Folklore in Nineteenth-Century Periodicals*. Austin: University of Texas Press, 1967.

Jelks, Randal Maurice. "Race, Respectability and the Struggle for Civil Rights: A Study of the African American Community of Grand Rapids, Michigan, 1870–1954." PhD diss., Michigan State University, 1999.

Jenkins, Ron. *Acrobats of the Soul: Comedy and Virtuosity in Contemporary American Theatre*. New York: Theatre Communications Group, 1988.

Jenkins, Wilbert L. *Climbing Up to Glory: A Short History of African Americans during the Civil War and Reconstruction*. Wilmington, DE: SR Books, 2002.

Johnson, Walter. *Soul by Soul: Life Inside the Antebellum Slave Market*. Cambridge, MA: Harvard University Press, 1999.

Jones, Jacqueline. *Labor of Love, Labor of Sorrow: Black Women, Work, and the Family, from Slavery to the Present*. New York: Basic Books, 1985.

Jones, LeRoi (Amiri Baraka). *Blues People: Negro Music in White America*. New York: W. Morrow, 1963. Reprint, New York: Perennial, 2002.

Kasson, Joy S. *Buffalo Bill's Wild West: Celebrity, Memory, and Popular History*. New York: Hill and Wang, 2000.

Kelley, Robin D. G. "How the West Was One: The African American Diaspora and the Re-Mapping of U.S. History." In *Rethinking American History in a Global Age*, edited by Thomas Bender, 123–47. Berkeley: University of California Press, 2002.

King, Wilma. "Multicultural Education at Hampton Institute–The Shawnees: A Case Study, 1900–1923." *The Journal of Negro Education* 57, no. 4 (Autumn 1988): 524–35.

Klein, Christina. *Cold War Orientalism: Asia in the Middlebrow Imagination, 1945–1961*. Berkeley: University of California Press, 2003.

Kolchin, Peter. *Unfree Labor: American Slavery and Russian Serfdom*. Cambridge, MA: Belknap Press of Harvard University Press, 1987.

Krauthamer, Barbara. "In Their 'Native Country': Freedpeople's Understandings of Culture and Citizenship in the Choctaw and Chickasaw Nations." In *Crossing*

Waters, *Crossing Worlds: The African Diaspora in Indian Country*, edited by Tiya Miles and Sharon P. Holland, 100-120. Durham, NC: Duke University Press, 2006.

Lahti, Janne. *The American West and the World: Transnational and Comparative Perspectives*. New York: Routledge, 2019.

Landrum, Cynthia L. "Kicking Bear, John Trudell, and Anthony Kiedis (of the Red Hot Chili Peppers): 'Show Indians' and Pop-Cultural Colonialism." *American Indian Quarterly* 36, no. 2 (Spring 2012): 182-214.

Larson, Erik. *The Devil in the White City: Murder, Magic, and Madness at the Fair that Changed America*. New York: Vintage Books, 2004.

Larson, John Lauritz. "Pigs in Space, or What Shapes American Regional Cultures?" In *The American Midwest: Essays on Regional History*, edited by Andrew R. L. Cayton and Susan E. Gray, 69-77. Bloomington: Indiana University Press, 2001.

Lavers, Katie. "Horses in Modern, New, and Contemporary Circus." *Animal Studies Journal* 4, no. 2 (2015): 140-72.

Lawrence, A. H. *Duke Ellington and His World*. New York: Routledge, 2001.

Lehuu, Isabelle. *Carnival on the Page: Popular Print Media in Antebellum America*. Chapel Hill: University of North Carolina Press, 2000.

Levine, Lawrence W. *Black Culture and Black Consciousness: Afro-American Folk Thought from Slavery to Freedom*. New York: Oxford University Press, 1977.

Lewis, Robert M., ed. *From Traveling Show to Vaudeville: Theatrical Spectacle in America, 1830-1910*. Baltimore, MD: Johns Hopkins University Press, 2003.

Lewis, Steven. "Untamed Music: Early Jazz In Vaudeville." Master's thesis, Florida State University, 2012.

Lindfors, Bernth. *Early African Entertainments Abroad: From the Hottentot Venus to Africa's First Olympians*. Madison: University of Wisconsin Press, 2014.

———. "Ethnological Show Business: Footlighting the Dark Continent." In *Freakery: Cultural Spectacles of the Extraordinary Body*, edited by Rosemarie Garland Thomson, 207-18. New York: New York University Press, 1996.

Lindsey, Donal F. *Indians at the Hampton Institute: 1877-1923*. Urbana: University of Illinois Press, 1995.

Littlefield, Daniel F., Jr. *The Cherokee Freedmen: From Emancipation to American Citizenship*. Westport, CT: Greenwood Press, 1978.

Litwack, Leon F. *North of Slavery: The Negro in the Free States, 1790-1860*. Chicago: University of Chicago Press, 1961.

———. *Trouble in Mind: Black Southerners in the Age of Jim Crow*. New York: Alfred A. Knopf, 1998.

Lively, Adam. *Masks: Blackness, Race, and the Imagination*. Oxford: Oxford University Press, 1998.

Logan, Rayford W. *The Negro in American Life and Thought: The Nadir, 1877-1901*. New York: Dial Press, 1954.

Lomawaima, K. Tsianina. *They Called It Prairie Light: The Story of Chilocco Indian School*. Lincoln: University of Nebraska Press, 1994.

Lomawaima, K. Tsianina, and Theresa L. McCarty. *To Remain an Indian*. New York: Teachers College Press, 2006.

Lott, Eric. *Love and Theft: Blackface Minstrelsy and the American Working Class*. New York: Oxford University Press, 1993.

Madison, James H. *The Indiana Way: A State History*. Bloomington: Indiana University Press, 1986.

Manser, Rodney N. *Circus: The Development and Significance of the Circus, Past, Present, and Future*. Blackburn, UK: Richford, 1987.

Mark, Mary Louise. *Negroes in Columbus*. Columbus: Ohio State University Press, 1928.

Mathes, Valerie Sherer. "Helen Hunt Jackson and the Ponca Controversy." *Montana: The Magazine of Western History* 39, no. 1 (Winter 1989): 42–53.

Maxwell, Anne. *Colonial Photography and Exhibitions: Representations of the 'Native' and the Making of European Identities*. London: Leicester University Press, 1999.

May, Earl Chapin. *The Circus from Rome to Ringling*. New York: Duffield and Green, 1932.

McAfee, Ward M. *Religion, Race, and Reconstruction: The Public School in the Politics of the 1870s*. Albany: State University of New York Press, 1998.

McCaskill, Barbara, and Caroline Gebhard, eds. *Post-Bellum, Pre-Harlem: African American Literature and Culture, 1877–1919*. New York: New York University Press, 2006.

McCaul, Robert L. *The Black Struggle for Public Schooling in Nineteenth-Century Illinois*. Carbondale: Southern Illinois University, 1987.

McDonnell, Janet A. *The Dispossession of the American Indian, 1887–1934*. Indianapolis: Indiana University Press, 1991.

McKechnie, Samuel. *Popular Entertainments through the Ages*. New York: Benjamin Blom, 1969.

McKee, Irving. *The Trail of Death: Letters of Benjamin Marie Petit*. Indianapolis: Indiana Historical Society, 1941.

McKennon, Joe. *Logistics of the American Circus: Written by a Man Who Was There*. Sarasota, FL: Carnival Publishers of Sarasota, 1977.

McNamara, Brooks. "The Indian Medicine Show." *Educational Theatre Journal* 23, no. 4 (December 1971): 431–45. https://doi.org/10.2307/3205750.

———. *Step Right Up*. Rev. ed. Jackson: University Press of Mississippi, 1995.

McNenly, Linda Scarangella. "Foe, Friend, or Critic: Native Performers with Buffalo Bill's Wild West Show and Discourses of Conquest and Friendship in Newspaper Reports." *American Indian Quarterly* 38, no. 2 (Spring 2014): 143–76. https://doi.org/10.5250/amerindiquar.38.2.0143.

———. *Native Performers in Wild West Shows: From Buffalo Bill to Euro Disney*. Norman: University of Oklahoma Press, 2012.

Meier, August, and Elliott Rudwick. *Along the Color Line: Explorations in the Black Experience*. Urbana: University of Illinois Press, 1976.

Middleton, George. *Circus Memoirs: Reminiscences of George Middleton as Told to and Written by His Wife*. Los Angeles: HardPress Publishing, 2012.

Middleton, Stephen. *The Black Laws: Race and the Legal Process in Early Ohio*. Athens: Ohio University Press, 2005.

Miles, Tiya. *The House on Diamond Hill: A Cherokee Plantation Story*. Chapel Hill: University of North Carolina Press, 2010.

---. *Ties That Bind: The Story of an Afro-Cherokee Family in Slavery and Freedom.* Berkeley: University of California Press, 2005.

Miles, Tiya, and Sharon P. Holland, eds. *Crossing Waters, Crossing Worlds: The African Diaspora in Indian Country.* Durham, NC: Duke University Press, 2006.

Mintz, Sidney W., and Richard Price. *The Birth of African-American Culture: An Anthropological Perspective.* Boston: Beacon Press, 1992.

Mitchell, Michael. *Monsters: Human Freaks in America's Gilded Age: The Photographs of Chas Eisenmann.* Toronto: ECW Press, 2002.

Moore, Opha. *History of Franklin County, Ohio, Illustrated.* 3 vols. Topeka, KS: Historical Publishing Company, 1930.

Morgan, Jennifer L. *Laboring Women: Reproduction and Gender in New World Slavery.* Philadelphia: University of Pennsylvania Press, 2004.

Morgan, Philip D. *Slave Counterpoint: Black Culture in the Eighteenth-Century Chesapeake and Lowcountry.* Chapel Hill: University of North Carolina Press, 1998.

Morgan, Thomas L., and William Barlow. *From Cakewalks to Concert Halls: An Illustrated History of African American Popular Music from 1895 to 1930.* Washington, DC: Elliot and Clark, 1992.

Morris, Thomas D. *Southern Slavery and the Law, 1619-1860.* Chapel Hill: University of North Carolina Press, 1996.

Moses, L. G. *Wild West Shows and the Images of American Indians: 1883-1933.* Albuquerque: University of New Mexico Press, 1996.

Moy, James S. "Entertainments at John B. Ricketts's Circus, 1793-1800." *Educational Theatre Journal* 30, no. 2 (May 1978): 186–202.

Murphy, Jacqueline Shea. "Antidance Rhetoric and American Indian Arts in the 1920s." In *The People Have Never Stopped Dancing: Native American Modern Dance Histories,* NED-New edition, 81. Minneapolis: University of Minnesota Press, 2007.

Nash, Gary B. *Red, White, and Black: The Peoples of Early North America.* Englewood Cliffs, NJ: Prentice-Hall, 1974.

---. *The Urban Crucible: Social Change, Political Consciousness, and the Origins of the American Revolution.* Cambridge, MA: Harvard University Press, 1979.

Neihardt, John G. *Black Elk Speaks: Being the Life Story of a Holy Man of the Oglala Sioux, as told through John G. Neihardt.* Albany: State University of New York Press, 2008.

Neirick, Miriam Beth. "When Pigs Could Fly: A History of the Circus in the Soviet Union." PhD diss., University of California, Berkeley, 2007.

Nesper, Larry. "Remembering the Miami Indian Village Schoolhouse." *American Indian Quarterly* 25, no. 1 (Winter 2001): 135–51. https://www.jstor.org/stable/1186010.

Nicoll, Allardyce. *Masks, Mimes and Miracles: Studies in the Popular Theatre.* New York: Cooper Square, 1963.

North, Henry Ringling, and Alden Hatch. *Circus Kings: Our Ringling Family Story.* Garden City, NY: Doubleday, 1960.

Norton, Mary Beth. *Founding Mothers and Fathers: Gendered Power and the Forming of American Society.* New York: Alfred Knopf, 1996.

Padgett, Chris. "Evangelicals Divided: Abolition and the Plan of the Union's Demise in Ohio's Western Reserve." In *Religion and the Antebellum Debate over Slavery*, edited by John R. McKivigan and Mitchell Snay, 249–72. Athens: University of Georgia Press, 1998.

Parezo, Nancy J., and Angelina R. Jones. "What's in a Name? The 1940s–1950s 'Squaw Dress.'" *American Indian Quarterly* 33, no. 3 (2009): 373–404. http://www.jstor.org/stable/40388470.

Parkinson, Tom. *The Circus Moves By Rail*. Boulder, CO: Pruett Publishing, 1978.

Payne, Charles M. *I've Got the Light of Freedom: The Organizing Tradition and the Mississippi Freedom Struggle*. Berkeley: University of California Press, 1995.

Pearce, Susan M. *Museums, Objects, and Collections: A Cultural Study*. Leicester, UK: Leicester University Press, 1992.

Penn, Irvine Garland. *The Afro-American Press and Its Editors*. Springfield, MA: Willey, 1891.

Peretti, Burton W. *Lift Every Voice: The History of African-American Music*. Lanham, MD: Rowman & Littlefield, 2009.

Pfening, Fred Jr. "Black Animal Men." Unpublished manuscript, last modified 16 September 2007.

———. "Black Loyalty to Circuses." Unpublished manuscript, last modified 27 July 2003.

———. "Black Performer Notes." Unpublished manuscript, last modified 23 July 2003.

———. "Black Performers." Unpublished manuscript, last modified 4 August 2003.

———. "Black Show Owners." Unpublished manuscript, last modified 27 July 2003.

———. "Black Side Show Performers Including Zip and Mungo." Unpublished manuscript, last modified 3 August 2003.

———. "Black Workingman Notes." Unpublished manuscript, last modified 23 July 2003.

———. "Blacks in the Circus." Unpublished manuscript, last modified 11 June 2003.

———. "Pfening Text of Af Am Article." Unpublished manuscript, last modified 21 July 2003.

———. "Sells Brothers." Unpublished manuscript, last modified 21 July 2003.

———. "Side Show Bands; Black Bands." Unpublished manuscript, last modified 20 October 2016.

Philbrick, Francis S., ed. *The Laws of Indiana Territory, 1801–1809*. Springfield: Illinois State Historical Library, 1930.

Porter, Joy. *To Be Indian: The Life of Iroquois-Seneca Arthur Caswell Parker*. Norman: University of Oklahoma Press, 2001.

Prucha, Francis Paul. *The Great Father: The United States Government and the American Indians*. Lincoln: University of Nebraska Press, 1984.

Pulley Hudson, Angela. *Real Native Genius: How an Ex-Slave and a White Mormon Became Famous Indians*. Chapel Hill: University of North Carolina Press, 2018.

Rafert, Stewart. *The Hidden Community: The Miami Indians of Indiana, 1846–1940*. Indianapolis: Indiana Historical Society Press, 1982.

———. *The Miami Indians of Indiana: A Persistent People, 1654-1994*. Indianapolis: Indiana Historical Society Press, 1996.

Reeder, Warren A. *No Performances Today: June 22, 1918, Ivanhoe, Indiana*. Hammond, IN: North State Press, 1972.

Reiss, Benjamin. *The Showman and the Slave: Race, Death, and Memory in Barnum's America*. Cambridge, MA: Harvard University Press, 2001.

Renoff, Gregory J. *The Big Tent: The Traveling Circus in Georgia, 1820-1930*. Athens: University of Georgia Press, 2008.

Research Department of the Association for the Study of Negro Life and History. "Free Negro Owners of Slaves in the United States in 1830; Together with Absentee Ownership of Slaves in the United States in 1830." *Journal of Negro History* 9, no. 1 (1924): 41-85. https://www.jstor.org/stable/2713436.

Richardson, Heather Cox. *The Death of Reconstruction: Race, Labor, and Politics in the Post-Civil War North, 1865-1901*. Cambridge, MA: Harvard University Press, 2001.

Rinehart, Melissa A. "Miami Indian Language Shift and Recovery." PhD diss., Michigan State University, 2006. https://doi.org/doi:10.25335/3ved-ph94.

Robinson, Gil. *Old Wagon Show Days*. Cincinnati: Brockwell Company Publishers, 1925.

Royster, Jacqueline Jones, ed. *Southern Horrors and Other Writings: The Anti-Lynching Campaign of Ida B. Wells, 1892-1900*. Boston: Bedford/St. Martin's, 1997.

Rydell, Robert W. *All the World's a Fair: Visions of Empire at American International Expositions, 1876-1916*. Chicago: University of Chicago Press, 1984.

Rydell, Robert W., and Rob Kroes. *Buffalo Bill in Bologna: The Americanization of the World, 1869-1922*. Chicago: University of Chicago Press, 2005.

Sampson, Henry T. *The Ghost Walks: A Chronological History of Blacks in Show Business, 1865-1910*. Metuchen, NJ: Scarecrow, 1988.

Saxon, Arthur. H. *P.T. Barnum: The Legend and the Man*. New York: Columbia University Press, 1989.

Sayers, Isabelle S. *Annie Oakley and Buffalo Bill's Wild West*. New York: Dover, 1981.

Schenbeck, Lawrence. "Music, Gender, and 'Uplift' in the *Chicago Defender*, 1927-1937." *The Musical Quarterly* 81, no. 3 (Autumn 1997): 344-70. https://www.jstor.org/stable/742322.

Schmalenberger, Sarah. "Shaping Uplift through Music." *Black Music Research Journal* 28, no. 2 (Fall 2008): 57-83.

Schwalm, Leslie A. *Emancipation's Diaspora: Race and Reconstruction in the Upper Midwest*. Chapel Hill: University of North Carolina Press, 2009.

———. *A Hard Fight for We: Women's Transition from Slavery to Freedom in South Carolina*. Urbana: University of Illinois Press, 1997.

Scott, James C. *Weapons of the Weak: Everyday Forms of Peasant Resistance*. New Haven, CT: Yale University Press, 1985.

Shapiro, Nat, and Nat Hentoff. *Hear Me Talkin' to Ya: The Story of Jazz as Told by the Men Who Made It*. New York: Dover, 1966.

Shriver, Phillip R., and Clarence E. Wunderlin Jr., eds. *Documentary Heritage of Ohio*. Athens: Ohio University Press, 2000.

Simmons, David. *The Circus in Ohio*. Columbus: Ohio Historical Preservation Office, 1976.

Sleeper-Smith, Susan. *Indian Women and French Men: Rethinking Cultural Encounter in the Western Great Lakes*. Amherst: University of Massachusetts Press, 2001.

———. "Resistance to Removal: The 'White Indian,' Francis Slocum." In *Enduring Nations: Native Americans in the Midwest*, edited by R. David Edmunds, 109–23. Urbana: University of Illinois Press, 2008.

Slout, William L. *Olympians of the Sawdust Circle: A Biographical Dictionary of the Nineteenth-Century American Circus*. San Bernardino, CA: Borgo, 1998.

———. *A Royal Coupling: The Historic Marriage of Barnum and Bailey*. San Bernadino, CA: Emeritus Enterprise, 2000.

Smith, Felipe. "'Things You'd Imagine Zulu Tribes to Do': The Zulu Parade in New Orleans Carnival." *African Arts* 46, no. 2 (2013): 22–35. https://doi.org/10.1162/AFAR_a_00063.

Smith, Shawn Michelle. *Photography on the Color Line: W. E. B. Du Bois, Race, and Visual Culture*. Durham, NC: Duke University Press, 2004.

Sobel, Michal. *The World They Made Together: Black and White Values in Eighteenth-Century Virginia*. Princeton, NJ: Princeton University Press, 1987.

"Social Security Death Index." Indiana State, number 306-26-3905. 1 November 2010. https://www.ssa.gov/dataexchange/request_dmf.html.

Sollors, Werner. *Neither Black nor White Yet Both: Thematic Explorations of Interracial Literature*. New York: Oxford University Press, 1997.

Sorisio, Carolyn. "Playing the Indian Princess? Sarah Winnemucca's Newspaper Career and Performance of American Indian Identities." *Studies in American Indian Literatures* 23, no. 1 (2011): 1–37. https://doi.org/10.5250/studamerindilite.23.1.0001.

———. "Sarah Winnemucca, Translation, and U.S. Colonialism." *Reading, Writing, and Recognition* 37, no. 1 (Spring 2012): 35–60.

Sotiropoulos, Karen. *Staging Race: Black Performers in Turn of the Century America*. Cambridge, MA: Harvard University Press, 2006.

Southern, Eileen. *The Music of Black Americans: A History*. 3rd ed. New York: W.W. Norton, 1997.

Spangenberg, Kristin L., and Deborah W. Walk, eds. *The Amazing Circus Poster: The Strobridge Lithographing Company*. Cincinnati: The Cincinnati Art Museum and The John and Mabel Ringling Museum of Art, 2011.

Speaight, George. *A History of the Circus*. New York: A. S. Barnes and Company, 1980.

Stephens, John H. *History of Miami County*. Peru, IN: John H. Stephens Publishing House, 1896.

Stevenson, Brenda E. *Life in Black and White: Family and Community in the Slave South*. New York: Oxford University Press, 1996.

St. Leon, Mark. *The Circus in Australia: The American Century, 1851–1950*. Penshurst, NSW: Mark St. Leon & Associates, 2006.

Stoddart, Helen. *Rings of Desire, Circus History and Representation*. Manchester: Manchester University Press, 2000.

Stoler, Ann Laura. *Haunted by Empire: Geographies of Intimacy in North American History*. Durham, NC: Duke University Press, 2006.

Strange, Carolyn, and Tina Loo. "Spectacular Justice: The Circus on Trial and the Trial as Circus, Picton, 1903." *The Canadian Historical Review* 77, no. 2 (June 1996): 159–84.

Streeby, Shelley. *American Sensations: Class, Empire, and the Production of Popular Culture*. Berkeley: University of California Press, 2002.

Strobel, Christoph. *The Testing Grounds of Modern Empire: The Making of Colonial Racial Order in the American Ohio Country and the South African Eastern Cape, 1770s–1850s*. New York: Peter Lang, 2008.

Stuckey, Sterling. *Slave Culture: Nationalist Theory and the Foundations of Black America*. Oxford: Oxford University Press, 1987.

Sturm, Circe. *Blood Politics: Race, Culture, and Identity in the Cherokee Nation*. Berkeley: University of California Press, 2002.

Tait, Peta. "Danger Delights: Texts of Gender and Race in Aerial Performance." *New Theatre Quarterly* 12, no. 45 (1996): 43–49. https://doi.org/10.1017/S0266464X00009611.

Takagi, Midori. *Rearing Wolves to Our Own Destruction: Slavery in Richmond, Virginia, 1782–1865*. Charlottesville: University of Virginia Press, 1999.

Tanner, Helen Hornbeck. *Atlas of Great Lakes Indian History*. Norman: University of Oklahoma Press, 1987.

Thayer, Stuart. *Annals of the American Circus*. Seattle, WA: Dauven & Thayer, 1986.

———. "The Out-Side Shows." In *American Circus Anthology: Essays of the Early Years*, edited by William L. Slout, 2005. Circus Historical Society. Stuart Thayer's American Circus Anthology: Part One: Generic History. http://www.classic.circushistory.org/Thayer/Thayer1e.htm.

Thornbrough, Emma Lou. *Indiana Blacks in the Twentieth Century*. Bloomington: Indiana University Press, 2001.

———. *The Negro in Indiana: A Study of a Minority*. Indianapolis: Indiana Historical Bureau, 1957.

———. *The Negro in Indiana Before 1900: A Study of a Minority*. Indianapolis: Indiana University Press, 1993.

Thornbrough, Gayle, and Dorothy Lois Riker, eds. *Readings in Indiana History*. Vol. 36 of Indiana Historical Collections. Indianapolis: Indiana Historical Bureau, 1956.

Thurman, Kira. *Singing Like Germans: Black Musicians in the Land of Bach, Beethoven, and Brahms*. Ithaca, NY: Cornell University Press, 2021.

Towsen, John H. *Clowns*. New York: Hawthorn Books, 1976.

Troutman, John W. *Indian Blues: American Indians and the Politics of Music, 1879–1934*. Norman: University of Oklahoma Press, 2009.

Truzzi, Marcello. "The Decline of the American Circus: The Shrinkage of an Institution." In *Sociology and Everyday Life*, 312–22. Englewood Cliffs, NJ: Prentice-Hall, 1968.

Turner, John M. *Victorian Arena: The Performers: A Dictionary of British Circus Biography*. Vol. 2. Formby, UK: Lingdales Press, 2000.

Vinson, Robert Trent, and Robert Edgar. "Zulus Abroad: Cultural Representations and Educational Experiences of Zulus in America, 1880–1945." *Journal of Southern African Studies* 33, no. 1 (March 2007): 43–62. https://www.jstor.org/stable/25065170.

Voegeli, V. Jacque. *Free but Not Equal: The Midwest and the Negro during the Civil War.* Chicago: University of Chicago Press, 1967.

Von Eschen, Penny M. "Globalizing Popular Culture in the 'American Century' and Beyond." *OAH Magazine of History* 20, no. 4 (2006): 56–63.

———. *Satchmo Blows Up the World: Jazz Ambassadors Play the Cold War.* Cambridge, MA: Harvard University Press, 2004.

Waite, Cally L. "The Segregation of Black Students at Oberlin College after Reconstruction." *History of Education Quarterly* 41, no. 3 (2001): 344–64. https://www.jstor.org/stable/369200.

Walker, Juliet E. K. *Free Frank: A Black Pioneer in the Antebellum Frontier.* Lexington: University Press of Kentucky, 1983.

Wallis, Michael. *The Real Wild West: The 101 Ranch and the Creation of the American West.* New York: St. Martin's Press, 1999.

Walsh, Martin W. "The 'Heathen Party': Methodist Observation of the Ohio Wyandot." *American Indian Quarterly* 16, no. 2 (Spring 1992): 189–211. https://doi.org/10.2307/1185429.

Watkins, Clifford E. *Showman: The Life and Music of Perry George Lowery.* Jackson: University of Mississippi Press, 2003.

Weisenburger, Francis P. *The Passing of the Frontier, 1825–1850.* Vol. 3 of *A History of the State of Ohio.* Columbus: The Ohio Historical Society, 1968.

Wells, Samuel J., and Roseanna Tubby, eds. *After Removal: The Choctaw in Mississippi.* Jackson: University Press of Mississippi, 1986.

Wexler, Laura. *Tender Violence: Domestic Visions in an Age of U.S. Imperialism.* Chapel Hill: University of North Carolina Press, 2000.

Wickett, Murray R. *Contested Territory: Whites, Native Americans, and African Americans in Oklahoma, 1865–1907.* Baton Rouge: Louisiana State University Press, 2000.

Wilkins, David Eugene. *American Indian Politics and the American Political System.* Lantham, MD: Rowman and Littlefield, 2006.

Williams, Loretta J. *Black Freemasonry and Middle-Class Realities.* Columbia: University of Missouri Press, 1980.

Wilson, Benjamin C. *A Rural Black Heritage between Chicago and Detroit, 1850–1929.* Kalamazoo: New Issues Press, Western Michigan University, 1985.

Winger, Otho. *The Last of the Miamis: Little Turtle.* North Manchester, IN: L. W. Schultz, 1961.

Wittmann, Matthew. *Circus and the City: New York, 1793–2010.* New York: Bard Graduate Center, 2012.

Wolfe, Patrick. "Land, Labor, and Difference: Elementary Structures of Race." *American Historical Review* 106, no. 3 (June 2001): 866–905. https://doi.org/10.2307/2692330.

Woodson, Carter G. *The Mis-Education of the Negro*. Washington, DC: Associated Publishers, 1933.

Zapff, Gerhard. *Jumbo auf dem Drahtseil — Elefantendressuren von gestern und heute*. Berlin: Henschelverlag, 1984.

# Index

Page numbers in *italics* refer to illustrations.

acrobats, 32, 72
*Afro-American Press and Its Editors, The* (Penn), 56
after shows, 17, 26
Ailey, Alvin, 154
Alabama Minstrels, 50
Al G. Barnes Circus, 90, 91, 145
Allen, A. G., 46, 53
American Circus Corporation, 10, 41, 60, 85, 87, 90, 106, 145
American Horse, 107
American Indian Brotherhood, 71
American Indian Movement, 13
Anderson, Joseph, 34
Anderson, Priscilla, 134
Anglo-Zulu War (1879), 68
animal acts, 17, 22, 31
Antioch Baptist Church, 133–34
Apache Nation, 113
Arapaho Nation, 98
Armstrong, Louis, 52, 62, 153
Askew, Thomas, 55
assimilation, 57, 119–21, 123
Astley, Philip, 20

Baartman, Sarah, 78
Badger, Bill, 73
Bailey, Buster, 46
Bailey, James, 9, 31, 85, 135
Bailey, Lewis, 21
Baldwin, Louise Bottineau, 124
"Ballad of John Henry," 35
Ballard, Ed, 85, 145
ballyhoo, 29
bandleaders, 38–47
Baraka, Amiri, 47

Barclay, Jenifer, 83
Barnum, P. T., 31, 78–79, 150; African exoticism and, 68, 69, 75; buffalo hunt staged by, 29–30; Chappelle likened to, 2; colonialism and, 97
Barnum's American Museum, 75, 82
Barrett Show, 73
Battle of Isandlwana (1879), 67, 68
Battle of Little Big Horn (1876), 98, 99, 108
Battle of Rorke's Drift (1879), 68
Battle of Rosebud (1876), 108
Battle of Slim Buttes (1876), 108
Beatty, Clyde, 143
Beaver, 105
Bechet, Sidney, 46
Benjamin, Frank, 88–89
Bethune, Thomas Green Blind Tom, 34
Beyoncé, 62
Big George Bell, 75
Big Hawk, 105
*Billboard*, 58–59, 71–72, 85, 88, 91
*Birth of a Nation, The* (film), 4, 68
Black America pageant, 24
Black Arts movement, 154
*Black Atlantic* (Gilroy), 154
Black Bull, 105
Black Elk (Oglala Lakota man), 102, 127
*Black Elk Speaks* (Neihardt), 102
blackface, 11, 24, 25–26, 38, 53, 70
Black Hussar Band, 10
Black newspapers, 39, 55–60 *See also specific newspapers*
Blind Tom (Thomas Green Bethune), 34
blues, 11–12, 32–36, 38, 46–48, 61
Booker, Ada, 80

199

Bostock and Bailey's Menagerie, 73
Bowen, Benjamin, 133, 134
Bowen, Della, 133
Bowen, Katie, 133
Bowen, Leslie, 133
Bowen, Lotta, 133
Bowen, Minnie, 133
Bowen family, 131
Bower, Bert, 89
Bowers, Bert, 85, 145
Bowles, George, 85
Boy Scouts of America, 121
Brandon, Hezikiah, 134
Breckinridge, Clifton, 68
Brennan, John R., 119
Bright Eyes (Susette La Flesche Tibbles), 110, 126–27
Brister's Boy's Band, 34
Brown, Gertrude, 80
Brown, Harry, 149
Brown, J. Purdy, 21
Brown, Minnie Lee, 80
Brown, Tom, 149
Bruell, Andy, 143
Bucktooth, Ernest, 94
Bucktooth, James, 94
Buffalo Bill (William F. Cody), 8, 58, 71, 99, 104, 108, 111, 120; Black Elk and, 102; death of, 123; defense of Native Americans, 109; in Indian Wars, 99; Lakota-Ojibwa meeting and, 30; Sitting Bull's view of, 107; as Wild West show innovator, 99–100; women's races staged by, 105
Buffalo Ranch, 120
Bull Bear (Cheyenne chief), 101
burlesque, 79
Bushell, Garvin, 46–47
Butler, William, 90

*Cain Raisers* (Cox), 49
Caldwell's Minstrels, 42
calliopes, 21
canvasmen, 84, 85, 86, 87
Carnegie Institute, 113

Castello, Dan, 22
Cetshwayo, King, 67, 68
Chappelle, Pat, 1, 2–3
Cherokees, 143
Chesapeake and Ohio Railroad, 141
Cheyenne Nation, 101, 106
*Chicago Defender* (Black newspaper), 39, 57, 58, 80
Chicago World's Fair (World's Columbian Exposition, 1893), 97–98, 100, 111
Chindahl, George, 130
*Christian Recorder*, 57
Christine, Millie, 81
Christy, George W., 91–92
Christy and His Wonder Show, 91
Chude-Sokei, Louis, 25
citizenship, 5, 54, 66–67, 117–24
Clarke, Ed, 88
classical music, 56–57, 119–20, 153
Clayton, Elias, 90
*Clorindy, or the Origins of the Cakewalk* (musical comedy), 36
Cloud, Henry Roe, 121
clowns, 10, 21
Coca-Cola Corporation, 153
Cochran, Stewart S. (pastor), 134
Cody, William F. *See* Buffalo Bill
Cold War, 153
Cole Brothers, 42, 51
Colin (horse), 21
*Colored World, The* (Back newspaper), 56
Columbia Records, 49
comedians, 10, 24, 26, 32
contortionists, 72
cooch dancing, 79
Coolidge, Calvin, 44
Cooper, Edward E., 56
Cooper and Bailey, 75
Coup, W. C., 68, 75
Cox, Ida, 49, 80
Cradic, Richard, 134
"Crazy Blues" (Mamie Smith), 47
Crazy Horse, 98, 108
Los Cubanos, the Three Garcia Brothers, 67

cultural imperialism, 152–53
Curtis, Bill "Cap," 84–85, 130
Custer, George Armstrong, 98, 99, 100, 106

Dahomey Giant, 75
dance bands, 7
Davis, Angela, 47–48
Davis, Janet, 8
Dawes Act (1887), 5
De Cora, Angel, 124
Decosta, Littela, 44
Degas, Edgar, 79
Delaware Nation, 132, 143
Dellah, William (Dehl Montano), 73
Deloria, Philip, 8, 99, 101
Deloria, Vine, 8, 107
Dodds, Johnny, 47
Dorsey, Thomas A., 3
Douglass, Frederick, 24, 54
Douglass, Joseph, 24
"Down Hearted Blues" (Bessie Smith), 49
*Drama of Civilization, The* (Wild West show), 100
Drew & Campbell's Sideshow, 71
Drury, Mary, 134
Du Bois, W. E. B., 26, 54–55, 74
Dudley, S. H., 36
Dunbar, Paul Laurence, 24
Dundy, Elmer S., 110
Duprey, E., 9

"Eagle Rock Rag" (Phillips), 46
Eastman, Charles, 121
Edward VII, King, 108
elephants, 9, 74, 130, 150, 151
Ellington, Duke, 153
Elliott, Ernest, 47
eugenics, 55, 97
Excelsior Seat Company, 129

Fairbanks, Douglas Sr., 102
Ferris, Bismark, 58
Fields, Ezekiel, 133
Fields, Joshua Ellsworth, 133

Filipino people, 98, 100, 105
Fisk Jubilee Singers, 35, 37, 38, 110, 154
Fitzgerald, Ella, 62
"Florida Blues, The" (Phillips), 46
Florida Orange Blossom Minstrels, 48, 49
Forepaugh, Adam, 150
Forepaugh, Addie, 150
Forepaugh, Patsy, 74
Forepaugh Circus, 150
Forepaugh-Sells Circus, 39, 42, 73–74, 76, 84, 132, 135
Fourteenth Amendment, 110
Frances Victoria Alexandra (Native American child), 104
freak shows, 16, 21, 23, 26, 53, 68, 74, 78
Fred Harevy Company, 114
*Freedom's Journal*, 56

Gabriel (drummer), 3
Gaines, Al, 48
Gardner, Cheerful, 106
Garvey, Marcus, 26
Georgia Jazz Band, 3
Georgia Minstrels, 38, 154
Geronimo, 100–101
Ghost Dance Movement, 107–8
Ghost Dog, 102
Gibraltar (horse), 20
Gillespie, Dizzy, 153–54
Gilman, Cornelius, 134
Gilmore, P. S., 23
Gilroy, Paul, 154
Ginger Band, 44
Glascoe, Percy, 46
Godfroy, Francis, 138, 139–41, 147
Godfroy, Gabriel, 129, *138*, *139*, 141
Goings, Frank C., 71
"A Good Man Is Hard to Find" (Lizzie Miles), 52
Good Robe (Native American woman), 104
Goodwin, Samuel H., 88
Grant, Ulysses S., 107, 111
Great Farini, The (William Hunt), 69, 75
Great Migration, 12

Index  201

Great Northern Railroad Show, 63
Great Pan American Shows, 88
Great Wallace Circus. *See* Wallace Circus (Hagenbeck-Wallace Circus)
Green, Silas, 48, 49, 53, 59, 64, 65
Gruenwald Café (Minneapolis), 44
"Gulf Coast Blues" (Bessie Smith), 49

Hagenbeck, Carl, 10–11
Hagenbeck-Wallace Circus. *See* Wallace Circus
Hale, Jennie, 65
Hall, James Reynolds, 131
Hamlin's Wizard Oil Company, 27–29
Handy, W. C., 46
Harigan, John J., 89
Harlem Renaissance, 6, 12, 60, 61
Harris, Eli, 134
Harvey, Fred, 114
Hay-o-Wei (Cheyenne chief), 99
Hearns, Lewis, 134
Hennessey, Pat, 101
Herndon, Coy, 58–60, 80, 82
Heth, Joice, 78–79, 82
Hicks, Charles B., 38, 149
"High Ball Rag" (Phillips), 46
High Bear (Oglala Lakota man), 104
Hightower, Willie, 46
Hocking Valley and Toledo Railroad, 129
hoedown, 25
Hollis, Orin L., 22
Holy Blanket (Oglala Lakota woman), 104
Hopi Nation, 113
horses, 6, 9, 18, 32, 40, 99, 130; in early circuses, 17, 20–21, 31; handlers of, 84; Native Americans and, 105, 116, 143, 144
Howell, Isaac, 134
Howes' Great London Show, 73, 89, 145
Howling Crow, 105
Huggard, William, 69
Hughes, Harley, 134
Hunt, William (The Great Farini), 69, 75
Hyers Sisters, 22, 31, 32, 35, 36, 38

*In Dahomey* (musical comedy), 36, 75
*Indianapolis Freeman* (Black newspaper), 39–46, 56–58
*Indianapolis Leader* (Black newspaper), 56
*Indianapolis World* (Black newspaper), 66
Indian princess figure, 114–15
Indian Removal Act (1830), 132
International Circus Hall of Fame, 147
Interstate Commerce Commission, 2–3
"It's Right Here for You," (Mamie Smith), 62

Jackson, Bill, 69
Jackson, Elmer, 90
Jackson, Helen Hunt, 110
Jackson, J. A., 58–59, 71, 79–80, 83
Jay Circus, 69
Jay-Z, 62
jazz, 11–12, 32, 34, 38, 46–47, 52, 153
Jenkins Orphanage Band, 47
Jezebel stereotype, 24
John L. Sullivan (elephant), 74, 150
John Robinson Circus, 44, 85, 90, 91
Johnson, Edward "Yellow," 88
Johnson, Lonnie, 62
Johnson, William "Bunk," 46
Johnson, William Henry (Zip the What Is It?), 44, 74–75
Jones, Joseph, 80
Jones, Ovie O., 134
Jones Brothers, 42, 50–51
jubilee singers, 9, 35
jugglers, 7, 26, 32

*Kansas Herald* (Black newspaper), 39, 57
Kasson, Joy, 8
Kelley, Robin D. G., 152
Kewley, Fred, 46–47
Kickapoo Indian Medicine Company, 27, 29
Kicking Bear, 103, 108
*King and I, The* (musical comedy), 153
kinkers, 12, 13, 66, 72–75, 78
Kirk, Frank, 17
Kit Carson Wild West Show, 91

Kline, Tiny, 75, 87
Ku Klux Klan, 4, 91

La Flesche Tibbles, Susette (Bright Eyes), 110, 126–27
Lakota Nation, 30, 98, 106, 110, 143
LaVilla, FL, 2
"Lawdy, Lawdy Blues" (Cox), 49
Leadbelly, 52
Leon's Southern Minstrels, 44
Leopold, Jessie Amelia Kelly, 151
*Life among the Piutes* (Winnemucca Hopkins), 126
*Life in Sellsville* (Robinson), 10
Little Chief Ogallala, 104
Littlejohn's (minstrel company), 38
Little Woman, 105
Lone Wolf, 102
Lopez, Maxine, 80
Louisville and Nashville Railroads, 2
Lowery, P. G., 9, 33, 39–42, 44, 55, 61, 62, 134
Luca family, 38
Lynch, George, 80
lynching, 4, 88, 89, 90

Madden, Thomas "Curly," 91
magicians, 22, 23
Main, Walter L., 84
Major Lillie's Far East, 71
Malaley, W. H., 101
"Mama Doo Shee Blues" (Cox), 49
Mammy stereotype, 24
Ma Rainey, 3, 48, 49, 62
Mariotini, Cayetano, 21
Marks, Charles, 105–6
Marks, LaMoine, 105, 143
Marshall, Harriet Gibbs, 57
Martin, Katie, 134
Martin, Sara, 62
Mason, Max, 90–91
Master Duffee, 21
McCall's Minstrels, 42
McClain, Billy, 149
McDaniel, Hattie, 7

McGhie, Isaac, 90
McKoy, Christine, 82
McKoy, Jacob, 82
McKoy, Millie, 82
McKoy, Monemia, 82
McLaughlin, James, 108
Meadows, Herbert T., 45–46, 54
medicine shows, 11, 23, 27, 29
Mellinger, Susie Tucker, 106
menageries, 16–17, 23
Miami Nation, 7, 14, 106, 129, 137–45, 147–48
Mike York's Dog and Pony Show, 105
Miles, J. C., 50–51
Miles, Lizzie, 49–53, 62
Miles, Nelson A., 108
Miniconjou Lakota Nation, 108
Minnie Ought to Be, 105
minstrelsy, 4, 9, 11–12, 22, 23, 32, 53–54, 64; of Black-owned vs. white-owned companies, 36, 38; blues singers and, 48; classically trained musicians in, 57; respectability culture and, 55; typical sequence in, 24–25
Mississinewa Council, 138–39
Miss La La, 78, 79
Mitchell, Michael, 83
Mix, Tom, 102, 143
Montarno, Dehl (William Dellah), 73
Montezuma, Carlos, 123–24
Morgan, Thomas Jefferson, 108
Morris, Thomas, 69
Morton, Jelly Roll, 50, 53
Mrs. Frost, 105
Mugivan, Jerry, 60, 90–91, 141, 145
Mulligan, Jerry, 85

Nadir, 4
Nashville Exposition (1897), 34
National Association for the Advancement of Colored People (NAACP), 90
*National Geographic*, 78
Navajo Nation, 113
*Negro World*, 57

Index   203

Neihardt, John, 102
Nelson, Barney, 113
Nelson, Dave, 3
Nelson, Francis, 71
Netzahualt, Nabor Feliz, 111, *112*, 113
New Orleans Minstrels, 53
*New York Age* (Black newspaper), 44, 51–52, 57, 58
*New York Clipper*, 85
Nickel Plate Railroad, 141
North, Henry Ringling, 84
Northern Cheyenne, 98
Northern Pacific Railroad, 106
Nubian (Black performer), 26

O'Brien Circus, 69
O'Bryant, Jimmy, 47
Ohio State University, 129
Ojibwa Nation, 30
Okeh Records, 47, 51, 62
olio (medley), in minstrel shows, 25
Oliver, King, 46, 50, 53, 62
101 Ranch, 100–101, 120
Onondaga Nation, 94
Ory, Kid, 50
Oskazuma, Prince, 70–72
*Out of Bondage* (musical comedy), 36
"outside show," 27, *28*
Owen, William, 91

Pacific Railway Act (1863), 21
parades, 16, *18*
Paramount Records, 48
Paris Universal Exposition (1893), 100
Parker, Arthur C., 94, 121–22, *123*
Parker, C. W., 48
Pawnee Bill's Wild West Show, 75, 105, 114
Pelton, D. K., 89
Penn, I. Garland, 56
Pepin & Breschard Show, 21
Petit, Buddy, 46
Pfening, Fred, Jr., 91
Phillips, William, 46
physical-culture movement, 77

Pitre the African (Peter the African, Young African), 20–21
Plato, Desseria, 24
*Plessy v. Ferguson* (1896), 136
Pocahontas, 114
Poindexter Village, 136–37, 146–47
Polkadot School (Sellsville), 134, *135*, 136
Pollack, Ed, 3
Ponca tribe, 109–10
Pope, Charles, 149
Pope, R. Roy, 44–46
Potawatomi Nation, 137
Pratt, Richard H., 118
Princess Standing Holly, 114
Princess Wee Wee (Harriet Elizabeth Williams Thompson), 44, *81*, 83
prison songs, 35
Professor Williams' Consolidated American and German Railroad Shows, 63
protectionism, 153
Pueblo Nation, 113

Rabbit's Foot Minstrels, 2, 48, 49, 53
race records, 38, 61, 62
ragtime, 7, 12, 38
Rahman, Abdul, 70
railroads, 11, 21–22, 31, 113, 129, 141
railroad songs, 35
Rainey, Gertrude "Ma," 3, 48, 49, 62
Rainey, Will, 48
Ralston, Alex, 143
razorbacks, 84
Reconstruction, 4
recording industry, 7, 34, 48
Redmond, Charles, 91
Red Shirt (Oglala man), 102
Reed, Lucy, 134
respectability culture, 53–55
Richards and Pringles' Georgia Minstrels, 41
Rickett, John B., 20, 21, 85
Ringling Bros. and Barnum and Bailey Circus, 8, *19*, 31, 44, 145; Black

employees and patrons of, 27, 28, 40, 42, 45, 75, 84, 85, 87, 88–89; consolidation of, 135; Native American performers of, 105
ring shout, 35
Rink, Sidney, 73, 91
Robinson, Alvin "Zoo," 46
Robinson, Aminah, 10, 136, 146
Robinson, Gil, 69, 72
Robinson, John, 27, 71, 72
Robinson's Famous Shows, 145
Roosevelt, Franklin D., 136–37
Roosevelt, Theodore, 101, 116–17
roustabouts, 84
Russell Brothers, 38

"Salty Dog" (Lizzie Miles), 52
Sambo stereotype, 24
Santa Fe Railroad, 113
Sapphire stereotype, 24
Sawyers Cabin Singers, 75
Schayinsky, Alexander, 52
Schlitz Palm Garden (Milwaukee), 44
Second Great Awakening, 76
Sells, Ephraim, 9, 84, 134, 136
Sells, Lewis, 9, 84, 135
Sells, Peter, 9, 84, 145
Sells, William Allen, 9
Sells and Downs Circus, 42
Sells and Gray Circus, 42
Sells and Renfrow Circus, 42, 71
Sells Brothers Circus, 8, 14, 31, 120, 145–46; Black musicians employed by, 39, 40; geographic reach of, 22; labor pool used by, 7, 128; origins of, 9; racial strife and, 91
Sells-Floto Circus, 18, 46, 99, 145
Sells-Forepaugh Circus, 39, 42, 73–74, 76, 84, 132, 135
Sellsville (Columbus, OH), 7, 9–10, 14, 31, 128, 129–37, 146
Sellsville Clippers, 134
Sellsville Sluggers, 134–35
Short Bull, 103
Sioux, 110

Sitting Bull, 8, 98, 106–8
Skerbeck, Frank, 63
slavery, 4, 33, 47–48, 95, 117, 118
Smart Set Minstrel Show, 38, 80
Smith, Bessie, 48, 49, 50, 53
Smith, Charles H., 68
Smith, John, 114
Smith, Joseph Pearson, 82
Smith, Mamie, 47, 61–62, 80
Social Darwinism, 4
Society of American Indians (SAI), 5, 13, 94, 95, 120–24, 127
*Souls of Black Folk, The* (Du Bois), 54
*South Before the War, The* (musical comedy), 36
*South Pacific* (musical comedy), 153
Soviet Union, 153
Sparks Circus, 145
spirituals, 35
squaw figure, 114, 115
Standing Bear, 102, 105, 109–11, 127
Standing Bear, Alexandra Birmingham Cody, 109
Standing Bear, Luther, 102, 108–9, 127
*Standing Bear v. Crook* (1879), 110
Standing Rock Reservation, 106, 107–8
Starr, Milton, 36
Stewart, Doc, 134
St. Louis World's Fair (1904), 98
Sun Woman, 105
Swallow (purported Sioux man), 105
Sweatman, Wilbur, 46
Sweeney and Royer (knockabout act), 71
Swinger, George, 88

Talbott, John, 141
Tarver, James G., 75
tents, 21
Terrell, Mary Church, 54
Theater Owners Booking Agency (TOBA), 36, 49
"This Thing Called Love," (Mamie Smith), 62
Tibbles, Thomas Henry, 110
tightrope walking, 22

Index   205

Thompson, Ephraim (Eph), 73, 74, 150–51
Thompson, Harriet Elizabeth Williams (Princess Wee Wee), 44, *81*, 83
Thornton, Clara, 134
Thornton, I. A., 134
Tinsley, Pedro, 34
Tolliver's Circus and Musical Extravaganza, 48
Trans-Mississippi and International Exhibition (1898), 101
trapeze artists, 22, 32, 67
*A Trip to Coontown* (musical comedy), 36
Troup, Robby, 52
Tubbee, Okah, 70
Tucker, Dave, 89
Tucker, Gabe, 106
Tucker, Mary, 106
Turner, Frederick Jackson, 98–99
*Types of American Negroes, Georgia, USA* (photo collection), 55

Uncle stereotype, 24
Underwood, Charlie, 139
United Monster Shows, 68

vanishing Indian myth, 5, 97, 117–18
vaudeville, 13, 17, 26, 38, 48
ventriloquists, 22
Victoria, Queen, 68, 82, 102, 108–9

Wabash Railroad, 141
Walker, Frank, 49
Walker, George, 61, 131, 134
Walker, Laura Brown, 131, 134
Walking Girl, 105
Wallace, Benjamin, 41, 129, 140, 143
Wallace, Robinson, 10–11
Wallace, Sippie, 62
Wallace Circus (Hagenbeck-Wallace Circus), 8–9, *18*, *19*, 43; Black employees and performers at, 41, 71, 84, 87, 89, 128; consolidation of, 10; Lowery and, 40–42; Miami Nation and, 7, 10, 14, 137–45; ownership of, 105, 147
Wallace Quarters (Peru, IN), 137–45, 147
Washington, George, 20
Waters, Ethel, 80
Weisenberger, Susie Ticker, 106
Weisheimer Brothers Flour Mill, 129, 131
Wells, Al, 67
Western Concert (equestrian show), 106
White, Princess, 80
White, Solomon, 9
White and Clark's Black and Tan Minstrels, 49
White Bird, 105
White Cow, 105
White Eyes, 105
Whitman Sisters Company, 44
Wickliffe, John, 44
Wild West shows, 23, 26, 71, 94–109, 113–14, 117–24; Black talent and, 17, 38; colonialism and expansionism links to, 96–99, 105, 152–53; Native Americans and, 11, 13, 27, 30, 32, 99–102; origins of, 29–30, 99–100; in Sells Brothers Circus, 9; sideshow bands in, 34; stereotypes in, 5–6, 27
Williams, Bert, 61
Williams, Ephraim, 63–64, 65
Williams, Lewis, 1–2
Williams, Mamie, 80
Willis, Louis, 72–73
Wilson's Three-Ring Circus, 50
Winnemucca, Sarah, 124, 126, 127
Wolfscale, Dennis, 42
Wolfscale, Esther, 42
Wolfscale, James, 42, *43*, 44, 46, 58, 62
Wolfscales, Roy, 44
women's suffrage, 78
Woods, Neil, 134
Woodson, Emanuel, 79
Woodward, Sidney, 24, 35
World's Columbian Exposition (1893), 97–98, 100, 111
world's fairs, 11, 23–24, 95, 97–98, 152

Worther, Nellie, 80
Wounded Knee Massacre (1890), 102, 108
Wovoka (Paiute holy man), 107, 108
Wright, P. T., 42
Wyandot Nation, 132
Wynn, Albert, 3

Yellow Robe, Chauncey, 121, 122
"You Can't Keep a Good Man Down," (Mamie Smith), 61–62
Young African (Pitre the African, Peter the African), 20–21
Young Buffalo's Wild West Shows, 71
Young Men's Christian Association (YMCA), 121

Zimmerman, Edward, 131
Zip Coon stereotype, 24
Zip the What Is It? (William Henry Johnson), 44, 74–75
Zulu peoples, 67–72, 98, 100

www.ingramcontent.com/pod-product-compliance
Lightning Source LLC
Chambersburg PA
CBHW021856230426
43671CB00006B/407